# THE GROUNDWORK OF
# CHRISTIAN ETHICS

*N. H. G. Robinson*

# THE GROUNDWORK
# OF CHRISTIAN
# ETHICS

**COLLINS**
*St James's Place, London, 1971*

William Collins Sons & Co Ltd
London · Glasgow · Sydney · Auckland
Toronto · Johannesburg

First published 1971
© N. H. G. Robinson, 1971
ISBN 0 00 215283-5
Set in Monotype Garamond
Made and Printed in Great Britain by
Cox & Wyman Ltd, London, Fakenham and Reading

# CONTENTS

# CONTENTS

To
Frazer, Gordon, Catherine
and Maureen

# PREFACE

This essay on Christian ethics is not primarily concerned with particular ethical problems which confront the contemporary Christian nor with their solution. That in any case is the task and responsibility of the individual Christian and his fellows as they directly encounter these problems. Rather what is aimed at here is the articulation of the understanding of the moral life itself intrinsic to Christian faith, and of course the attempt is made in critical dialogue with other efforts to bring to clear expression this understanding. Otherwise it would have been doomed to failure. I am acutely conscious of my debt to other thinkers in this field, and not least when I am compelled to disagree and diverge. I am aware too of my debt to former students with whom I have had the privilege of discussing these matters, mainly in Rhodes University, Grahamstown, South Africa, but also for a few weeks in 1961 in the Presbyterian College, Belfast. It seems to me, however, that the investigation of the fundamental problems of Christian ethics is by no means irrelevant to the general task of systematic theology in the contemporary situation which has chiefly claimed my attention in recent years. Indeed it may well be that the Christian ethical question is the concealed axis around which the contemporary theological debate tends to revolve in uncertain dialectic.

St Mary's College,                          N. H. G. ROBINSON
The University,
St Andrews.

*Chapter 1*

# ETHICS AND THEOLOGY

## (a) Christian ethics a normative science within theology

The subject that is here to be investigated is what is commonly known as Christian ethics, and it is customary to assign to it a separate space in the total schematism of theological thought. Thus it is not uncommon to divide the field of Christian truth into apologetics, dogmatics and ethics. In itself this division of the field is unobjectionable and indeed necessary. The task of theological study would be hopelessly confusing unless some such division were observed. None the less in making this division we are abstracting elements from a total whole and we should, therefore, be aware that we have abstracted, so that the very process of abstraction may not be allowed to lead us into errors. 'Religion', says Professor Hendrik Kraemer in a significant passage,[1] 'is nowhere in the world an assortment of spiritual commodities that can be compared as shoes or neckties. This sounds frivolous, nevertheless it is a point of such overwhelming importance that it can hardly be over-estimated. It ought never to be forgotten in the treatment of religious subjects – but it constantly is – that religion is the vast and desperate effort of mankind to get somehow an apprehension of the totality of existence, and therefore every religion is an indivisible, and not to be divided, unity of existential apprehension. It is not a series of tenets, dogmas, prescriptions, institutions, practices, that can be taken one by one as independent items of religious life, conception or organization, and that can arbitrarily be compared with, and somehow related to, and grafted upon, the similar item of another religion.' 'Every religion', he continues, 'is a living, indivisible unity.'

It is easy enough to forget this within dogmatics itself, in dealing with one doctrine, for example, in isolation from all the others; but nowhere is the temptation so strong, nowhere does it carry such disastrous consequences if we yield to it, nowhere is it so fatally easy to be misled by the necessary division of theological

11

study and the inevitable process of abstraction, as is the case in dealing with ethics. Here, perhaps more than anywhere else, we can be compelled to err almost in spite of ourselves and to end in vague and ill-defined affirmations or aspirations.

In his essay, *What is Christian Civilization?*, John Baillie once argued that 'the Christian civilization of the past has not . . . been a civilization all or even most of whose members had come under such a saving conviction of Christian truth as to work renewal in their inward man, leading them to observe in all things the Christian standards of conduct. It was rather', he continued, 'a civilization in which nearly all acknowledged the authority both of that truth and of these standards, accepting in their minds even what they delayed to take to heart, and trembling when they were farthest from obeying.'[2] That was the situation in the past, but nowadays, he held,[3] 'modern life is no longer carried on within the setting of the Christian world-view, but either is a pragmatic business lacking any general setting, or attempts to conform itself to a new complex of ruling ideas having their centre in the dogma of racial progress.' 'We cannot . . . say that our moral practice gives us the right to think of our present society as Christian, but', he went on, 'I believe the case to be different when we turn our attention to our *professed moral standards*. So far as our civilization is still Christian, it is this principally in respect of the fact that its *conscience* is still recognizably Christian, that we judge other men and nations, and to a less extent allow ourselves to be judged, by norms of conduct which Christianity introduced into the world.'[4]

Undoubtedly there are contexts in which these observations have considerable point and an unquestionable validity. When Sir Winston Churchill described the period in which the United Kingdom stood alone against her enemies in the last war as one which held the greatest danger for what he called Christian civilization, he was not using words at random and without a meaning; and in relation to this somewhat problematical subject of Christian civilization Baillie's statements in the essay from which I have quoted are legitimate and even helpful. Especially in a context in which the concept of Christian civilization is explicitly called in question it seems perfectly proper to refer to a conscience and to professed moral standards as Christian, even when they have been divorced from the truth and the faith which have historically inspired them. That does not mean, however, that the Christian moralist can without qualification lift these statements from Baillie's discussion and transpose them into a discourse on Christian ethics, expecting them to have the same general value there which they had in their original context. In this new context, in a discourse on Christian ethics, it might very quickly appear that such statements are out of place and that, while in a sense it is proper enough to speak of a conscience and of professed moral standards as Christian even when divorced from the Christian faith and any apprehension of Christian truth, yet in another sense in that case the word 'Christian' should at least be put in inverted commas. The truth is that when the word 'Christian' is applied to actions and behaviour and even to conscience and moral standards it is ambiguous, for there are two quite different senses in which it may be used, it may be used either descriptively or normatively.

In his essay, *What is Christian Civilization?*, Baillie was using the term descriptively. He was using it with reference to an area of human life and achievement which was in some recognizable sense Christian. He was applying it to the standards acknowledged in our contemporary society, acknowledged if not always or even frequently observed, in a society which historically had received them from, or at any rate had produced them under the influence of, Christianity. Admittedly Baillie had in mind, not the actual behaviour of people, not their normal practice in the surrounding society, but the standards, the norms which they acknowledged; and he was saying that these standards were in some sense Christian, they were derived from Christianity, in his own words, they were 'norms of conduct which Christianity introduced into the world'. That is to say, he was dealing with empirical Christianity, with what passes for Christianity in our time, and accordingly his use of the word 'Christian' in this connection was a descriptive use. Moreover, it was precisely because he was using the word in this way that he could justifiably speak of a conscience and of professed moral standards as Christian although admittedly they had been divorced completely from Christian faith and Christian truth.

On the other hand, when we use the word 'Christian' normatively and apply it in this sense to actions or to standards we do not have in mind what passes empirically for Christianity, we mean rather what *ought* to pass for Christianity; and when we use the word in this way it is very doubtful whether we may speak of a conscience or of behaviour as Christian which has lost touch with Christian truth. Could there possibly be a way of life or a system of practical principles which was irreligious, which was compatible with any religious outlook or no religious outlook at all, and which yet deserved to be called a Christian way of life or a system of Christian practical principles? The supposition seems manifestly absurd, and I find that Professor Kraemer has admirably expressed the point I have in mind. 'The Christian ethic', he says,[5] 'is radically religious and theocentric and Christocentric.' 'The neglect of this dominant point', he says,[6] '. . . has resulted in the production of many ethics, which are specimens of a philosophy of cultural life, shot through with stronger or weaker Christian threads. In these cases other ethical systems, all fundamentally anthropocentric and not theo- and Christocentric, were the points of orientation, while the Christian ethic only contributed elements, a procedure which resulted in an adjustment of the Christian ethic to other ethics.' 'The Christian ethic', he maintains,[7] 'is . . . never abstract; it is never the application of abstract principles belonging to a moral order, of which God is the Custodian and Maintainer, but the concrete doing of the will of the living, ever-active God.'

If all this is sound it is an error, and no small error, to put our Christian dogmatics and our Christian ethics into separate and watertight compartments. Doubtless it is necessary to distinguish between them for the sake of orderly and systematic study, but that does not imply that in content dogmatics and ethics may ever fall apart. We simply cannot have the fruits of the Spirit without the gift of the Spirit. We cannot have the works without the faith of which they are the works; and if none the less the works become separate and self-contained they cease to be the works of this faith.

Just as the Christian faith is not merely an intellectual system of propositions which have no immediate connection with life, so the Christian life cannot be understood apart from the faith by which it lives. A faith which cannot be lived is not the Christian faith. As D. M. Baillie put it with regard to the Incarnation, 'if we try to isolate absolutely the mystery of the Incarnation, failing to connect it with the all-round paradox of our Christian faith and experience, we shall end by having on our hands a mystery which is not a *religious* mystery at all and has no bearing upon our actual religious life'.[8] Similarly, a life which does not above all other things express the Christian faith is not the Christian life. It may, as Kraemer admits, be a life, and behind the life a system of practical principles, which historically and empirically owes this item and that one to historical and empirical Christianity; but none the less the life and the system are not specifically Christian if the governing, organizing and unifying principle is not, in fact, the Christian faith. If, however, whatever else it is, the Christian life is essentially a life of faith, then Christian ethics can never properly be divorced from Christian dogmatics, and the separation between them is no more than a methodological device for the sake of orderly and systematic study.

This seems a sound and incontrovertible principle, and one so important that it ought to be stated at as early a point as possible in the discussion. None the less it has not always been accepted, and in fact it is only in comparatively recent times that it has gained serious and substantial recognition. As we have allowed, the word 'Christian' can indeed be applied to human behaviour and standards of conduct, considered in separation from Christian faith and truth; but then the word is being used descriptively, and, although this is a perfectly legitimate use in certain contexts, it is not legitimate in a discussion of Christian ethics, for the proper concern of such discussion is not with what passes for Christian behaviour and Christian standards, but with what ought so to pass. Quite explicitly Christian ethics is concerned with the normative use of the word 'Christian'. It sets itself the task of giving a systematic account of the life that Christians ought to live, of the claim that God in Christ makes upon them; and it is not immediately and directly concerned with this life and this claim as they are refracted, watered down and compromised in the actual historical life of this society and century or that. And yet to some extent earlier thought has failed to rise to the clear and explicit enunciation of this principle. This is not to say that hitherto the necessary connection between dogmatics and ethics has always been denied. Sometimes indeed it has; but at other times, and within theological outlooks not disposed to make this denial, it has too often been overlaid, minimized in one way or another, and obscured. Nor does it simply mean that in earlier ages a clear distinction was lacking between a normative ethical discussion and a purely descriptive one, for although that may be largely true no great harm was done because of it. In fact the normative use of ethical terms came much more readily to men's lips and their merely descriptive use was a much more recent achievement.

The basic handicap was rather a failure to apprehend the fundamental problem of Christian ethics, a failure to appreciate its fundamentally problematical character; and this in turn was due to the fact that for so long Christian ethical discussion took place in the shadow and the shelter of one *de facto* authority or another, the Church or Scripture, which was simply there, unquestioned and so unvindicated. The truth is, however, that neither the Church nor Scripture introduced moral terms into human language. Men are moral beings apart from Church and Scripture, and when Christian thought takes the form of Christian ethics it does not lead men into an entirely new country where a quite different language has to be learned, it does not land them on the moon but enters a field already occupied. The Christian is certainly in some sense a new creature, but that clearly means, not another species altogether, but a creature, a man transformed or renewed, whose transformation and renewal cannot be articulated apart from some understanding of his existence as a creature independently of that renewal. No more then can the ethical side of that transformation be understood apart from some comprehension of the human condition which is the subject of renewal. In other words Christian ethics cannot get under way in any adequate and fundamental fashion unless it comes to terms with, and relates itself to, natural man's understanding of his own moral existence, his own existence as a man.

It will not do at this point to rely exclusively upon the characteristically picturesque language of Karl Barth when, recognizing the original inhabitants of the land which theological ethics enters, he declared that annexation was the only correct policy and that 'there must be no armistice with the peoples of Canaan and their culture and their cultus'.[9] Indeed it is to be noted that, whether paradoxically or not and whether consistently or not, Barth on the same page did say that 'theological ethics can and must estab-

lish a continuous relationship of its thinking and speaking with
the human ethical problem as a whole'. This by itself may not be
satisfactory, but at least the problem is in sight; and the immediate point is that, so long as the Christian ethical discussion proceeded on the basis of a *de facto* authority, whether Church or
Scripture, the original inhabitants were not even recognized and
the problem they created not even grasped.

Too often in the past, even when the word 'Christian' was
being used normatively, one or another of several things has
happened. For one thing, sometimes the ethical side of Christianity has not received adequate consideration at all and its treatment has been dispersed and dissipated throughout the discussion
of the Christian faith and has therefore remained incidental and
unsystematic. Sometimes, again, a considerable and concentrated
attention has been paid to the ethical aspect of the Christian
religion but without yielding a systematic treatment worthy to
be called Christian ethics, and this because the predominating
concern has been with specific ethical or practical problems, or
with particular Christian virtues and duties, and consequently the
treatment has been very largely of an *ad hoc* character, providing
what has sometimes been called a 'situational' ethics. In this
category might be placed the rules for Christian living enumerated
by Basil of Caesarea in the fourth century and rather inappropri-
ately described by him as the principles of ethics, and the more
extensive treatment offered by Bishop Ambrose of Milan under
the title *De Officiis Ministrorum*. Also to be placed in this class,
however, is what may fairly claim to be the great successor of
such pioneer endeavours, namely, the entire enterprise of moral
theology, both as it developed and continued on Catholic soil
and as it was transplanted and cultivated on Protestant soil, which
characteristically understood the Christian life in a directly *ecclesiastical* rather than *theological* context. Indeed moral theology developed as the Church attempted to save its members from sin and
to regulate its administration of the sacrament of penance; and
accordingly by the nature of the case moral theology is distinguished from Christian ethics because it is bound to posit and
presuppose the *de facto* authority of the Church.

Alongside these and in the same class must be seen the more
radically Protestant view which seeks to understand the Christian

life in a severely Scriptural context as distinct from an ecclesiastical or a theological one, finding the rule of life for the Christian man in the explicit precepts of holy writ. Yet for two reasons it will be desirable to treat this view as providing one of the main types of specifically Christian ethical outlook. This is so because, for one thing, this view can readily be understood as an explicitly theological kind of ethical system through the identification of Scripture as such with the revelation of God, and because, further, it appeared historically as one strand in what was potentially a much more profound outlook, both theological and ethical, being as it were the fundamentalist strain in Calvin's thought in particular and in Reformed teaching in general.

There is indeed some truth in the verdict of A. B. D. Alexander that 'as a separate branch of study Christian Ethics dates only from the Reformation. It was natural', he added,[10] 'and perhaps inevitable that the first efforts of the Church should be occupied with the formation and elaboration of dogma. With a few notable exceptions . . . the Church fathers and schoolmen paid but scanty attention to the ethical side of religion.' It was not simply, however, preoccupation with other matters which prevented the earlier appearance of Christian ethics, for a systematic treatment of the subject worthy of the name required not just an orderly discussion of the various topics but also an apprehension of the basic problem of Christian ethics or of the problematical character of Christian ethics as a whole, and this was not forthcoming.

Prior to the Reformation the Church did indeed produce two very notable approximations to Christian ethics, from the pens of St Augustine and St Thomas Aquinas; but in neither does the problematical character of Christian ethics come clearly into view. On the contrary, both proceeded on their respective ways without any apparent awareness of the questionable nature of what they were doing. None the less what they were doing might have suggested the problem and the need for a less simple, a more profound solution to it; and accordingly the developed Catholic view, as Barth has said, 'merits the closest attention'[11] and provides 'a very imposing, indeed in its way a classical, attempt at a solution'.[12] On the one hand, St Augustine simply *superimposed* or superimpressed his Christian insight upon the ethical outlook of Platonism, identifying virtue with 'the perfect love of God' and holding that the virtues recognized by Platonism were varying forms of this essential virtue. For St Augustine 'the happiness which is the aim of human endeavour consists', says John Burnaby in his distinguished study of St Augustine's thought, *Amor Dei*, '. . . in a relation of knowledge and love which binds the soul to the one immutable Reality';[13] and he is quite emphatic about the strong Platonic influence which lay behind this identification of the Good and behind St Augustine's other-worldliness which was but the other side of the same coin. 'No Christian Father is more uncompromising', he says,[14] 'in his other-worldliness than is Augustine. But his other-worldliness is not a piece of traditional homiletic: it can only be appreciated in its intimate connection with his Platonic metaphysic.'

On the other hand, St Thomas Aquinas, following the analytic philosophy of Aristotle rather than the synthetic philosophy of Plato, looked for a unity of mere aggregation, and consequently, instead of superimposing his Christian insight upon the ethical outlook of Greek philosophy, he was content to *juxtapose* the two, setting the virtues and moral rules of the one alongside those of the other. But, whether by assimilation (St Augustine) or by bare addition (St Thomas Aquinas), the fundamental problem of Christian ethics, in all its problematical character, is obscured and Christian ethics on a properly conceived foundation, as a thoroughly integrated and single-minded discipline, fails to appear.

The birth of Christian ethics, however, does come nearer with the Reformation and especially with the work of Martin Luther and John Calvin. It is true that in Calvin especially there was a streak of fundamentalism which when separated off yielded an ill-grounded conception of the Christian life; but this was by no means the whole of Calvin's ethical thought. In his *Institutes*, for example, he devoted several chapters of Book II and, later on, several chapters of Book III to practical matters of Christian life, and in the second of these sections especially he provided a treatise within a treatise of which the subject was Christian ethics. Here he expounded God's law as one of self-denial which, he said,[15] 'relates partly to men, but partly, and indeed principally, to God', whereby a man may wholly resign 'himself to the Lord', leaving all the parts of his life to be governed by God's will and commanding even his reason 'to give place and submit to the Holy Spirit'. More important, however, even than the systematic treatment and articulation of the single theme of self-denial is the theological context in which this treatment had its place, for Calvin had already outlined a doctrine of the total depravity of natural man, he had represented faith as 'the principal work of the Holy Spirit',[16] and had insisted that 'faith can in no wise be separated from a devout disposition'.[17] He had further declared emphatically that 'it is vain to cry up righteousness without religion. This', he had said, 'is as unreasonable as to display a mutilated, decapitated body as something beautiful.' 'Whatever equity, continence, or temperance men practise among themselves is in God's sight empty and worthless.'[18] And if, apart from the self-denial of the Christian, he then repeated,[19] 'there is any semblance of virtue, it is vitiated by depraved lusting after glory' and accordingly Paul 'commands us to put off our own nature and to deny whatever our reason and will dictate'. Moreover all this Calvin was still to place within a theological environment of divine predestination. Thus, whether in an acceptable form or not, Calvin did achieve a conception of the Christian life which is thoroughly integrated with the essential affirmations of the Christian faith as he understood them.

Here then, with a considerable degree of clarity and firmness, are the outlines of a specifically, severely and purely Christian conception of the good life; but running through it all is a streak of ethical fundamentalism. Perhaps Calvin was too much involved in controversy with an infallible Church to transcend effectively the rival conception of an infallible Scripture; but whatever the reason the streak of fundamentalism is there. Moreover, so far as Calvin's representation proves to be one-sided and fails to ring quite true to the life of the Christian, that streak of fundamentalism is likely to work itself free or to become more prominent, and so to provide a much less profound conception of the Christian ethic. Further, the effort to correct this less profound and almost mechanical conception of the Christian life may well, and in fact did, produce fresh articulations of it which exhibited an increasing independence of the theological context. Here we catch sight of the main justification for stressing at an early point in the discussion the close connection between Christian ethics and Christian dogmatics, and the principal way, additional to those already noted, in which so-called Christian ethics can fail to be true to its own nature. The history of Protestant ethical thought compels this emphasis. It was on Protestant soil, we may say, that Christian ethics arose as a distinguishable and systematic discipline; but it was also on Protestant soil that it was given a degree of independence of theology in general which obscured its own true nature. This did not happen in Calvin himself, and yet it was out of the Reformed theology that the dilemma arose, either fundamentalism or liberalism.

The truth, however, lay with neither; and the debate has been carried further in the nineteenth century by Schleiermacher and by certain of the followers of Ritschl, and has come to a climax in the quite remarkable contributions of the twentieth century, in the work of Karl Barth, Emil Brunner, Anders Nygren, Reinhold Niebuhr and others. In these contributions the range of possibilities has been narrowed and attention has been more closely concentrated on a specifically Christian ethic; but in them, as we shall see, there has emerged another dilemma, narrower and, one might say, more Christian than that which derived from the Reformation, but none the less sharp.

### (b) Past forms of Christian ethical thought

This development has taken time, and it is not possible to understand it adequately without recognizing the various phases through which the process has gone, even if some of the positions which it has thrown up no longer speak effectively and significantly to the contemporary world. Within Protestantism (1) perhaps the earliest type of treatment which morality received involved the collection and systematic presentation of the practical injunctions and exhortations to be found in Scripture. This is the kind of thing that even Calvin appears to have had in mind when he said that 'It will be useful to collect from various places of Scripture a rule for the reformation of the life, that they who cordially repent may not be bewildered in their pursuits'. This task Calvin deemed not impossible but indeed necessary, for, he said, 'as the philosophers have certain principles of rectitude and honour, whence they deduce particular duties and the whole

THE GROUNDWORK OF CHRISTIAN ETHICS

circle of virtues; so the Scripture is not without its order in this respect, but maintains an economy superlatively beautiful, and far more certain, than all the systems of the philosophers', although, as he at once admitted, 'the Spirit, whose teaching is void of affectation, has not so exactly or perpetually observed a methodical plan; which nevertheless, by using it in some places, he sufficiently indicates ought not to be neglected by us'.[20]

Thus the design of a systematic ethics is defended; but the method invoked, that of collecting from Scripture and of presenting systematically the various practical injunctions and exhortations contained in Scripture, clearly carries with it certain definite presuppositions of a fundamentalist nature, in particular that Scripture itself is uniformly the word of God and is without qualification to be identified with his self-revelation. Thus, not only is this view of the Christian life itself superficial and even mechanical, but it is tied to a whole fundamentalist theology which is no more profound. On the other hand, it does answer in some measure to the reality of the Christian life, it has served the Christian community at certain stages of its development, and it falls therefore to be noted as one historically important conception in the field of Christian ethical thought. Into the bargain, in Calvin himself, as his discussion of self-denial amply shows, it was always on the point of breaking out into an understanding much more profound, and so it acted as a pointer in that direction.

(2) The second main approach which has appeared on Protestant soil is to be found in the entire enterprise which is known as philosophical or natural ethics, the discussion of morality on the basis not of revelation at all but of reason and conscience, the discussion of morality in complete divorce from the beliefs and dogmas of religious faith, as we find it in such diverse thinkers as John Stuart Mill and Immanuel Kant, James Martineau, Henry Sidgwick and Hastings Rashdall. It may seem that since morality is here discussed in total independence of religion the investigation cannot be of immediate interest to the student of theology and ought not to find a place in an essay on Christian ethics; but there are certain considerations which militate decisively against any such assumption.

For one thing, for the Christian mind religion has the most intimate possible connection with morality; and if the teaching of Scripture is not reducible without remainder to *moral* teaching it has none the less an all-pervasive moral quality. An amoral interpretation of Christianity would *ipso facto* be a misinterpretation and certainly unbiblical. In the Bible the moral and transmoral are inextricably intertwined. The evidence for this is to be found on almost every page of the Bible, and it rises to an impressive height when St John declares that 'this is the work of God, that ye believe on him whom he hath sent', and when St Luke suggests that Christ 'ought . . . to have suffered these things, and to enter into his glory'.[21] In this moral dimension of Scriptural teaching which pervades, while it does not exhaust, that teaching, is to be seen the justification for explicitly theological affirmations of the close and intimate connection between morality and religion; and even if, as Barth suggested, Ritschl introduced a journalistic note into theology, it remains highly unlikely that morality, which to some reductionist minds is the final refuge of the religious outlook, has no central place in the total picture painted by a more accurate and adequate brush.

Thus John Baillie held that 'religious knowledge has the distinguishing mark of always being relevant to our *ultimate* ends of desire and action. And that', he said, 'is the same as to say that it is relevant to our *ethical* ends, and that no knowledge or belief can be regarded as authentically religious in character unless it possesses this ethical relevance.'[22] Similarly, H. R. Mackintosh firmly declared that 'there will always be metaphysic in theology, but it is the implicit metaphysic of faith, moving ever within the sphere of conscience'.[23] If, however, there is this close connection between morality and religion the study of theology may never be indifferent to the study of morality. The student of theology may not simply turn his back upon the thesis that morality is wholly self-contained and its proper doctrine totally independent. Such a thesis impinges directly upon the theologian's understanding of the Christian religion, and it matters much to him whether in fact the thesis is true or false. Unless indeed, either explicitly or unwittingly, he takes it that ordinary morality and Christian morality are two wholly separate and independent things; but that is to reckon seriously with neither, for morality is one and self-consistent or else it is not morality, and there is a finality about the insight that I ought which *in the last resort* brooks no plurality of claims.

In the second place, and perhaps even more important in the present connection, the moralists themselves do not regard their work as properly a matter of indifference to theology. They make certain claims which the theologian for his part may regard as intolerably pretentious but of which plainly he ought to take account. Kant, for example, thought that morality provided the gateway to religion; while John Stuart Mill believed that his ethical theory had caught the very essence of Christianity. 'In the golden rule of Jesus of Nazareth', he said,[24] 'we read the complete spirit of the ethics of utility.' It is interesting to note too that Mill believed that 'others besides utilitarians have been of opinion that the Christian revelation was intended, and is fitted, to inform the hearts and minds of mankind with a spirit which should enable them to find for themselves what is right, and incline them to do it when found, rather than to tell them, except in a very general way, what it is; and that we need a doctrine of ethics, carefully followed out, to *interpret* to us the will of God'.[25]

It is of course possible for a philosopher to study morality while believing that every theistic view, including the Christian view, is quite mistaken; but this belief concerning the truth or falsity of theism is clearly another matter, and it is plain that many moralists would accept the outlook indicated in the statement which I have quoted from Mill. They would agree in other words that what Mill calls 'a doctrine of ethics' is a self-contained and independent topic to be investigated solely in its own light, and in its finished form to be handed over to, and presumably to be accepted by, the student of religion and theology. This conception of the relationship between morality and religion and of the relationship between ethics and theology may not of course be sound; but whether it is sound or unsound it is plainly not irrelevant to the study of theology. Indeed, on the face of it, there is considerable point in the criticism of certain theological systems that they run counter to what as ordinary moral beings we are bound to believe and must therefore, as one writer has put it,[26] 'stand discredited at the bar of ethics'. In the last resort it may not be true that ethics here has the last word, but the suggestion that it has is one that theology would do well to note. In the end theology may have to dismiss the suggestion for reasons that are in part dogmatic; but to dismiss for dogmatic reasons is one thing and to dismiss dogmatically without any reasons is quite another.

The third position to be found amongst the various systematic and extensive treatments of morality which have flourished on Protestant soil is in some ways not very different from the one just mentioned which accords to the study of morality an absolute, ultimate and complete independence; but it is not inappropriate to indicate it in passing and to assign to it a place of its own. This is so because, while the earlier position is based upon a self-contained understanding of morality, the other properly stems from a particular interpretation of religion and, especially, of Christianity, and moves not from morality to religion but from religion to morality. Bishop Butler gave noteworthy expression to it in the eighteenth century when he declared in his *Analogy of Religion* that Christianity is a republication of natural religion; and Bishop Herbert Hensley Henson echoed the moral side of this theory when he argued in his Gifford Lectures at St Andrews, published under the title *Christian Morality* in 1936, that 'Christian morality is, in unique and plenary sense, natural, the expression of natural theology'.[27]

The suggestion is that morality can be studied by itself, that it is best studied in the form of Christian morality for Christian morality *is* morality at its completely natural and at its best, and that Christian morality is most clearly seen in the teaching and example of Jesus of Nazareth. In a way this view resembles the first one because it insists on bringing Christianity into the picture, although it differs in that it concentrates attention, not on the words of Scripture as such, but on the teaching and example of Jesus. More significantly it is similar to the second view for it believes that in that example and teaching is to be seen *natural* morality at its most sublime, and yet, because it is natural, it can be examined in abstraction from any detailed theological context. Bishop Henson, moreover, was able to quote from John Stuart Mill's *Three Essays on Religion* to the effect that the teaching and example of Jesus are such that even an unbeliever would be hard put to it 'to find a better translation of the rule of virtue from the abstract into the concrete than to endeavour so to live that Christ would approve our lives'.[28]

Such a view may readily expose itself to theological criticism. It may run foul of the theological contention that, even on the moral side of his being, it does not take a sufficiently high view of Jesus, and that in order to do so it would require to take account of the whole Christ, the moral and also the trans-moral and theological. Our concern at the moment, however, is not to criticize, it is rather to grasp, to distinguish, and so more fully to understand. Further, if it is thought that this theory does not demand serious attention, since either morality is natural and then no figure such as Jesus can be given a unique and final position in relation to it, or else Jesus has a unique and final position in the moral life and so Christian morality is not really natural in Bishop Henson's sense at all, it ought to be borne in mind that Henson himself believed that the account he had given did leave room for the finality of Jesus. 'Natural morality', he said,[29] 'can never become obsolete, for obsoleteness would prove that it is not genuinely natural.' Further, he held, 'the authority of Jesus is final because it is limited to the sphere of personal morality'. 'He is not the Universal Teacher bringing all knowledge within the reach of His disciples, but He is the Ideal Man, in whom all men can see the true version of their own manhood.'[30] Theologically this may not prove a very stable position, and its implications, when followed out, may well lead to its rejection; but many have found in it or in something like it an adequate and effective account of the Christian life.

(4) The last of the four main types of roughly Protestant position is one of which three things can be said. In the first place, it does not make the clear-cut and absolute division between ethics and dogmatics characteristic of the second and third positions to which reference has already been made. Secondly, however, it does not, like the first position mentioned, simply unite ethics and dogmatics in what is mainly a purely formal manner, as having the same source in Scripture. And yet, in the third place, it too can be accused of assigning to Christian ethics an undue independence. It is a position which has had a fairly continuous history from the time of Schleiermacher. It affirms in principle

the necessary connection between dogmatics and ethics if the ethics is to be specifically Christian; but it tends to maintain this connection, not just formally, but none the less statically. That is to say, it takes over certain *ideas* from the Christian faith and from Christian dogmatics, and then in the field of Christian ethics it tends to immobilize the revelation upon which it professes to depend.

Thus A. B. D. Alexander said of dogmatics and ethics that 'though it is convenient to regard these separately they really form a whole, and are but two aspects of one subject'.[31] 'Dogmatic theology', he said,[32] 'when divorced from practical interest is in danger of becoming mere pedantry; and ethical inquiry, if it has no dogmatic basis, loses scientific value and sinks into a mere enumeration of duties.' On the other hand, Alexander also maintained that Christian ethics – this Christian ethics which forms a single whole with dogmatics – 'Christian Ethics is a branch of general Ethics'; and this suggests that, so far as ethics is concerned, all that Christianity contributes is additional content and further material, in much the same way as, according to one interpretation, in early Eastern theology Christianity was regarded as simply providing new material for the general philosophical enterprise to assimilate. If Christian ethics is held to be but a branch of general ethics, the implication seems to be that Christian ethics *is* general or philosophical ethics coming to grips with some new material of a Christian origin, which in being placed at the disposal of general ethics in this way is immobilized. Thus Alexander spoke of 'the doctrinal postulates or assumptions with which Ethics starts', and held that, amongst other things, 'Ethics assumes the Christian *idea of God*'.[33] It is difficult, however, to believe that in Christian ethics justice can be done to the Christian life if God is represented, not as a living reality in whom men live and move and have their being, but as a doctrinal postulate or assumption, as a necessary presupposition, as in one way or another *an idea*.

Theodor Haering too maintained, regarding dogmatics and ethics, that 'on external grounds of convenience they are separately treated but they form one whole';[34] and yet Alexander regarded Haering as one of several who 'accentuate the difference'[35] between the two disciplines. Another writer from the same period, Newman Smyth, held that 'Christian Ethics natur-ally follows Christian theology',[36] but that 'whatever postulates Christian Ethics may borrow from Christian theology it must bring these to its own moral tests and judgments'.[37] If, however, on a wide scale the dogmatic contribution to Christian ethics is represented in the form of postulates or ideas, it is necessary to acknowledge this fourth main approach to the subject, which is then distinguished by the fact that it recognizes the necessary connection between dogmatics and ethics but it combines this recognition with the assertion of a relative independence of the latter which has the effect of immobilizing or fossilizing the insights drawn from the former.

Christian ethics, it is clear, is a complex subject which manifests very different methods of approach. Four main types of treatment have been singled out; and it is to be noticed that they have been distinguished in respect of their representation of the *form* of the Christian life rather than of its *content*. A classification on the basis of content is certainly possible; and on that basis it might be necessary to distinguish theories which understand the Christian ethic as primarily an individualistic ethic, those which understand it primarily as a social ethic, as when Haering uses 'the term "Kingdom of God" for the highest good of Christian Ethics',[38] and again these theories which seek to transcend this division between the individual and society in some, perhaps more abstract, but more comprehensive concept, as in Alexander's concentration upon *life* and his definition of salvation as 'nothing else than the restoration, preservation, and exaltation of life'.[39] These differ-ences are not by any means unimportant, and a complete discus-sion of Christian ethics would certainly have to take account of them; but even so the investigation of the formal side has its own significance and discloses questions which are quite fundamental for a correct understanding of the Christian life.

Indeed it is primarily on the formal side that the various Pro-testant versions of morality come into clearest conflict with the understanding that prevails in Roman Catholicism. Whatever the rational ethical theory which lies behind that understanding and may be held in some measure to justify it, and however important that theory is in its own place, this understanding necessarily assigns a central and supreme place to the *de facto* authority of the

Church. Accordingly it is difficult to see how, in keeping with the place thus given to the Church, the Christian life can be understood within Roman Catholicism as other than essentially a life of obedience to the Catholic Church, regarded as the vicar of Christ. Roman Catholic writers do not hesitate to speak not only of 'the natural standard of ethics' but also of the 'Christian revelation' and, *as of no less weight*, of the 'positive law of the Church'. There is still point therefore in Haering's contention that 'if we seek out comprehensive phrases we may say that the moral action of the Roman Catholic is legalistic and that it is not independent and so, of course, it is also fragmentary and external'.[40] It ought, however, to be added that such strictures should not exclude the possibility that in reality the action of the Roman Catholic may very well belie the theory, and it is the theory or the conception which is in question. Moreover, the source of this conception is to be found in the understanding of the Christian salvation. 'It is not', says Haering, 'personal communion with a personal God . . . but the impartation of heavenly powers, a participation in the ineffable mystery of the divine life.' And 'such a content', he adds,[41] 'can only find its point of contact with the will in the form of an outward law . . . and the further claim is that the same Church which has the control of the means of grace has the regulation of all moral endeavour.'

No doubt in modern Catholicism strenuous efforts are being made to transcend the reality of the past of which such critical comments may be valid; but there is a point which seems to resist and withstand all such efforts to transcend and that is the point at which there is combined a rational theory and the recognition of a visible, *de facto* and inviolable authority.[42]

Accordingly for Roman Catholicism, so long as it remains in continuity with its historic past, the good life is at root a life of obedience to the visible Church; but for the various trends and tendencies which have arisen outside, this is not so. In one form the good life appears as a life of obedience, not to the visible Church, but to the word and letter of holy writ; in another it appears as essentially a life lived by the light of man's moral understanding, his moral consciousness. In still a third it is a life lived according to the pattern of the teaching and example of Jesus; while in the fourth it is a life lived in terms of the theological framework of all human existence, with due regard for the fundamental *ideas* of the Christian revelation. The alternative to Roman Catholicism is not simple, nor is it single. The Christian moralist is confronted by several possibilities, and yet it may appear in the end that no one of these is entirely satisfactory.

## Chapter 2

# ETHICS AND NATURAL MORALITY

### (a) The unique character of the moral consciousness

One of the distinctive marks of human life is what is called the
moral consciousness, that is to say, the awareness of falling under
a certain judgment or a certain standard, of being the appropriate
subject of certain peculiar distinctions which we all recognize
even if we might be hard put to it to give a rational account of
them, the moral distinctions. We share with the brute creation
the fact that we as much as the animals can be accounted either
short or tall, light or heavy, strong or weak, and so on. We, like
them, are subject to physical distinctions; but we and not they
can be adjudged good or bad in a moral sense, and our actions
right or wrong. It is not even indisputably clear that reason is
confined to human beings, but so far as we can see it is only
human beings who are aware of moral distinctions and who
therefore possess a moral consciousness. Human beings may not
all be aware of these distinctions with the same degree of acute-
ness, nor are they by any means all agreed on the incidence of
these distinctions, on what actions, for example, are right and
what wrong. There are differences of moral code, and even
within the same moral code different people hear its demands
with a greater or less degree of clarity and urgency; but neither
of these differences upsets or challenges the fact that all normal
human beings possess as one of their distinctive marks a moral
conscience.

Moreover, although in Scripture the place of the moral consciousness is to a large extent occupied by the law given to the
Jews, a principal task of the great prophets of Israel was to
secure a genuinely moral interpretation of the law and the rejection of any undue nationalist exclusiveness and pride, in other
words, to affirm the law indeed but to affirm it within the moral
order of all mankind. St Paul too in his day could speak of the
law written in the hearts of the Gentiles, of their conscience and

31

of their thoughts, as accusing or excusing them. Jesus himself could conduct what are plainly moral arguments and controversies with the people whom he encountered, as when he declared, 'If ye then, being evil, know how to give good gifts unto your children . . .'[1] – an argument which clearly hinges on the duties of parents to their children. Indeed it is not too much to say that Scripture as a whole treats men throughout as moral beings, so that Karl Barth was not only wrong-headed but unbiblical when he allowed himself in his Gifford Lectures to classify morality with chance as an arbitrary factor in human life.[2] Whatever changes the Christian religion may work in the moral outlook of men, and however radical these changes may be, morality, it would plainly seem, is not the product but the indispensable presupposition of the Christian revelation and the Christian gospel.

Accordingly, Christian ethics cannot afford to ignore morality, nor the general ethics which has the task of investigating it. Indeed at a later stage careful consideration will have to be given to the question of the relationship between general ethics and Christian ethics; but in the first instance some account must be taken of natural morality itself, partly because, as we have seen, some moralists have maintained that morality, when it is examined, turns out to be a self-contained phenomenon to be studied in its own light, and that, while presumably religion and theology are free to accept, and perhaps to add to, the findings of ethics, they may not alter them; but partly also because, unless the intolerable doctrine is to be entertained that there are two entirely independent moralities, there must be some common ground between natural morality and Christian morality.

The suggestion of a plurality of moralities *is* intolerable because, if we understand the uniqueness of the moral claim in its character as absolutely categorical and categorically absolute, that is, as brooking no argument and so no alternative, we can see that it would not be the peculiar claim that it is if it were not single and self-consistent. There may be several equally legitimate ways of going from St Andrews to Edinburgh *if* I wish to go there; but when I am confronted by the moral demand, the categorical rather than the hypothetical imperative, by 'thou shalt' or by 'I ought', there is *in some sense* only one road I may properly travel. This peculiarity is one aspect of the uniqueness of the moral, and it underlines the fact that, while morality presupposes freedom, it constitutes a limitation of freedom by indicating and commanding one use of freedom in contrast to all others.

The trouble is <u>this moral claim reveals itself in all sorts</u> of <u>different ways</u> and we express it in a great variety of moral judgments which do not at once exhibit their single self-consistent character as moral judgments. None the less, as I have just said, if they are moral judgments the claim which they express is bound to be, in the last resort, a single self-consistent claim. The aim of ethics then is to reduce to order and system the different judgments which the ordinary moral consciousness is accustomed to make. This task is by no means an easy one since there are on the face of it so many different kinds of moral judgment, as, for instance, the judgments that this act is right and that one wrong, that a certain man ought to behave in a certain way in a certain situation, and that it is his duty to do so, that a certain state of affairs is good in contrast to another which is bad, and that a certain individual is a virtuous person and a man of upright character. These are only a few of the moral judgments that we regularly make, and yet even they reveal a remarkable variety of moral epithet. 'Right', 'wrong', 'good', 'bad', 'virtuous', 'vicious', 'dutiful', 'obligatory', 'upright' – there is an embarrassing wealth of moral terms, and it is difficult to see how they are to be reduced to order and system and put in their proper relationship one to another, since, although they all point to the same sphere, they are not simply synonymous.

On the other hand, to acquiesce in sheer diversification is virtually to accept the disintegration of morality. In the past many moralists have shirked the complete ethical task and have been content either to treat the various moral terms as if they were synonymous or else to ignore a large proportion of moral judgments (which are, however, in their entirety the moralist's preliminary data). The result has been that, attending to what is no more than a part of the field, such moralists have constructed what was bound to be a partial or one-sided ethical theory, though offering it doubtless as if it were the whole and final truth. At the very end of the seventeenth century, for example, the Earl of Shaftesbury wrote a lengthy treatise on the subject in which he concerned himself with virtues and vices, that is to say, with the components of good character and bad, but paid little or no attention to right actions and wrong, and left his readers to guess what should be said of them. In more recent times, however, moral philosophers have come more closely to grips with the ethical problem and have recognized more clearly the need to develop a theory which would cover the whole extent of the moral life and not merely a part of it. In consequence they have at least acquired a new sense of the magnitude of the ethical task.

It is true, however, that this problem is not quite so unmanageable as it might appear at first sight, for although the many different moral terms employed by the ordinary moral consciousness are not simply so many different words for precisely the same thing, yet there are distinct groups of more or less synonymous words amongst them and the multiplicity of terms can be reduced to three main sets, one applied to actions, another applied to motives and character, and a third applied to states of affairs. By itself this understanding of the situation does not solve the ethical problem, but it does accomplish a considerable simplification of the field which it is the task of ethics to investigate systematically. Some moralists even take a further step, maintaining that one of these three sets of moral terms is really a special case of one of the other two and should therefore be placed as a sub-set within it. In particular the suggestion is that the moral goodness which is attributed to human motives and characters is just a specially interesting and important instance of the general goodness of states of affairs, although admittedly in ordinary usage the word 'virtuous' is a synonym of 'morally good' and not of 'good' in general and would be applied to motives and characters but not to other states of affairs. Thus the wide variety of moral terms and judgments can be reduced to two fundamental groups, those which affirm that actions are right or wrong, and those which declare that states of affairs, including the characters of men and women, are good or bad.

If this is a legitimate reduction of moral judgments it involves a substantial simplification of the ethical problem. This problem is then largely concerned to set in their due relationship to each other the idea of rightness and the idea of goodness, the idea of moral rule and that of moral end. When the moral life is interpreted in terms of rightness it is conceived as essentially a life of obedience to moral rules, laws, commandments, imperatives. When it is understood in terms of goodness it is regarded as a life in which moral ends or goods are pursued, whether they be external goods such as a good state of affairs in this context or in that, a nobler order of society perhaps, or interior goods such as fine qualities of mind and spirit and a high character. And to a large extent the ethical task is to achieve a view of morality which integrates these two interpretations of it.

In the history of ethics sometimes the moral life has been understood almost exclusively in the one way, sometimes in the other. The Greeks, for example, favoured the conception of a good or an end as the central idea in any attempt to understand the moral life. Aristotle began his *Ethics* with a well-known sentence which laid it down that 'every art, and every science reduced to a teachable form, and in like manner every action and moral choice, aims, it is thought, at some good; for which reason a common and by no means a bad description of the Chief Good is "that which all things aim at".'[3] As the Greeks saw it, the moral life consisted in nothing else than the pursuit of this Chief Good, and the task of ethics was to make clear in a systematic fashion what it involved and of what it was constituted. This was the prevailing ethical conception in the ancient world of Greece as expressed by one philosopher after another.

In the course of history, however, other influences came into play, 'influences Stoic, Roman, Christian, and other, under which', as one writer has put it,[4] 'the idea of that which it is Right to do, of a Rule according to which men should direct their conduct tended to take the place of the idea of an End or form of goodness to be realised in life'. In this passage Muirhead has stressed Stoic, Roman and other influences alongside the Christian, but it would be difficult to exaggerate the importance of the Hebrew–Christian tradition in propagating the idea of the moral life as essentially one of obedience to law, to moral rule and commandment, and in so giving to the medieval and modern worlds an alternative to the Greek conception of the moral life as basically the pursuit of the Good. It requires little more than a casual acquaintance with the literature of the Old Testament to discover that amongst the Hebrews the dominant moral idea was that of law, the divine commandment, in keeping with which men were required to live their earthly lives. Through Christianity that ethical conception came to permeate European culture, so that the medieval world was debtor both to the Hebrews and to the Greeks.

No doubt different moralists may find one side of this twofold inheritance more congenial than the other and are thus tempted to ignore the latter and to provide a theory which can only be deemed one-sided. In such circumstances ethics can indeed survive, for the multiplicity of ends, or of laws, challenges the moralist to penetrate beneath the mere multiplicity and to disclose the secret, the inner meaning, of morality as it appears along this particular approach. To be content with a mere accumulation of duties, or, it may be, of goods, is simply to forego the task of ethics; but that task, one would think, cannot be complete until both moral rule and moral end are grasped together, until morality is seen as a whole and its basic terms and ideas, its fundamental types of judgment, set in their due relationship one to another. To fall short of this, to acquiesce in sheer diversification, even at this advanced stage, is still to accept, whether one likes it or not, disintegration.

## (b) St Thomas Aquinas and Immanuel Kant

One of the first thinkers to attempt to take into account both the moral end and the moral law was the outstanding intellectual figure of the medieval age, St Thomas Aquinas. In his *Summa Theologica* Aquinas is to be found treating first of all of goodness and then, later on, of law; and in this way, already in the thirteenth century, he had the wit to see something of the basic ethical problem and provided a pattern for any subsequent comprehensive ethical theory. On a rough reading, it is true, he may seem to leave the impression that although the two basic ideas of morality have both found a place in his system of thought, they have simply been set down side by side and have not been brought into effective relationship one to another. Certainly over a wide area, so far as the discussion of morality is concerned,

St Thomas is chiefly regarded as an exponent of the theory of natural law. To acquiesce in this impression, however, is seriously to underestimate the cohesion of St Thomas's thought, for in his mind the whole range of natural law is derived from the concept of man's natural good, and that good can virtually be read off from man's nature. Thus man's sexual nature is objectively oriented towards the propagation of the race as its natural good, and, according to this way of thinking, what is law in this sphere can readily be inferred from that fact. More generally St Thomas can say that 'the precepts of the natural law are many in themselves, but are based on one common foundation'. 'This is', he continues,[5] 'the first precept of law, that good is to be done and ensued, and evil is to be avoided. All other precepts of the natural law are based upon this.'

In this way the ethical concept of law or right or duty, although it bulks very largely in the thinking of St Thomas, is ultimately subordinated to that of good, which, in turn, is contained in the very idea of man's nature. It is because this is so that Etienne Gilson is justified in saying that 'Thomist morality is unquestionably autonomous', and can maintain that for St Thomas the will remains 'master of itself' even 'when external legislation imperiously prescribes its end'.[6]

The tight cohesion of this ethical system is undeniable and it impressed itself upon succeeding generations. Yet at various points it was open to serious question. It was questionable especially whether the diversity of natural laws was validly deducible from the concept of good; and it was questionable further whether the concept of man's good was so clearly to be derived from the idea of his nature. What in any case is meant by human nature? Can we really achieve a clear and stable conception of it?

As a matter of fact when in the late seventeenth and eighteenth centuries the modern ethical debate had its beginnings in England, there lay behind it a very different view of human nature from the rather abstract one accepted by St Thomas Aquinas. Indeed the discussion largely arose in reaction against the approach of Thomas Hobbes, whose concept of man was radically opposed to the Thomistic one. For one thing it was less exalted and even cynical, for Hobbes thought that each man can do no other than seek persistently his own private ends, defined not by the objective orientation of his abstract nature but by the subjective bent of his particular desires. Hobbes even declared that 'these words of Good, Evill and Contemptible, are ever used with relation to the person that useth them, there being *nothing* simply and absolutely so'.[7] More than that, his concept of man was less abstract, more concrete, than that of St Thomas, and he saw man invariably in relation to his fellows, from the beginning in the context, if not the society, of his fellow-man. Although he spoke of laws of nature they boiled down to the prudential consideration that, since in the state of nature the life of man was necessarily 'solitary, poore, nasty, brutish, and short',[8] men ought as a matter of self-interest to create a settled society under law wherein, surrendering some of his desires, each would ensure for himself a larger measure of satisfaction than the state of nature could ever afford.

It was against this background that in the England of the eighteenth century ethical discussion revived, for if the thirteenth-century Thomas was too sanguine for a more modern age the seventeenth-century Thomas was as yet too cynical; and the subsequent debate produced not a few distinct types of ethical theory. It produced, for example, the school of sentimentalism which, however its detailed affirmations may vary from one exponent to another, holds essentially to a theory of morals which concentrates attention upon virtue and the particular virtues, upon good character and its component parts, and which accordingly suggests that the fundamental moral judgment is that which describes certain motives, and likewise certain habitual dispositions to act from certain motives, as good and virtuous and others as bad or vicious. The ethical discussion further produced the school of intellectualism or intuitionism which emphasizes the fact that for the moral consciousness certain kinds of act are right and others wrong, and which tends to understand this moral consciousness as a kind of moral reason capable of apprehending by intuition, as rationally clear and self-evident propositions, that it is wrong to appropriate someone else's goods, that it is right to keep a promise that one has made, and so on. It is as if in morals reason operates as it does in mathematics when it apprehends as axiomatic that the shortest distance between two points is a straight line. Changes in the understanding of mathematical truths may weaken the parallel or render it ambiguous; but there are still moralists who would hold that when we make moral judgments about particular acts 'it is not by deduction but by direct insight'[9] that we see them to be right or wrong.

One of the most popular schools, and perhaps in practical matters one of the most influential, has been that which attracted to itself the name of utilitarianism and which directed the main attention, not to the motives from which actions are done, not to the character of the acts themselves, but to their consequences. Sometimes the relevant consequence of acts was found exclusively in their effect upon the general happiness, sometimes it was more broadly conceived in terms of a larger goodness than happiness alone. In either case, implicitly or explicitly, the concept of right was subordinated to that of good, and one utilitarian even held, at one stage in the development of his ethical theory, that '"right" does and can mean nothing but "cause of a good result".'[10]

No doubt the characteristic tenets of these three schools of thought would reflect more or less adequately the ethical convictions of many moralists, but it would be perilous indeed to suggest that between them they account for all; and again and again questions crop up in ethics on which the discussion tends to blur the clear-cut frontiers that these schools acquire when they are abstracted from the ongoing ethical debate. Moreover, from time to time ethical theories appear which have affinities with more than one, and indeed the dominant aim of the ethical inquiry must be to hold together the truth contained in each. Obviously the moral field is a complex one which it is very difficult to comprehend in its various aspects within the compass of a single ethical theory; and it is this fact which gives such great importance to the attempt of Immanuel Kant to construct an integrated and yet comprehensive ethical theory.

Kant's contribution stands out as one of the great attempts, and perhaps even as the classical attempt, to achieve an account of morality at once adequate and complete; and, if even a brief reference to it is to be tolerably just, attention must be paid to three elements in it, namely, what Kant had to say about goodness, what he had to say about rightness or moral law, and what he conceived to be the relationship between these two factors. So far as goodness is concerned, Kant laid down one clear and emphatic principle that there is nothing whatsoever absolutely good except one thing, the good will. Everything else, including the consequences of acts upon which utilitarianism lays so much stress, if it is good at all, is so only relatively and conditionally, not absolutely. It is good for those who desire it and their desiring it makes it good. The good will on the other hand is not dependent for its goodness on being desired, it is good absolutely for all rational beings as such, in a sense it commands them whether they like it or not.

What then is the good will and how is it to be described? To this question too Kant had a clear and emphatic reply. The good will is one which does not allow itself to be moved by individual desires for this, that and the next thing, but is moved only by respect for law, for law as such, not for this law or that law, but for law in general, the form of law. To the mind of Kant it was clear that a rational being, acting rationally, would act on principle according to a law applicable to all rational beings; and it would not matter what the principle or law laid down in particular, for the important thing is that it should be a principle, a law, something *universally* valid. It is the form of law, the lawfulness of a rational act which makes it peculiarly appropriate to a rational being; and only a will which steadfastly respects law in general, the form of law, can be described, according to Kant, as an absolutely good will.

Thus Kant summed up the moral law in the imperative: Always act on that maxim which can without contradiction be made into a universal law. In this way Kant contrived to bring the idea of good and that of moral rule or law into the most intimate relationship to each other, and was able to hold that the notion of duty already 'includes that of a good will, although implying certain subjective restrictions and hindrances'.[11] To be good a will must act rationally, to act rationally is to act on principle, according to law, and the notion of duty is that of a command so to act against all the contrary solicitations of sense and desire. To act according to law is the essential characteristic of a rational will, and a rational will acting in that way must be judged good, and indeed, Kant maintained, the only unconditional and absolute good there is.

Even in its barest outline this moral theory of Immanuel Kant stands out as a notable attempt to give an integrated and com-

prehensive account of morality. In comprehensiveness it equals
and in cohesiveness it may even excel the ethics of St Thomas
Aquinas. It rules out utilitarianism as a false account of morality,
and it tries to combine the insights of sentimentalism and intuitionism. In the field of ethics it is one of the most significant
productions of the Protestant world; and there can be no doubt
that Kant in this unusually comprehensive account of morality,
positing as it did a kingdom of persons, each an end in himself,
and all acknowledging the rule of law in their conduct and in
their mutual relations, contrived to give to the modern world an
idea and an ideal which in many respects rang true to the ordinary
moral consciousness and proved itself capable of guiding the
technicalities of its thinking in one practical sphere after another.[12]

On the other hand, Kant's ethical theory does not say the last
word, and in fact two main charges have been persistently preferred against it, the charge of rigorism and the charge of formalism. Of these the former concerns itself with Kant's understanding
of the good will and the latter with his account of the moral law.
The good will, for Kant, is not moved by particular desires but
rather against them. Then, however, according to the critics, it
will not be a will for it will not be moved at all. Morality may
forbid the indulgence of single and excessive desires, but it does
not seek to abolish desire altogether; and if it does, as in Kant it
seems to do, it accomplishes only its own destruction. On the
other side, Kant's conception of the moral law, the critics have
held, is exclusively and therefore excessively formal, because in
the end it is empty and this in spite of Kant's penultimate emphasis
upon respect for persons and a kingdom of ends. To act morally,
the criticism runs, is certainly to act on principle or according to
law; but some principles and laws are moral, others are not, and
the difference between them is not just that the former do not
contradict themselves when put in the form of universal law while
the latter do.

### (c) The legitimacy of the ethical inquiry

Enough has been said to establish the ethical inquiry as a legitimate
and genuine one in which some arguments are valid and others
invalid; and, since the Christian revelation addresses men specific-

ally as moral beings, it is an inquiry of interest and concern to the Christian moralist and theologian. Emil Brunner rightly said[13] that 'in the last resort . . . moral scepticism, like all scepticism, is a flight from one's own reality and a form of self-deception'; and, if I am not mistaken, the revelation attested by Scripture, taken as a whole, holds us to our reality as moral beings and would have been decisively different from what it is if that had not been so. From these considerations alone the importance of the ethical inquiry for the tasks of the Christian moralist and the Christian theologian would seem to follow as a matter of course.

Indeed there are at least four aspects of morality with which ethics has from time to time concerned itself and regarding which the findings of the ethical inquiry would seem to be of interest and importance both to Christian ethics and to theology. The first of these is the *possibility* of morality as investigated in the ethical inquiry concerning freedom and responsibility. About this topic much has been written within the sphere of general or secular ethics, and the argument seems relevant to the work of theologians who, in elaborating their doctrine of sin, have frequently found themselves in a dilemma on this very matter, being driven now almost to deny freedom and responsibility in order to do justice to the universality of sin, now to modify that universality in order to restore a genuine responsibility which the very concept of sin seemed to posit.

Again, ethics has on occasion concerned itself with the *purity* of the moral, imperilled, it is thought, by such confusions as that contained in Bishop Butler's well-known statement that 'when we sit down in a cool hour we can neither justify to ourselves this or any other pursuit, till we are convinced that it will be for our interest, or at least not contrary to it',[14] and defended afresh by such arguments as those found in H. A. Prichard's famous article in *Mind*, 'Does Moral Philosophy Rest on a Mistake?', and in his inaugural lecture on *Duty and Interest*. This too it is exceedingly difficult to regard as properly a matter of indifference to Christian moralist and theologian, as if, contrary to the dominant teaching of Scripture, a concern for pure and undefiled religion were not also at the same time a concern for pure and undefiled morality.[15]

In the third place, ethics has again and again been concerned with the question of the *objectivity* of the moral order, and although the suggestion has been made frequently that moral distinctions are relative and subjective, the suggestion has always provoked, sooner or later, a considerable ethical controversy. Finally, as we have already noted, right at the centre of the ethical inquiry there is the question of the *coherency* and self-consistency of the moral claim, with which many of the most notable contributions to the subject have been directly engaged.

The discussion of all these matters, it would appear, is highly relevant to the work of the theologian, concerned as it is with the divine self-revelation and the divine claim upon human life, if in truth that revelation and that claim hold men fast, as I think they clearly do, to their reality as moral beings. Ethics, in taking this reality seriously in all its aspects as a fit subject of investigation, and especially in respect of the four aspects I have mentioned, is manifestly on the side of the angels – unless indeed the intolerable supposition is to be entertained that there are two quite separate, independent and absolute claims upon human life, the divine claim and the moral claim. The case for the recognition of some intimate and interior connection between these two, even if it falls short of complete and unqualified identification, and therefore the case for admitting the relevance of the ethical inquiry to theological investigation, seems to me quite overwhelming, so that only deep-seated confusion can obscure its massive strength.

To say that man is inescapably a moral being, to say with Brunner that moral scepticism is 'flight from one's own reality and a form of self-deception', is not to say that man always does his duty, nor even that he always knows beyond any shadow of doubt what it is his duty to do. It is not to say that man is a being who carries about with him as an inalienable possession a single unchanging code of conduct, nor that he always understands his own reality in the same way. On the contrary, he is an historical being whose outlook invariably, in greater or less degree, reflects the historical situation in which he lives; and moreover he is capable of almost unlimited self-deception. Yet, at the very centre of his being, he is aware of a peculiar claim; however obscured, overlaid and distorted it may be, he remains 'a man under authority', and he knows the moral meaning of 'ought' in its uniquely categorical and absolute character, even if that character comes to him through a mist, a veritable fog of inconsistencies and relativities. This claim may be understood by some men as simply the moral claim; but it does not seem possible seriously to suppose that in this ultimate sphere, at the very core of man's being, there can in fact be two quite independent claims. Yet, however it is understood, whether as simply moral or as also divine, man can no more escape from it than he can from his own reality.

## (d) The theological attack upon ethics

In view of all this it is strange indeed that in his important work on Christian ethics, *The Divine Imperative*, Emil Brunner allowed himself to make certain strictures upon general ethics which were intended to bring the whole ethical inquiry under judgment from the point of view of Christian faith. Strange or not, however, the attack was a serious and sustained one; and because it articulates a negative attitude toward general ethics that is widespread in Protestant thought it demands very careful consideration.

Having agreed that 'the moral precedes every kind of ethic',[16] Brunner none the less went on to hold that 'Western morality is just as much determined by ethics as ethics by morality. Ethics does not merely express the self-interpretation of a period; it is also one of the outstanding forces which have shaped it'.[17] From any point of view this is a most extraordinary thesis, for although it is clear that morality determines ethics or is presupposed by it, it is by no means clear that ethics in any way determines morality. It is much more likely that changes in moral outlook and standard have their source elsewhere, almost anywhere else except ethics. If ethics on minor points, for example in the direction of a greater consistency, does effect changes in moral outlook it is because on the whole it accurately reflects, and answers to, the already existing moral climate.

Brunner, however, was prepared to go even further, for he was prepared to insist that the *aim* of philosophical ethics was 'the erection of a standard for the will and for conduct which can be established in accordance with reason'.[18] What philosophical ethics always promised was 'a rational argument for morality'.[19] 'The philosophical ethic of reason . . . has arisen out of the need

44

to give greater security to ethical thought than it possesses in its popular form.'[20] According to Brunner, therefore, the purpose of general ethics is to erect and defend a moral standard, a rational moral standard; and Brunner's whole treatment of general ethics, as an introduction to his discussion of Christian ethics, is governed by this remarkable conviction. If this fundamental contention is ignored his argument fails to make sense; and yet it is no more plausible to say that the function of ethics is to erect a moral standard than it would be to maintain that the purpose of theology is to create a religion. 'The owl of Minerva', said Hegel,[21] 'takes its flight only when the shades of night are gathering.'

As a matter of fact, apart from exceptions which prove the rule, ethics has never fulfilled the function which Brunner assigned to it, although many moralists have confused and mingled their proper task with what may well be an improper one. For they have sometimes tried, not indeed to invent and erect a moral standard, but to commend and defend the existing one. The Earl of Shaftesbury, for example, whose chief contribution to the ethics of his time was his insistence on the reality of public affections as against the thorough-going egoism of Thomas Hobbes, none the less devoted a long section of his *Enquiry Concerning Virtue* to an attempt to prove that in doing only what was in the public interest a man was promoting also his own interest. Even Bishop Butler held that 'when we sit down in a cool hour we can neither justify to ourselves this or any other pursuit, till we are convinced that it will be for our interest, or at least not contrary to it'. The occurrence of such passages, however, does not support the thesis that the overruling function of ethics is to commend an existing standard, still less that it is to contrive and impose another; and it is much more likely that H. A. Prichard was right when he argued that the appearance of such discussions within the field of ethical discourse was really due to a confusion of thought.

Indeed when moralists have in fact avoided the proper task of ethics and have sought instead simply to defend moral standards on other than moral grounds they have been guilty of an aberration which more careful thought has been able to expose. Still more, when on a rare occasion moralists have tried to disclose and erect moral standards, as Brunner held it was the function of ethics to do, and as, for example, the evolutionary moralists, Herbert Spencer and Leslie Stephen, did try to do, when they endeavoured to extract a new moral code from the evolutionary conception of life at large, they have manifestly fallen away from the main stream of ethical discussion and have failed to speak and argue ethically at all.

Accordingly there is not much to be said in favour of Brunner's contention that the aim of philosophical ethics is 'the erection of a standard for the will and for conduct which can be established in accordance with reason', and there seems to be a great deal that can be said against it. On the other hand, it must be allowed that our consideration of this matter has proceeded by inspection and analysis of ethical discussion, whereas it is possible that the real grounds for Brunner's verdict on ethics are not to be found in this way, that ethical analysis cannot even make contact with them. It may be in other words that Brunner would not have disputed anything that has so far been said about ethics and its ostensible aim and function, and that what he was really saying was that, in spite of the truth of all this so far as the appearance of the matter goes, none the less in reality the ethical inquiry is sustained by a deep-seated and hidden motive which seeks for self-dependent and self-sufficient reason, morality, man, a greater security than otherwise they possess. Along these lines, as it seems to me, there can be achieved an understanding of Brunner's point of view on this matter which is both more sympathetic and more adequate; but it is not an understanding which finally disposes of the controversy between Brunner and his critics in favour of the former. On the contrary, it raises a fresh batch of critical questions.

For one thing, if it is true that what Brunner was alleging was that, although ostensibly the ethical inquiry is not an attempt to impose, from within human reason alone, a moral standard upon men, none the less, in its underlying reality, it is an inquiry in which man seeks sinfully to assert and secure his independence over against God, the question at once arises whether Brunner's entire criticism of general ethics was not after all a vast *argumentum ad hominem* and therefore fallacious. To diagnose a man's motives, it is well known, is neither to assess nor to meet his arguments; and this distinction is valid whether the diagnosis is correct or not. Indeed, further, it may not be greatly amiss to think of

Brunner's criticism of general ethics in terms of an *argumentum ad hominem*, provided that it is unambiguously conceded that this particular *argumentum ad hominem* is not arbitrary, self-willed and vituperative, but follows objectively from certain dogmatic convictions regarding the sinfulness of natural humanity. In other words, it is because Brunner believed on dogmatic grounds that natural men are thoroughly sinful and that their sinfulness extends to all their activities, that he could describe ethics and the ethical inquiry in the way that he did. Natural man for Brunner was man in revolt against God, and in revolt in all parts of his being and so in all his activities. Consequently it seemed to Brunner that in his natural ethics man was really seeking, not an objective and adequate account of some subject-matter standing over against himself, but, first and last, above everything else, his own security in independence of God.

The matter, however, is neither as simple nor as one-sided as Brunner tended to suppose. Certainly there may be considerable truth in his contentions, so far as they take seriously the reality of sin, and consequently they cannot just be ignored. On the other hand, while in the vigorous revival of modern Protestantism, to which Brunner made his own contribution, the reality of sin has been seriously recognized, the recognition has too often been accompanied by an almost totally negative concept of sinful man, so that it becomes a question whether the humanity of man has not been destroyed by his sin. This negative concept does not answer well to the dynamic reality of man in the world nor to his multifarious activities with the variety of norms and standards by which they are governed. Into the bargain it has its own repercussions within the field of dogmatics, for if sinful man is so conceived that there is in him no point of contact for the redeeming work of divine grace then grace ceases to be grace and becomes sheer creation, and, contrary to the whole tenor of Scripture and of evangelical religion, a second book of Genesis takes the place of the Gospels.

Brunner's own position in this exceedingly complex and highly controversial matter was that, although in intention he affirmed a point of contact, he failed to give it sufficient substance to make it credible;[22] and this self-imposed dilemma reveals itself at different points in the development of Brunner's thought. So far as the verdict on natural ethics is concerned it is only the excessively negative view of sinful man which would justify the allegation that in his ethics man seeks above all else his own security in independence of God. That is to say, the verdict on general ethics is in line with Brunner's actual theological achievement rather than his theological intention. The latter might have required a more discriminating verdict and an account of ethics which represented it as fundamentally an attempt to give an adequate and objective account of moral reality, within of course whatever limitations might be imposed by natural man's rebellious outlook, an account which might certainly be the instrument of man's sinful pride, but which, like a system of mathematical truth, would not be tied to the act which produced it but might enjoy a semi-independent existence, might therefore be reviewed by others, and would always be open to assessment in respect of its validity or invalidity. It is, however, the view of ethics as exclusively or basically an attempt by man to secure his independence of God and as therefore tied to the sinful act which produces it, which permits those who hold it to take a drastic short-cut with the ethical inquiry and with ethical arguments of every description, not assessing them on their merits, not reckoning with them, but in effect simply dismissing them. And it is this course which Brunner followed.

It is true that Brunner had much more to say about the detail of ethical discussion, but his treatment was governed by the outlook and the presuppositions already described, and he did take a drastic short-cut with the debate between different types of ethical theory. In his opinion there are in the last resort in ethics only two main alternatives, naturalism on the one side and idealism on the other. Under the former head he grouped all those theories which find the principle of right conduct in happiness, in the satisfaction of desire, whether desire is regarded as always selfish or as sometimes altruistic. According to this type of theory 'the sense of obligation and the "moral laws" are abbreviated forms of the experience of humanity in respect of that which I find useful and pleasant'.[23] This theory can certainly fill the moral life with a rich content, but it has not really any room for its moral character, since, as Brunner saw it, the ultimate principle is desire and not something which checks or controls desire. In the end 'the choice before the naturalistic moralist is either to deny the existence of such a "sense of ought" or to give up his naturalism'.[24]

The principal alternative to naturalism is idealism and especially the ethical theory of Immanuel Kant, wherein the sense of obligation is wonderfully recovered, but at an immense cost, the emptying of the moral law and the moral life of all content. 'It describes the "form" of the "good will", but it cannot say what should be done.'[25] Thus, to the mind of Brunner, in seeking to erect and impose a moral standard, ethics in the long run inevitably finds itself in a dilemma, advocating either lawlessness or else obedience to law in general which is no law in particular, life without law or law without content. In the final analysis the message of general ethics is either that men should do what they like, should follow their natural desires, or else they should obey a law which commands neither this nor that but only obedience as such.

From this dilemma ethics has sought again and again to escape, and the result has been the ethics of self-realization, the ethics which finds a basis in the actual 'superindividual process of the development of Spirit', and that which rests upon what Brunner called 'substantial yet spiritual values';[26] but the precise identification of the ethical theories which Brunner had in mind at this point is less important than his conviction that in every case the attempt to escape ends in failure. As he saw it, the ethical inquiry in all its phases remains firmly and inescapably in the grasp of the dilemma, either a content for life without law or a law for life without content, either the reign of natural desire or the rule of empty law.

In this way Brunner dealt with the apparently intractable material provided by the ethical inquiry in its different stages and forced it into the neat mould he had prepared for it. Thus, he thought, he was able to sustain his thesis that in general or philosophical ethics man seeks first and last to secure his independence over against God by finding for himself a law to govern his life. The treatment thus given to ethics is open to serious criticism in itself;[27] but what is important in the present connection is the fact that Brunner was really taking a drastic short-cut with general ethics and that, within the system of his thought, the justification for it is to be found, not in ethical considerations and arguments at all, but in his underlying conviction regarding human sin and its effect, and in his consequent, excessively negative view of natural or sinful man. Unless Brunner's view of sinful man can be accepted his treatment of general ethics cannot carry any conviction but must stand condemned. It is here in their judgment of natural man that catholic and evangelical interpretations of Christianity may be said to diverge. In itself Brunner's drastic short-cut with ethics has nothing to be said for it; and its justification must be sought elsewhere in the interpretation and articulation of Christian truth and, in particular, of the doctrine of sin. On the other hand, even if made ultimately on dogmatic grounds, the rejection of philosophical ethics is so radical a step that Protestantism itself has always grown restless with it and accordingly it demands the most critical evaluation.

### (e) The attitude of Karl Barth

I have concentrated attention so far on Emil Brunner because in fact it is he more than any other neo-Protestant who took account in some detail of the general ethical discussion. Yet his final attitude to that discussion is closely matched by the attitude of the distinguished pioneer of neo-Protestantism himself, Karl Barth. In one respect after another Barth's theology has frequently been attacked on ethical grounds, and certainly he was always at pains to stand aside from the Ritschlian school of theology, which he regarded as no more than an episode in the development of theology and as introducing a journalistic note.

None the less Barth himself, it must be said, was capable of grasping the unique character of the moral with a clarity to which moral philosophers might well aspire. 'The ethical question', he wrote,[28]

is the question as to the basis and possibility of the fact that in the multitude and multiplicity of human actions there are certain modes of action, i.e., certain constants, certain laws, rules, usages or continuities. It is the question as to the rightness of these constants, the fitness of these laws. It is the question as to the value which gives any action the claim to be the true expression of a mode of action, the fulfilment of a law – the right to

be repeated and in virtue of its normative character to serve as
an example for the actions of others ... There are all sorts of
questions about modes of human behaviour, about the law and
rule and continuity of human action, which do not so far, or
any longer, have anything to do with the ethical question in
itself. ... If we try to equate the ethical question unequivocally
and consistently with the psychological, or historico-morpho-
logical, or politico-juridical, or philosophico-historical question
– to which the actuality of human behaviour may also be
subject – this means that we have not yet put to ourselves the
ethical question, or have ceased to put it. ... The ethical question transcends those other questions ... in relation to those ·
other questions the ethical question is the supremely critical
question. It is supremely critical because it questions not only
individual human actions from the standpoint of general modes
of action, but also general human modes of action from the
standpoint of the good.

On the other hand, and no less emphatically Barth maintained
that Christian ethics must adopt a thoroughly negative attitude
to the entire exploration of this supremely critical question as we
find it in general ethics. 'Man', he said,[29]

derives from the grace of God, and therefore he is exposed
from the very outset to this question. ... But ... man is not
content simply to *be* the answer to this question by the grace of
God. He wants to be like God. He wants to know of himself
(as God does) what is good and evil. He therefore wants to *give*
this answer himself and of himself. So, then, as a result and in
prolongation of the fall, we have 'ethics,' or, rather, the multifarious ethical systems, the attempted human answers to the
ethical question. But this question can be solved only as it was
originally put – by the grace of God, by the fact that this allows
man actually to *be* the answer. Revelation and the work of
God's grace are just as opposed to these attempts as they are to
sin.

Here then is precisely the same affirmation as that made by
Brunner, that the general ethical discussion is 'as a result and in
prolongation of the fall', and accordingly the whole inquiry must

by theology be set aside as a presumptuous intruder, presumptuous with the presumption and pride of sin. To this inquiry and all its answers theological ethics must simply say 'No', and if – by grace – it also says 'Yes', 'it does so by completing its own answer to the ethical problem in active refutation, conquest and destruction of all human answers to it'.[30]

It is difficult to believe, however, that this drastic short-cut with philosophical ethics is in the end defensible. For one thing, as we have seen, it commits the fallacy of *argumentum ad hominem*, and this fallacy seems no less fallacious when it takes the form of an *argumentum ad humanum*. To refuse to enter the ethical debate, to decline to undertake the task of weighing and assessing in respect of validity and adequacy the various ethical theories that have arisen, and to do this from the outset, *a priori* as it were, as an implication of a theological doctrine of sin, is surely to cast doubt upon the understanding of that doctrine.

Moreover this cavalier dismissal of general ethics leads directly to contentions which are highly questionable and ambiguous. Thus Barth maintained that man 'is exposed from the very outset' to the ethical question, and yet he also maintained that theology must say a comprehensive and unqualified 'No' to all human answers to this question, and that the true answer is to be found 'in the knowledge of Jesus Christ'[31] and nowhere else. But these are exceedingly difficult theses to hold together, and they seem to resist every attempt to integrate them into a single, self-consistent standpoint. They appear to posit, *per impossibile*, that one can be significantly said to be exposed to a certain question without any grasp whatsoever of the reality to which the question refers and which gives rise to the question, and indeed – if one bears in mind Barth's intransigently hostile attitude to the very idea of general revelation – without being exposed to that reality.

This is a thoroughly unstable position, and in fact an impossible one. Yet, it would seem, Barth was driven to embrace it as a necessary paradox because he could conceive of no third alternative to the two courses he saw confronting him in ethics, either to dismiss general ethics from the theological discussion of morality as never anything but a presumptuous intruder or else to surrender to general ethics and its general principles and to accept whatever area these principles would allow for the articulation of

Christian ethics – either an outright offensive or a tame submission. 'Theological ethics', he wrote,[32] '. . . will cease to be what it is, if it dares to free itself from this offensiveness, if it dares to submit to a general principle, to let itself be measured by it and adjusted to it.'

We may not lightly depart from Barth at this point for he was well aware of the errors of the past, the Babylonian captivity in which theology had been enthralled; but no more may we concede to him the simple, somewhat undiscriminating dilemma with which he would confront us. Suffice it to say at this stage, to admit the relevance of general ethics is not by any means to proclaim its sovereignty.

Whatever the diverse accounts which ethics may offer of it the natural morality of man is a fact and reality with which theology and, in particular, Christian ethics ought seriously to reckon. In any given expression of it there may be any number of arbitrary and relative elements, elements that are historically and socially conditioned, but running through it all there is an ineradicable sense of oughtness and some glimpse of an ideal without which human life would scarcely be human at all. As one writer has put it,

> Wanton murder, injustice, betrayal are absolutely wrong, all of us believe. The wrongness, all of us hold, does not depend on how we happen to judge such acts; it is not jeopardized by changes in customs or morality, by shifts in goals or in the nature of our chosen ultimate ends. These acts are essentially wrong, intrinsically wrong; they and wrongness together make an irreducible ethical fact which it would be folly to deny. He who does not know such facts, who does not know that peace is good, that the world is not the best possible and should be improved, that men can be guilty for crimes committed years ago, that love is better than hate, is insincere or mad. Or so we all believe, and many of us say.[33]

Human history may exhibit again and again, as it has done in the present century, atrocities greatly exceeding the evil imagination of an average man; but man himself, even the average man, is capable of condemning and disowning them in the name of his humanity. This fact, this moral reality, may not properly be ignored.

No more, one would think, may the ethics which seeks as far as may be to interpret and to understand it. It pursues what is on the face of it an entirely legitimate inquiry; and, although theology is not committed to accept uncritically all its findings, it can hardly as itself a rigorous intellectual discipline dismiss them as total error or the inquiry itself as an act of sinful rebellion, a kind of unilateral declaration of independence like that of Southern Rhodesia in 1965. In his search for truth man can, and ought to be, much more discriminating than is always possible for him in his political actions.

# Chapter 3

# THE ABDICATION OF ETHICS

## (a) Subjectivism in ethics

The development of the general ethical inquiry is by no means easy to characterize. Brunner saw in it the gradual articulation of a dilemma, either life without law or law without life and content; but the argument has something of the nature of special pleading and the analysis, divorced from its theological premiss in the doctrine of sin, is hardly convincing. Moreover, it is almost as if nothing had happened in ethics since the eighteenth century, or perhaps the nineteenth, whereas in fact the present century has already seen some new exciting ventures in ethical thought and moral theory. It is arguable, and it may even be true, that the development of ethical thinking is away from the intolerable abstractness of Greek thought in the ancient world and of the definitive medieval conception in St Thomas Aquinas, in the over-all direction of a greater concreteness and, in particular, of a more vivid awareness of the historical character of human existence, and so of the moral being. Perhaps to make this suggestion is to adopt the role of prophet as well as student, although it may be that a line can be traced from the ancient conception of the good of human nature in the abstract, through Kant's idea of the conduct appropriate to a rational being, to the sight of the human individual engaged in the concrete issues of historical existence.

There is, however, another possible interpretation, for it might be suggested that the movement towards a greater concreteness involves more fundamentally a gradual loosening of the metaphysical ties which have traditionally been assigned to morality, and even a liberation of morality from an ancient captivity. It might thus be suggested that this movement has already begun when ethical theory begins to think in terms, no longer of human nature in the abstract nor of the being of man as timelessly the same, but rather of concern for others as a normal motive of human conduct or of life in earthly society as involving a duty to

55

keep the promises one has made. It might also be suggested, however, that at this stage the movement has still a long way to go, and that in fact it is only in recent ethical thinking that it has achieved something like an ultimate clarification in the revival of what can only be regarded as ethical subjectivism.

Some such interpretation, I say, might be suggested. If it were it would have to face the fact that over important areas, whether long in time or intense in interest, the ethical debate gives little support to this view; but doubtless the main appeal would be to more recent developments. For the fact is that, whereas a generation ago moralists were fiercely divided as to whether the ultimate moral category was rule or end, right or good, but were virtually unanimous that whatever the correct resolution of this question ethical subjectivism was dead and objectivism established, in more recent times – however unlikely or indeed impossible it seemed thirty years ago – precisely ethical subjectivism has achieved a new and vigorous lease of life.

The basic issue between subjectivism and objectivism concerns the interpretation of the ordinary morality with which we are all familiar, the mass of opinions, judgments and other elements which we use the word 'morality' to indicate and of which one indispensable feature seems to be, in the broadest sense of the word, some kind of standard or standards of judgment and evaluation. Any attempt to interpret this morality is bound sooner or later to face the question: Is this underlying standard or are these underlying standards purely subjective, relative to the individual or the social group in which they are found, variable with different individuals and groups, and expressing no more than subjective likes and dislikes, subjective preferences for this rather than that? Or is there behind all the undeniable variations something objective, something independent of the moral agent, alone or in the mass, which he in his moral judgments endeavours to grasp and apply? In other words, is morality a purely human phenomenon or does it have an indefeasible trans-human reference, a reference beyond all actual men and the empirical groups to which they belong, by which both men and groups are in some sense finally judged?

## (b) The emotive theory

A generation ago, we have said, it may have been the case that those engaged in the most influential ethical debate of the time were prepared to assume that, whatever problems and points of divergence remained, at least the case against subjectivism had been established; but it is precisely this assumption that the subsequent years have proved to be mistaken. Indeed a quite radical change has come over the scene, and it is now ethical objectivism that has been seriously called in question. Subjectivism is in the ascendant and may seem to some to be sweeping everything before it. Yet there is one aspect of this situation which is worthy of note, and that is that for the most part the resurgence of subjectivism has come, not through an independent examination of morality on its own merits, but through a treatment of morality from the standpoint of an already established philosophy which has derived its distinguishing features elsewhere. If there is a hidden theological premiss behind the rejection of philosophical ethics already considered, there is very often a hidden philosophical premiss behind its abdication from any metaphysical or theological role.

Thus one of the earliest and most notable instances of this fresh approach to the subject of morality came from the philosophical school of logical positivism or radical empiricism and, in particular, in 1936, from the pen of Professor A. J. Ayer. At the risk of seeming to whip a dead horse – and one perhaps which Professor Ayer himself is no longer willing to ride – it is instructive to note some of the characteristics of the treatment this afforded to morality. In his *Language, Truth and Logic*, which made a profound impression upon the philosophical world, Ayer declared that 'it is our business to give an account of "judgments of value" which is both satisfactory in itself and consistent with our general empiricist principles',[1] and, he went on to say, 'we shall set ourselves to show that in so far as statements of value are significant, they are ordinary "scientific" statements; and that in so far as they are not scientific, they are not in the literal sense significant, but are simply expressions of emotion which can be neither true nor false'.[2]

What he had in mind here was explained a little later in the statement that 'a complex sign of the form "*x* is wrong" may constitute a sentence which expresses a moral judgment concerning a certain type of conduct, or it may constitute a sentence which states that a certain type of conduct is repugnant to the moral sense of a particular society. In the latter case, the symbol "wrong" is a descriptive ethical symbol, and the sentence in which it occurs expresses an ordinary sociological proposition; in the former case, the symbol "wrong" is a normative ethical symbol, and the sentence in which it occurs does not, we maintain, express an empirical proposition at all'.[3] In other words, if Ayer's analysis here was correct, whenever I say that lying is wrong I may mean one or other of two things. I may be saying that in a certain society, the society of which I am a member or some other society, lying is frowned upon and is not an acceptable form of behaviour; and in that case my statement will be true or false according as lying is or is not frowned upon in the society in question. So understood, however, my statement is not really a moral statement, it is not a normative 'laying down the law' kind of statement, but is instead a purely descriptive one, descriptive of one aspect of the moral outlook of a certain society. In precisely the same way the statement that the Romans worshipped many gods may be perfectly true, as a descriptive statement about Roman religion, without saying anything one way or the other about the truth of polytheism and without advocating in any degree the practice of polytheism. On the other hand, when I say that lying is wrong I may be saying something quite different. I may not be talking in a detached way about the moral outlook of this, that or any society but may be giving expression to my own moral outlook, laying down the law as it were and making a normative and genuinely moral judgment. In this case, however, according to Ayer's analysis, my statement is neither true nor false for it simply expresses my moral disapproval of a certain type of conduct.

Whatever be Professor Ayer's present view of morality, he was perfectly clear in his own mind, when he wrote *Language, Truth and Logic*, about the adequacy and validity of what is sometimes called the emotive theory of values; and indeed no one could have expressed the main point more clearly. 'If I say to someone,' he wrote,[4] '"You acted wrongly in stealing that money," I am not stating anything more than if I had simply said, "You stole that money." In adding that this action is wrong I am not making any further statement about it. I am simply evincing my moral disapproval of it. It is as if I had said, "You stole that money," in a peculiar tone of horror, or written it with the addition of some special exclamation marks. The tone, or the exclamation marks, adds nothing to the literal meaning of the sentence. It merely serves to show that the expression of it is attended by certain feelings in the speaker.'

If this emotive theory of values were true, however, it would mean that morality is a purely human and subjective phenomenon, and it would then be difficult to see how the study of it could be directly relevant to the investigation of the Christian ethic, which is bound to reflect the claim of Jesus Christ, not just to represent one code of morals rather than another, but to be nothing less than *the* way, *the* truth, *the* life. Is the emotive theory, however, the whole truth? Certainly, emotions do attach themselves to moral judgments and may even provide some measure of the personal conviction with which these judgments are sometimes made; but to admit that is one thing, and it is a very different thing to hold that such judgments, like exclamation marks, do nothing else than express emotions. If this were really the case it would be difficult to believe that morality could possibly be what to all intents and purposes it is, a recognizable and distinctive reality which is fundamentally the same in spite of all sorts of diversities and variations in its content. It may even be the case that Ayer himself had some inkling of this deficiency, for it is worth noting that he did not suggest that moral judgments are the expression simply of any kind of approval or disapproval. Rather, he maintained, they are the expression of specifically *moral* approval or disapproval, as if one were to say 'You stole that money', not in any tone of horror but in a *peculiar* tone of horror, or as if one were to add to the written statement, not ordinary exclamation marks, but, as Ayer said, 'some *special* exclamation marks'.[5] The very problem, however, is just to identify this peculiar or special or, more specifically, moral element; and the more straightforward, the less circular, explanation seems to be that moral emotions acquire their peculiar quality from the moral judgments which they accompany. But if this is so, moral judgments cannot be simply the expression of moral emotions, and to fail to see this is rather like losing sight of the baby in the soap-suds.

## (c) The prescriptive theory

It has already been said that the theoretical treatment of morality currently given is highly sensitive to changes in the climate of general philosophical opinion; and consequently it is not surprising to find reflected in ethical theory one of the more important changes in general philosophy, namely, the supersession of logical positivism by the school of linguistic analysis. It had been held by Ayer in *Language, Truth and Logic* that so far as moral statements are significant they are simply descriptive of the moral outlook of this society or of that, and that so far as they go beyond such description they merely give expression to the speaker's moral approval or disapproval and 'are not in the literal sense significant'.[6] It is, however, a characteristic of philosophers who belong to the school of linguistic analysis that they are not nearly so prone to restrict significance or meaningfulness to those statements which are either true or false. On the contrary, their special advance may well be said to lie in the recognition of many more kinds of significant statement, regarding some of which it would be quite nonsensical to ask whether they are empirically verifiable or whether they are true or false, since by the nature of the case they make no such claim.

Thus commands, expressions of emotion, exhortations and many other kinds of statement are such that the question of their truth or falsity cannot logically arise; and yet linguistic analysts are quite clear that such statements are no less significant and that the denial of their significance was always an error. Accordingly these philosophers would not agree that statements which give expression to the speaker's emotions are without significance, but they would still hold, and quite rightly, that although significant they are neither true nor false. Thus they would maintain that genuinely moral statements, that is, statements which are more than sociological descriptions of the moral outlook of one society or another, must be understood, if they are correctly classified as statements which express a particular emotion, as significant statements which yet by their proper form and function dissociate themselves from any claim to enunciate truth.

So far as morality is concerned, however, many linguistic analysts would not accept the view that moral statements are significant in this particular way, as giving expression to certain emotions; and it is probably true to say that with such philosophers the prevailing interpretation of moral statements is that which holds, in the words of one moralist, that 'the language of morals is one sort of prescriptive language'.[7] It is one thing to make a statement of fact which may be true or false, it is another thing to express an emotion, and it is still another to issue a command or prescription or offer advice. No doubt these are quite different types of statement, no doubt they behave logically in very different ways; and a great deal of recent ethical activity has been devoted to the clarification of these differences. Unquestionably the problems thus raised and tackled by linguistic analysts have their own importance; but it seems to me no less important, to say the least, to endeavour to catch a view of the whole wood in spite of the multiplicity of its trees and so to learn what has happened to morality itself in the midst of much undoubtedly careful analysis.

According to the prescriptive view of morality genuinely moral statements are not statements which express the speaker's emotions but statements in which he issues commands or prescriptions and offers advice, but, like statements which do express the speaker's emotions, they are significant without being either true or false. On the face of it, this may seem anything but a revolutionary advance upon the view advocated by Professor Ayer in *Language, Truth and Logic*, for if meaningfulness has been restored to moral statements their claim to enunciate truth or to be in some way objective is still denied. On the other hand, it is worth noting that this is an advance in the general field of philosophy and not one confined to ethics. Further, so far as ethics itself is concerned, it may well be argued that the prescriptive theory does provide a much larger and more flexible mould for moral statements, in the sense that prescriptions are, one would think, open to a whole host of mutual rational connections to which the direct expressions of emotion are not. Prescriptions do not reflect the haphazard fluctuations of the speaker's emotional life but represent rather a rational attempt to guide conduct or to give practical advice, to answer the question 'What shall I do?'

Clearly, the change introduced by the prescriptive theory is by no means inconsiderable. On the contrary, it assimilates morality, no longer to a cheese-tasting function, but to the playing of a game with rules recognized by all the players and almost endless opportunities of mutual advice and exhortation. Indeed in the past it has often been assumed by moralists that to exhibit the rational character of moral judgments was at once to establish the objectivity of moral distinctions; and even if this assumption turns out to have been mistaken it may perhaps be granted that any theory that has grasped something of the rationality of moral judgments is closer to the distinctive and recognizable reality of the moral than one which has not.

On the other hand, it cannot be said that the prescriptive theory maintains the objectivity of moral distinctions. The rationality of moral judgments which it recognizes does not extend indefinitely, but appears mainly in the justification of particular prescriptions, particular pieces of practical advice. These particular moral judgments about what is right and wrong in particular situations are rationally justified by the prescriptive theory by reference to broader practical principles, which in turn find whatever justification they can in relation to a complete way of life of which they form an integral part. Sooner or later, however, a point is reached beyond which the justification cannot proceed; and so far as the objectivity of moral distinctions is concerned everything turns upon the way in which this process of rational justification is seen to come to an end.

The point here can be admirably illustrated from Professor R. M. Hare's eminently clear treatment of the subject in his book *The Language of Morals*. There he holds that 'if pressed to justify a decision completely, we have to give a complete specification of the way of life of which it is a part';[8] and by such a specification he seems to mean one which would consist of a system of prescriptions covering all the various kinds of situation with which in the course of life we may be called upon to deal. 'This complete specification', Professor Hare admits, 'it is impossible in practice to give; the nearest attempts are those given by the great religions, especially those which can point to historical persons who carried out the way of life in practice.' Yet suppose, he goes on, suppose for the sake of argument that we could give such a complete specification of our way of life, what would happen if we were asked in turn to justify that total way of life? If, says Professor Hare, 'the inquirer still goes on asking "But why *should* I live like that?" then there is no further answer to give him, because we have already, *ex hypothesi*, said everything that could be included in this further answer.' In other words, if Hare is right, we have already included in our complete specification of a total way of life every possible prescription which might be used to justify the particular decision that is in question, we have omitted no prescription which could conceivably be used in reply to this further demand for justification, and since it is a prescription that is to be justified it is only a prescription, or a system of prescriptions, that can provide the justification. The search for a justification therefore cannot possibly be carried any further, the end of the road has been reached.

Let us suppose, however, as seems not unreasonable, that the inquirer still deems it significant to ask 'But why?' 'Why should I accept for myself this total way of life which you have outlined, *per impossibile*, in your complete specification of it?' To such an inquirer, however, Hare tells us, there is little that can be said. 'We can only ask him', he says,[9] 'to make up his own mind which way he ought to live; for in the end everything rests upon such a decision of principle. He has to decide whether to accept that way of life or not; if he accepts it, then we can proceed to justify the decisions that are based upon it; if he does not accept it, then let him accept some other, and try to live by it.' In this way Hare describes the limits of rational justification in morals, and, as we shall see in a moment, his statement is a most important one and creates a very odd situation.

First of all, however, it is worth noting that the account given is seriously incomplete and that it is so for at least two reasons. One of these is that this account of the matter acknowledges a certain limit beyond which justification of moral decisions cannot be carried; but, short of this limit, it does allow the possibility of justification, ultimately in terms of a complete specification of a total way of life. Yet at the same time it suggests in passing that such a complete specification is after all not possible; and this

'impossible possibility' is in the present context exceedingly difficult to grasp. No doubt it would make sense to speak of some
independent reality which it is possible in theory but impossible
in practice to specify completely by *description*; but in the present
case, where *ex hypothesi* the argument has substituted *prescription*
for description, what is to be specified is not an independent
reality but a way of life, a system of practical precepts. It is,
however, difficult to understand how such a system of practical
precepts may be specifiable in theory but not in practice. If its
elements are not specified in practice how can they be specifiable
in theory? Are they involved in what *has* been specified? Then a
sufficient specification has already been given. Are they not so
involved? Then opportunism has become a principle and they
are not specifiable in theory until they are actually specified in
practice. In short, anything and everything practicable is prescriptible in theory, or else nothing is prescriptible in theory until it is
prescribed in practice. What the prescriptive theory needs at this
point is a genuine element of objectivity which might overflow
all our formulations of it, but that is precisely what it seeks to
avoid; and if there is nothing but our formulations there is
nothing to overflow them which might be the basis of a possibility in theory which is not a possibility in practice.

The second difficulty is even more serious. Behind the complete
specification of a total way of life there lies on this view a decision
upon which everything moral will rest; but on the face of it it
must be a decision without reason or principle for all relevant
reasons and principles are already contained in the complete
specification of a total way of life for which or against which a
man has been called upon to decide. This decision must be a
decision completely in the dark for all the guiding lights are
contained in that for which or against which a man must decide.
How is it possible to make such a decision for or against a total
way of life or perhaps between two alternative ways of life? How
can a responsible rational being possibly make such a decision no
matter how insistently Professor Hare demands that he decide?
Hare does indeed say that 'far from being arbitrary, such a decision
would be the most well-founded of decisions, because it would be
based upon a consideration of everything upon which it could
possibly be founded';[10] but by positing a 'consideration' behind

this ultimate 'decision' this statement introduces an objective element to which it is not entitled, and seems to forget that since the decision is at the end of the road it cannot be based or founded upon anything else, that being for or against everything it cannot be because of anything.

The criticism must, however, be pressed even further, for how in any case could a rational responsible being begin to make this decision one way or the other? Is he to decide in whatever way he wishes? Then desire is the ultimate factor in morality, individual variable desire is its final foundation, and moral codes are but complicated ways of getting what we want. If this were really what Hare intends it would have to be said that in certain respects his theory is not any advance upon the emotive theory and that at the end of the day it presents only a caricature of morality.

It seems quite clear, however, that this is not what Hare means. The trouble is that what he does mean is something which is not available to him, which is not open to him to mean. 'Decide,' he certainly says to the inquirer who persists, 'decide for yourself, you must decide'; but he does not say 'Decide whichever way you wish'. Rather what he actually says is that 'we can only ask him to make up his own mind which way he *ought* to live'.[11] The word 'ought' which I have emphasized deserves to be very carefully weighed and considered. It indicates that the ultimate decision is a moral one, and it serves the same purpose as the word 'moral' in the statement that moral judgments merely express emotions of *moral* approval or *moral* disapproval. It betrays in other words the circularity of the argument and the final inadequacy of this approach. If we can gather all prescriptions together into a complete specification of a total way of life and still ask significantly '*Ought* I to decide for this way of life or not?' then morality overflows the sum-total of prescriptions and cannot properly be explained by reference to them alone.

There is another but related deficiency in this representation of morality. It has already been argued that on this view morality is seen as something like a hierarchy of prescriptions but that the top-stone is a human decision for a total way of life, a decision without reason or principle, and consequently a decision which no rational and responsible being could rationally and responsibly make. In fact, however, morality does not have this thoroughly arbitrary character, although it is perfectly true that a member of any given society may find this particular aspect of its way of life or that aspect arbitrary for him. Morality does not have about it this ultimate and all-comprehending arbitrariness. It is not at all that without reason we decide in favour of a certain way of life but rather – as even Professor Hare's discussion tends to disclose at one point or another – that in deciding we recognize and acknowledge something objective, some sort of authority for man as man.

As it happens, Professor Hare does admit that as ordinarily encountered morality has indeed this element of authority or of objectivity, as if when I tell people that they ought to behave in a certain way 'it is not just I that am telling them; I am appealing to a principle that is in some sense there already; it is, as moral philosophers are constantly saying, objective'.[12] None the less in admitting this element of authority or objectivity in ordinary morality Hare is unwilling to take it at its face-value. Rather, he explains that if moral prescriptions are stable, if in a society for example the usual advice is to tell the truth and not to lie, in the course of time the phrase 'a good man' will come to include in its meaning the idea that he is a man who does not lie, and truth-telling as a duty will acquire authority and objectivity. This he calls 'the descriptive force which moral judgments acquire, through the general acceptance of the principles on which they rest', and this, he further maintains,[13] 'is quite sufficient to account for the feeling we have that, when we appeal to a moral principle, we are appealing to something that is there already. In a sense it is indeed there already, if our fathers and grandfathers for un-numbered generations have all agreed in subscribing to it, and no one can break it without a feeling of compunction bred in him by years of education. If everyone would agree – with complete conviction – that a certain kind of act ought not to be done, then in saying that it ought not to be done I do indeed speak with an authority which is not my own.'

This argument I find far from convincing, for it seems to suffer from two separate defects. For one thing, it is guilty of a confusion between the conservatism of the moral consciousness and the coerciveness of morality. That is to say, it may account for the so-called objectivity and authoritativeness of some men's moral convictions but not for that of others. It may account for the objectivity of second-hand moral convictions but not for the coerciveness of convictions held by pioneers and reformers, men who like Martin Luther take their fresh stand because they can do no other.

In the second place, this explanation starts the moralist off on an infinite regress. It is said that the authority of my moral principles is due to the fact that my father and grandfather held them too, but the authority of their principles must then be treated in the same way. So the moralist must pursue his search endlessly back along a process which, if the earlier criticism was sound, could not in any case have begun, since it required a totally blind decision. It seems much nearer the truth to say, with a theologian like John Baillie,[14] that no matter how far back we go into our childhood we cannot recall a time when we were not dimly aware that the guiding principles which we received from our parents expressed a law by which they themselves and their parents were bound – and that this is true of society as well as of the individual.

*(d) The uniqueness of the moral: non-natural quality, prescriptive linguistic form, divine imperative?*

If this critical examination of the contemporary emotive and prescriptive theories of morality is to be trusted, modern ethical theory is to be seen as following a peculiar pattern. It begins by rejecting any objective standard or element lying behind the varying, and to some extent subjective and relative, apprehensions of it; but in the end it is constrained, in spite of itself, wittingly or unwittingly, to posit and presuppose just such an element. This, if it is really the case, represents a curious state of affairs which demands some sort of explanation.

This explanation is perhaps to be found in the fact that, although contemporary ethical theory is plainly subjectivist in tendency and closely akin in outlook to the modern philosophical schools of logical positivism and linguistic analysis, it does relate itself positively to earlier ethical discussions and does seek to achieve a greatly clarified articulation of what was basically sound in these previous debates. If so, it may not be altogether surprising that what in the last resort does come to the surface is something for which the contemporary moralist did not bargain. A generation ago, I have said, almost everyone in what was probably the main ethical debate of the time took it for granted that the case against subjectivism in ethics had been established; and it is hardly to be expected that the contemporary moralist will find the strength of that earlier debate in this perception. Far from it. My suggestion is that the course of their own debate may well prove them to be wrong in this; but they themselves are more likely to concede that the strength of the earlier debate lay rather in its recognition of the uniqueness of the moral.

The situation, however, is complicated, if not confused, by the fact that a generation ago this might well have been understood as amounting to the same thing. In other words, it might well have been thought then that only in thorough-going ethical objectivism could the distinctive character of the moral be secured against any misleading assimilation to the non-moral.

In the nineteenth century John Stuart Mill had been guilty of such an assimilation and confusion when he laid down his notorious principle that 'the sole evidence it is possible to produce that anything is desirable, is that people do actually desire it';[15] and in the twentieth century it was G. E. Moore who described this error as the naturalistic fallacy, while H. A. Prichard, in his famous article 'Does Moral Philosophy Rest on a Mistake?', alleged that not only Mill but most other moralists of the past had been guilty of precisely this confusion. Thus between the Wars there were several ethical schools, locked in vigorous debate, which, whatever their disagreements, had clearly seen the error of deriving the moral from the natural or non-moral, the 'ought' from the 'is', and which were accordingly insistent upon the uniqueness of the moral claim. This insight was indeed closely and, one might say, inextricably associated with a belief in the objectivity of that claim; and it is this association and the failure to distinguish these two beliefs that the contemporary discussion has called in question.

That this is so is evident from Professor P. H. Nowell-Smith's argument in his book on *Ethics*. There he says, 'I shall criticize the intuitionist theory; but my purpose is not to show that it is wholly mistaken or that its attacks on the Naturalistic Fallacy are misplaced. Rather I shall try to show that, on the negative side, the points which the intuitionist makes against the naturalist are correct; but that his way of making these points, the logical terminology in which he couches his arguments, misrepresents the very truths that the arguments are designed to bring out and makes his positive thesis in its own way as misleading as an account of moral discourse as were the earlier, naturalistic theories.' 'The strength of intuitionism lies', he holds,[16] 'in its uncompromising insistence on the autonomy of morals.' Indeed, according to Nowell-Smith the recognition of this goes back to David Hume who noted the transition often made from propositions with the copula 'is' to propositions with the copula 'ought', and who argued that 'as this *ought* or *ought not* expresses some new relation or affirmation, it is necessary that it should be observed and explained; and at the same time that a reason should be given for what seems altogether inconceivable, how this new relation can be a deduction from others that are entirely different from it'.[17]

In line with these contentions contemporary moralists who employ the method of linguistic analysis claim to have achieved an important clarification in the central thesis of the earlier schools of thought whose strength lay in their 'uncompromising insistence on the autonomy of morals'. Yet, as our own argument has demonstrated, this clarification has had the curious result that it has terminated in the quite serious ethical dilemma that, although traditional ethical objectivism is explicitly disowned, either the system of moral judgments is left suspended in mid-air until some objective element is inconsistently introduced, or else it is based incredibly upon a totally blind and thoroughly impossible decision which cannot plausibly be thought to define any autonomous sphere whatsoever.

None the less a clarification *was* necessary; and it is important to see why this was so. Once again Professor Nowell-Smith has accurately diagnosed the fault. This was the assumption that the autonomy of morals derives from the fact that moral adjectives stand for certain non-natural moral qualities, properties or characteristics. On this assumption it is taken that the statements that 'X is right' and 'X is obligatory' are properly to be 'construed as statements to the effect that X has the non-natural characteristic of rightness or obligatoriness, which we just "see" to be present',[18] that there are 'objective, non-natural properties',[19] that there is in fact 'a special "world" or "order" of values which man's moral consciousness apprehends or of special "qualities" (like yellow, yet so unlike yellow), that we are aware of, but not by means of the senses',[20] and that at the core of the moral consciousness there is an 'apprehension of non-natural qualities'.[21]

According to Nowell-Smith, G. E. Moore, having grasped the autonomy of morals, 'intended to mark an important difference in logical status and behaviour between "good" and "yellow". Yet this is precisely the sort of difference that is denied by calling goodness a property'.[22] Nor did intuitionists like H. A. Prichard and W. D. Ross fare any better, for they fell into exactly the same error. 'Opponents of the Naturalistic Fallacy', says Nowell-Smith,[23] 'have pointed out the logical errors. It is true that gerundive and deontological words cannot be defined in terms of pleasure, desire, or even purpose. . . . It is also true that gerundive judgments and value judgments do not follow logically from descriptive statements about what men like, enjoy, and approve of. But the reason for this is not that gerundive words and value words refer to special entities or qualities, but that a person who *uses* them is not, except in certain secondary cases, describing anything at all.'

This is a clear, careful and accurate analysis; but unfortunately the correct diagnosis is not always accompanied by the correct remedy, and the question remains an open one whether contemporary moralists have really achieved a reliable clarification and a more adequate understanding of the autonomy of morals. Indeed the argument has already demonstrated that this is not so; and the problem is to understand how, at a point where clarification was required and was seen to be required, the attempt to achieve it has not improved the situation but may have rendered it more untenable.

It is not in dispute, it should be noted, that the insight into the autonomy of morals is a sound one which is not to be controverted. The difficulty is to know how it is properly to be understood. Where a generation ago the moralist spoke of peculiar qualities or properties in this connection, specifically of *non-natural* qualities or properties, many contemporary moralists deem the *differentia* to be a logical one and lay all the weight upon a distinctive linguistic form. Where the former understood the autonomy of morals in terms of a unique kind of quality, the latter under-

stand it in terms of a unique kind of linguistic form. Yet the
argument has purported to show that the final result is even less
satisfactory, for the linguistic form is not peculiar to morality
and the moral has to be reintroduced to explain itself.

The trouble seems to be that the linguistic approach tends to
make certain assumptions which are difficult to justify when they
are made explicit and are brought under critical examination. In
particular, the linguistic approach seems to assume that there are
several simple, quite distinct linguistic forms, and that statements
which in some respects belong to one class and in other respects
to another are either mis-statements or mixed ones which can then
be broken down into several statements each of which is a pure
statement belonging to one class rather than another. Such an
assumption is not uncharacteristic of an analytic approach which
in its zeal may 'murder to dissect'. Language is a more flexible
and less mechanical instrument than the school of linguistic
analysis is prepared to recognize.

So far as moral language is concerned I cannot find that there
is any pure simple linguistic form which is *the* form *par excellence*
for morals, in terms of which the uniqueness of morality can be
adequately understood and expressed. Moral language is in certain
respects the language of prescription, and the realization that this
is so is a considerable aid in doing justice to the autonomy of
morals. If, however, this insight is made absolute and moral
language is treated as exclusively prescriptive the moralist lands
in the dilemma diagnosed. In fact, moral language has also, quite
irreducibly something like a descriptive or affirmative side, which
is not just an acquired element through uniformity of usage as
the prescriptive theory sometimes alleges.[24] Consequently, it is
not surprising to find that the same moral fact can be stated in
several different ways, one, for example, which brings out the
prescriptive side, and another which emphasizes the descriptive,
affirmative or objective side. Thus it may be said with reference
to a particular situation 'Do act X', or it may be said 'Act X is
right' or 'Act X is obligatory', or again 'You ought to do act X';
and it is by no means clear that the first is in any way more fundamental than the third nor that the third represents merely a verbal
rearrangement of the first.

On the contrary, the moral situation, which is the human

*But these
are not
descriptive!
Value - is.*

71

situation, is a highly complex one and all its facets cannot be comprehended by one linguistic form, although different forms may serve to underline one facet rather than another. The prescriptive theory oversimplifies this situation when it puts all its eggs into one basket and assumes that the uniqueness of the moral can be exhibited in terms of one linguistic form alone, that of prescription. It is perhaps unfortunate that more attention has not been paid to those words of Hume quoted by Nowell-Smith, for, said Hume in that passage, 'as this *ought* or *ought not* expresses some new relation or affirmation, it is necessary that it should be observed and explained'. 'Some new relation or affirmation', said Hume; and in fact it is *both*, not an incredibly peculiar quality but a relation, and although something of this relation can be conveyed by the language of prescription, it is not purely prescription but also affirmation.

If this analysis is correct it means that contemporary moralists are right when, in accepting the thesis of the autonomy of morals as defended by the intuitionists and ideal utilitarians of a generation ago, they yet contend that it requires clarification and reject the associated thesis that this autonomy is based on non-natural or moral qualities. On the other hand, these contemporary moralists are themselves no less mistaken when they propose to identify the unique character of morality with the unique characteristics and logical behaviour of a particular linguistic form, for then it is that which is to be clarified that is called in question, the autonomy of morals. If truth is to be attained we may not obscure the complexity of the moral situation in which I ought to do act A in relation to other persons, E, F, G, and – it may be, beyond all human persons – to X. It may not be easy to lay one's finger exactly upon whatever it is that makes this a distinctively moral situation; but it does seem clear that it is neither that the act in question has certain peculiar non-natural qualities nor that in this situation I may use the language of prescription. It is nearer the truth to say that in this situation I am under authority, that I am objectively directed, and, if I fail, objectively judged in terms of a standard which does not emanate from the will and decision of any man or group of men but brings all such men and groups under its own judgment. And at this point the theological interpretation of morality immediately becomes relevant.

## Chapter 4

# A NATURAL DOCTRINE OF ETHICS

## *(a) Is Kant the great Christian moralist?*

To enter the field of Christian ethics is to enter a field already occupied. Consequently if the fundamental problems of Christian ethics are to be discussed at all it is necessary to take cognizance of philosophical ethics and the general ethical inquiry. In turn any survey of this latter field, undertaken with a view to the problems of Christian ethics, is bound in due course to direct attention towards the predominantly negative treatment, the radical rejection, of philosophical ethics which is to be found in Brunner's account of the Christian ethic, and also to the self-effacing implications of the dominant schools in contemporary ethical theory. Simultaneously, however, there appears another theory, no less straightforward and no less radical, but quite opposite in intent and effect. It is the treatment of general ethics, *vis-à-vis* the projected system of Christian thought, in a way which is quite positive and affirmative, without qualification or reservation, in striking contrast both to Brunner's negations and to the explicitly anti-metaphysical temper of much modern ethical thought.

This alternative and positive account of the matter was sketched in outline by John Stuart Mill when he declared that 'others besides utilitarians have been of opinion that the Christian revelation was intended, and is fitted, to inform the hearts and minds of mankind with a spirit which should enable them to find for themselves what is right, and incline them to do it when found, rather than to tell them, except in a very general way, what it is; and that we need a doctrine of ethics, carefully followed out, to *interpret* to us the will of God'.[1] The suggestion seems to be that there is a natural, self-contained and independent doctrine of ethics by which Christian theology requires to be supplemented and which theology can do no other than accept. The same idea seems to lie behind the complaint of Professor H. D. Lewis that certain types

73

of theological system 'stand discredited at the bar of ethics',[2] as if here in ethics were to be found, hardly an unchanging yardstick, but at least one that can legitimately change only in terms of its own intrinsic logic and that certainly must be free from any tampering from the side of theology. It appears again in Professor W. G. Maclagan's forthright statement that 'the moral philosopher as such, starting with no theological presuppositions, is competent to tell us what morality is. His account, however it may be supplemented, is to be accepted so far as it goes, not just dismissed as necessarily a perversion of the truth.'[3]

John Stuart Mill did indeed think that it was his own utilitarian ethics which had captured the true spirit of Christianity and was therefore fitted to serve as an independent supplement to specifically theological thought. 'In the golden rule of Jesus of Nazareth', he said,[4] 'we read the complete spirit of the ethics of utility.' This is plainly a very large claim, and although Mill's thesis is intelligible enough the defence of it might require a good deal of special pleading. If there is an independent doctrine of ethics by which a theological system of thought is to be supplemented, probably a much stronger case can be made out for its identification, not with the utilitarian ethics, but with the moral theory of Immanuel Kant. Probably too a much more widespread support could be found for this identification than for the other, and indeed the case is not without considerable plausibility.

Thus Kant's rigorism can be matched by the ascetic side of St Paul's ethical teaching. Kant's first and formal articulation of the categorical imperative, 'Act only on that maxim whereby thou canst at the same time will that it should become a universal law', may be taken as at least moving in the same direction as the exhortation of Jesus, 'As ye would that men should do to you, do ye also to them likewise'. Kant's second and material formulation of the categorical imperative, 'So act as to treat humanity, whether in thine own person or in that of any other, in every case as an end withal, never as means only', may be seen as a rather more abstract rendering of the second great commandment of the Law which is like unto the first, 'Thou shalt love thy neighbour as thyself'. Finally, there may seem, superficially at any rate, to be an echo of the important idea of the Kingdom of God, central, many would say, in the New Testament conception of the good life, in Kant's final and complete formulation, which lays it down that 'all maxims ought by their own legislation to harmonise with a possible kingdom of ends as with a kingdom of nature'.[5]

On the face of it then there are not a few points of contact between the ethical teaching of the New Testament and the moral theory of Immanuel Kant; but the enumeration of these various points of contact is by no means sufficient to establish the thesis that there is an independent and natural doctrine of ethics and that it is to be found in the pages of Kant's ethical writings. On the contrary, certain serious difficulties remain.

For one thing, the points of contact between Kant's rigorism and St Paul's asceticism and between the first and second formulations of the categorical imperative and certain well-known Scriptural injunctions are points of contact only, in each case the one is reminiscent of or echoes the other, but there is no clear identity of meaning. Indeed an isolated point of contact and even a series of such isolated points of contact, impressive as the latter might well be, is insufficient to establish the thesis in question. Much would depend upon the total context in which they occurred, and in the last resort everything would depend upon whether or not the very framework of the one ethic was identical with that of the other.

Consequently, so far as these ethical frameworks are concerned, the question must be raised whether in truth Kant's idea of a kingdom of ends is identical with the biblical concept of the Kingdom of God. The precise characterization of the latter concept has been the subject of considerable controversy in the field of biblical scholarship, but the present issue is a fairly narrow one for which it is quite sufficient that, whatever else the biblical concept of the Kingdom of God may or may not involve, it does essentially contain the idea of God's rule and sovereignty. For it seems clear that that element is *not* included in Kant's idea of a kingdom of ends. So far as morality is concerned Kant's kingdom of ends is not really a kingdom but a republic, at the most a constitutional monarchy, whereas for Scripture and the Christian faith the Kingdom of God is unambiguously a kingdom and not a republic. Morally, for Kant, the difference between the good will and the holy will appears to be exclusively one of moral stature, not of moral status; and this remains the case even if the holy will is assigned both the power and the task of ensuring that victorious goodness is suitably rewarded.

For the biblical and Christian concept, on the other hand, God's sovereignty does not amount simply to an executive power, a peculiar and unique extension beyond a moral reality shared with men. It is not a restricted and constitutional sovereignty of this kind but an absolute and all-comprehending sovereignty, the sovereignty of the Creator, which must therefore include the idea, quite alien to Kant, of moral sovereignty. It might be argued that in Kant the idea of divine sovereignty, which played such an important role in the thought of the Reformation period, has been civilized and made constitutional; but it must be said that when this representation of the matter is confronted by the teaching of Scripture it is seen that in Kant something essential to the biblical idea of divine sovereignty has undoubtedly been lost. The early Barthian emphasis upon God as the 'wholly other' had certainly its dangers and its defects, but in all phases of his work Barth tried to keep clearly in view the difference and the disparity between the Creator and his creatures, and so to reaffirm the teaching both of Scripture and of the Reformation. Moreover it is only in relation to this distinction that the biblical idea of divine sovereignty can be appreciated as an absolute sovereignty. The Kingdom of God is the Kingdom of God the Creator; it is also a kingdom of salvation the proclamation of which is good news; and unless our thinking has room for such ideas as those of God the Creator and of Christ the Saviour, for such ideas as that of divine sovereignty and that of free sovereign grace, it is unlikely to do justice to the realities of the Christian life.

In the third place, to say all this is to emphasize one aspect of the fact that the Christian life, to be understood adequately, must be viewed in relation, not just to the message or ethical teaching of Jesus divorced from his mission, but to message and mission together in their intrinsic unity. Although Christ did give the commandment, 'Thou shalt love thy neighbour', he gave it explicitly as the second which is like unto the first, 'Thou shalt love the Lord thy God'; and, further, he who said, 'Do unto others . . .', also commanded and invited in a single exhortation, 'Come unto me'. When, however, the Christian life is related in thought to the message and mission of Jesus in their unity, the various points of contact which might be observed between his ethical teaching and the moral theory of Immanuel Kant tend to disappear and to leave in their place, not a point of contact, but a radical contrast.

## (b) The independence of ethics and the objectivity of morals

What I have been saying does not finally dispose of the general thesis that there is a natural, independent and self-contained doctrine of ethics, to be accepted by theology in its final form; but it does call in question the most plausible, and perhaps the most popular identification of such a doctrine, namely, with the ethical theory of Immanuel Kant. More than that, however, the criticisms advanced against this particular form of the thesis may contribute to a conclusion on the general question, since they have brought to attention a concept of crucial importance in the present connection, the concept of the divine sovereignty as absolute and therefore as including moral sovereignty.

This concept is relevant to the problem of the objectivity of moral distinctions. In the present discussion it has been argued that moral distinctions *are* objective, that they are not completely subjective and relative, although doubtless in any particular moral code there are subjective and relative elements. Indeed if moral distinctions were not objective it is difficult to see what *raison d'être* there could be for moral philosophy or the science of ethics, although they might have as their somewhat shadowy and insubstantial successor a study of a certain kind of language which, for the sake of continuity with earlier periods, might be called *moral* language.[6] Given the objectivity of moral distinctions, however, given that morality is not just a subjective phenomenon having its origin in human sentiments or human decisions and if man is essentially a moral being, if moral scepticism is always a flight from one's own reality and a form of self-deception, this *must* be given – the question soon arises as to where precisely the objective foothold of morality is to be found.

Some moralists have spoken as if moral qualities inhered in actions, motives and states of affairs, as if these entities carried about with them their moral attributes; but this has never been a

77

plausible theory. Kant placed the origin of morality in the rational will which as rational imposes a law of non-contradiction upon man's empirical will; but reason does not bring with it any necessary and authoritative rules of action, moral distinctions arise only in the act of living out of the concrete situations of life. The bare idea of lawfulness is insufficient to produce significant imperatives for living; and, into the bargain, to make the *human* rational will the legislator in the moral realm is apparently to distort the relationship between finite creature and infinite Creator and is to introduce God as no more than an appendix to man's moral realm. If, however, the objective foothold of morality is not in actions, motives and states of affairs, in the shape of attributes which objectively inhere in them, and if it is not in the nature of man's will as rational, it is not easy to see where it can be; and to speak vaguely at this point of what is called the nature of things is to evade the issue.

For the Christian moralist, on the other hand, there is available a solution to the problem in the concept of a divine sovereignty which is absolute, for that seems to carry with it the idea of moral sovereignty and so to imply that the ultimate origin of moral distinctions is no other than the will of God. In other words, it is God's will which holds together the various expressions of this peculiar claim upon human life as the single distinctive claim that it is. The grounds of this contention are not of course to be found in its success or failure in dealing with the problem of the objectivity of morals. It is not a mere hypothesis devised to meet this problem. It arises rather out of the idea of the Christian life and the attempt to understand it; but the contention does come to grips with general ethics in connection with the problem of the objectivity of moral distinctions. Here, the contention would be, is the required foothold in reality of these peculiar and peculiarly authoritative distinctions, in the sovereign will of God the Creator.

If this contention is sound it disposes of the general thesis that there is a natural and independent doctrine of ethics which theology is bound simply to accept, and it will then be necessary to say something of ethics and of the natural morality with which it deals, specifically from the standpoint of theology and so in the light of the Christian revelation and the Christian faith. Argu-

78

ments have been adduced, however, to show that the contention in question is anything but sound, and these ought first of all to be examined.

## (c) The ethical defence of independence

The case has been very carefully and forcibly argued by Professor W. G. Maclagan in his book *The Theological Frontier of Ethics*, and we cannot do better than review the position which he has set before us. The very title of the book suggests that there is a clear frontier between an independent and self-contained ethics on the one side and theology on the other and even that this frontier has from time to time been transgressed and overrun in theological sorties of one kind or another. Whether this case can effectively be made out is the issue that must now be resolved.

Professor Maclagan's starting-point is that 'morality itself is misunderstood by any who do not recognize that the concept of duty is cardinal in the interpretation of it',[7] and he proceeds to raise the question whether 'concepts of a theological nature do anything to elucidate' the authoritativeness of the moral law. If the answer to this question were in the affirmative the general thesis that there is an independent doctrine of ethics would certainly be in danger; but in the interests of clarity Maclagan holds that there are two different ways in which theological concepts may be thought to shed light upon the moral. 'We must differentiate', he says,[8] 'between two sorts of ways in which they may be supposed to do so. I label these respectively', he says, 'the *contextual* and the *aetiological* explanations of the claim of duty. They are not mutually exclusive: on the contrary, it is very natural, though not I think strictly necessary, to combine them. They are different kinds of explanation none the less.'

By the contextual type of theological explanation Maclagan means the supposition that the universe is friendly towards the practice of morality, either as rewarding such practice or as facilitating it and rendering it possible, that is, as being on the side of morality. Moreover either form of the supposition may be understood as thus providing a practical support to the moral claim so that without it no one could reasonably be expected to respond to that claim, or even as giving 'a satisfying analysis of its nature'[9] and so as making the moral demand more intelligible. Maclagan's conclusion, however, is that 'the moral demand neither needs nor abides extraneous support from what I have called contextual considerations; neither do such considerations illuminate its nature. It must be left to stand on its own, and to make sense of itself.'[10] And this verdict is not unconvincing. Indeed it must be agreed that so far as this type of theological explanation really seeks to explain the moral in terms of the non-moral it is no more defensible because it is incipiently theological than it would be if it were not theological at all. Our concept of the moral must be such that in its purity it can go on shining by its own light when all around is darkness. If Bertrand Russell's thought is objectionable when he writes in a famous passage,

> Brief and powerless is Man's life; on him and all his race the slow, sure doom falls pitiless and dark. Blind to good and evil, reckless of destruction, omnipotent matter rolls on its relentless way; for Man, condemned to-day to lose his dearest, to-morrow himself to pass through the gate of darkness, it remains only to cherish, ere yet the blow falls, the lofty thoughts that ennoble his little day[11]

—if Bertrand Russell's thought here is objectionable it is so, it must be said, not on ethical grounds, but on theological.

Further, Professor Maclagan seems to be right when he holds in effect that when the contextual explanation posits a friendly universe in the sense of one that is on the side of morality, there may very well be a connection between the friendliness of the universe and moral practice, but it is a connection involving a movement, not from the friendliness of the universe to the practice of morality, either to support the latter or to illuminate it and make it reasonable, but from the practice of morality to the friendliness of the universe. That is to say, the friendliness of the universe does not illuminate or explain the claim of duty, but the claim and practice of morality may help to illuminate the nature of the universe and throw into relief its friendliness to right endeavour. As Bishop Butler expressed the point, 'morality is the nature of things'; and that meant that the moral throws a light upon the nature of reality. To use Professor Maclagan's terminology, it is not that 'the absoluteness of the moral demand' is

'absurd' until we see it in the context of a friendly universe, it is
rather that in the light of this absolute demand the absurdity lies
with any conception of the universe other than one which represents it as on the side of morality. The movement of thought
starts from the absoluteness of the moral demand and does not
lead up to it as to a conclusion. It is because the moral demand is
absolute, brooking no argument, suffering no escape from its
impact, it is because the moral demand is absolute in this way that
men find themselves constrained to think that the universe itself
is at least as moral as they find themselves inescapably commanded
to be.[12]

The recognition of this kind of connection is in line with the
thought of Immanuel Kant. It is in line with Butler's dictum that
'morality is the nature of things', which P. T. Forsyth found so
congenial that he placed it as a motto at the beginning of one of
his books. It is apparently in line with Professor Maclagan's own
thought on these matters; and in itself it is compatible with the
thesis that there is a natural and independent doctrine of ethics. It
does acknowledge an intimate connection between morality and
religion, but it is a one-way connection, from morality to religion,
not from religion to morality.

*In itself*, I have said, the recognition of this type of intimate
connection between morality and religion is compatible with the
thesis that there is properly a self-contained and independent
doctrine of ethics; but it may well be questioned whether this
recognition can remain by itself, static and impotent. If one is
compelled to travel along the road from morality to religion may
one not be constrained to retrace one's steps in the opposite
direction? A road has been opened up, but, except by an arbitrary
fiat, can this be maintained as a one-way street? There is certainly
one condition under which the movement between morality and
religion can be restricted to one direction, for if the movement in
question were the logical movement of inference and argument it
might be maintained that there is only one proper direction in
which to move, from premisses to conclusion, and that to attempt
to move back again to enlarged premisses would necessarily
involve at one point or another a *petitio principii*.

This view would be in keeping with the Kantian system, for at
this point, in connection with the movement from morality to

religion, to the postulates of God, freedom and immortality, there is no doubt that Kant relied upon a kind of rationalism to make the transition possible, a moral and practical rationalism, it must be admitted, not the kind of theoretical rationalism which he explicitly disowned, but a pure rationalism none the less. Thus the Kantian system would certainly not permit a valid movement in thought from the logical postulates of pure practical reason to a fresh view of morality. In this way, without any arbitrary fiat, a one-way traffic can be maintained; but it may well be thought that Kant's introduction of an element of rationalism, even of moral and pure practical rationalism, at this point in his system was one of its weaknesses.

Certainly Professor Maclagan explicitly excludes this way of dealing with the matter. He does allow that 'a conviction of the friendliness of the universe' may come the way of the moral agent, but 'it will not come to him', he says,[13] 'as the conclusion of an argument, but rather as an integral part of the very experience of demand and attempted response'. 'A man's moral experience', he holds, 'can take on a sort of religious quality; for it seems not improper to speak so of the vital sense that one is at once challenged and sustained by "ultimate reality".' Professor Maclagan has acknowledged the debt he owes to his reading of the works of Kant; but here in his emphasis upon what may be called an element of empiricism, although of course in no narrow sense, at a point where Kant relied upon an element of rationalism, he has not only left Kant behind but also the grounded assurance that the traffic can be in one direction only.[14] To represent the divine as a *logical* appendix to the moral is no doubt to disarm the divine beforehand, and it was because he thought of the matter in this way that Kant considered that 'to wish to converse with God is absurd: we cannot talk to one we cannot intuit; and as we cannot intuit God, but can only believe in him, we cannot converse with him'.[15] To substitute an *experiential* appendix, however, for the logical one is to surrender this protection and every guarantee that it will remain an appendix.

If moral experience is or can be at the same time an experience of being 'challenged and sustained by "ultimate reality",' there seems no good reason why this extension of moral experience should not in turn illumine the moral itself. If moral experience

82

breeds the conviction that the universe or ultimate reality is in some way moral or friendly to the moral and if the concept of this ultimate reality takes a theistic form, what is the relationship between God and morality? And how does the moral appear in the light of divine revelation, especially when by that revelation man is confronted by an absolutely sovereign claim upon his life? These questions, it would seem, are bound to arise and they are not without significance. They are real questions and, it may even be, tentative pointers, against which there is no *a priori* case. They require some answer; and one possible answer to them, and perhaps the neatest, and, it may be, the only one which avoids in the end the intolerable supposition of two absolute claims upon the same life, is that moral distinctions have their origin in God's will. Yet this suggestion, which falls within what he has called the aetiological explanation of duty, Professor Maclagan outrightly condemns as 'imaginatively natural . . . and conceptually indefensible'.[16]

This aetiological explanation, which, it should be noted, purports to deal not merely with the external context of morality, its environment, but with its origin and cause, its very nature, Maclagan describes as 'inept'; and to justify his criticism he distinguishes two main forms, one less radical, the other more radical, which the theory may assume. The former he describes as reducing all our duties to one solitary obligation, that of obeying the command of God; and this thesis, he holds, is not only contrary to fact and plainly false, but in departing abruptly from the truth it substitutes arbitrariness and contingency in moral matters for the intrinsic character which the ordinary moral consciousness recognizes as belonging, for example, to truth-telling, as if by a divine fiat dishonesty could be made the highest virtue. On this theory, as Maclagan points out, there is one duty which is not made so by the command of God, namely, the duty to obey God; and what the command of God effects is to fill this one independent duty with the richly varied content which any moral life or code is likely to reveal.

What the more radical form of the theory does is to deny the independence of this one duty and to hold that all obligation without exception is 'a product of the Divine Will';[17] and Maclagan's contention is that if this is taken as a definition of duty it

THE GROUNDWORK OF CHRISTIAN ETHICS

is a definition which eliminates the very element of the normative and reduces all to positive fact, whereas if it is not taken as a definition 'it means that what is our duty *becomes* such through God's command, and we are then faced by just the same objections to which the less radical version of the theory lies open'.[18]

Of the two forms of this theory in general it is the more radical form that is the more consistent. 'It has the courage, so to say, of its conviction that moral obligation cannot be left to stand on its own feet. If the conviction is erroneous, why the command theory at all? If the conviction is sound, why exempt any obligation from its scope?'[19] None the less it fails, according to Maclagan, in the way indicated whether it is taken as offering a definition or not; and although it has a certain advantage in point of consistency Maclagan cannot see that 'it is an improvement in any other respect', for either it simply eliminates the normative altogether or else it is open to the same criticisms as the less radical thesis.

The only apparent hope of evading this conclusion, Maclagan holds, lies in grasping the former horn of the dilemma and in trying to show, by emphasizing both that God is other than man and that the concept of command is not to be taken too anthropomorphically, that the normative has not after all been eliminated and reduced to positive fact. With this proposal, however, Maclagan has little sympathy; and the hope it offers, he maintains, is more apparent than real. In fact in so far as the defence succeeds at all it deprives the theory of any meaning. 'The fact is', says Maclagan,[20] 'that if we are not to use anthropomorphic concepts the theory cannot be stated, and if we are to use them it cannot be defended; and one or other we must do. There seems no escape from this dilemma.'

Thus Professor Maclagan has provided a very carefully argued and a very carefully stated presentation of the case against any identification of morality with the will of God, what I have already described as one possible answer to an inescapable problem, perhaps indeed the neatest answer, and, it may be, the only one which avoids the intolerable supposition of two ultimate claims upon the same life. Yet something more must be said.

The first point to be observed is a fairly mild one and really amounts to an attempted clarification of Maclagan's position. His argument was that in its more radical form the theory either eliminates the normative altogether or else it is open to the same criticisms as the less radical thesis. These criticisms were in effect two, that the theory substituted arbitrary and contingent connections for the intrinsic ones of ordinary morality, and that it reduced the multiplicity of duties to the single one of obedience to God; but clearly the more radical thesis cannot be accused of the second of these defects since by definition this is precisely what it did not do. Indeed Maclagan himself suggests that the more radical thesis really denies that there is a separate obligation to obey God. 'Obedience to God is not *a* duty but simply the abstracted common relational character of all duties.'[21] Thus Maclagan's contention is really that the more radical version either eliminates the normative altogether or else substitutes arbitrary and contingent connections for the intrinsic ones of ordinary morality. His contention is, further, that if an attempt is made to escape from this situation by emphasizing that God is other than man and that the concept of command must not therefore be taken anthropomorphically, the further dilemma is confronted that if we do not use anthropomorphic conceptions the theory cannot be stated whereas if we do it cannot be defended.

So stated the argument seems logically tight and escape-proof, but this appearance may prove to be deceptive. In particular there are two points at which questions must be raised, and perhaps it will aid clear understanding if they are taken in the opposite order to that in which they occur in Maclagan's discussion, as if we were pushing a way back over the hurdles he has erected. In this direction a question must be placed in the first instance against the simple dilemma: Either anthropomorphism or not. The truth is that while anthropomorphisms may be inevitable they need not be used uncritically. Rather they may be employed with the necessary correctives to hold them in check where left to themselves they would tend to mislead. There is therefore very little plausibility in the suggestion that when the word 'command' is applied to God either it means nothing at all or else it means precisely the same thing in every respect as it does when applied to a human being. The dilemma then is not nearly so simple as it appears at first sight but may very well permit a path to be beaten out between the opposing alternatives.

Along this way, in the second place, the question must be raised whether it is necessary to think of the command of God either as making actions into duties in a quite arbitrary and contingent fashion or as confronting man as a positive fact with nothing normative about it. In other words, is it really the case that any attempt to find the origin of moral distinctions in the will of God implies either that that which has in itself no moral significance may now suddenly acquire one or that genuinely moral significance itself has been eliminated, that 'I ought' has vanished and the merely factual 'X commands' has taken its place, no more normative than 'I desire' and so appearing by a kind of supernaturalistic fallacy? Maclagan's contention is that on any such hypothesis as we are considering we are indeed enclosed and imprisoned by these possibilities; but both alternatives seem to presuppose and to posit a certain view of God and his command which may not withstand examination. It is as if God and his command were elements in the world around us, as if God himself were another individual so that if the sum of moral agents is $x$, God's identity number, as it were, is $x + 1$, as if God and his command were items within the *created* universe. There may be theistic systems which could without discomfort assimilate such implications, but Christian theology with its conception of God as Creator is not one of them; and yet unless these implications are allowed to stand all talk of contingency and positive fact seems to be misplaced.

Unwittingly such language commits the error of treating God the Creator as a part of his own creation. Moreover, as I understand it, this theological interpretation of morality is not moved by any 'conviction that moral obligation cannot be left to stand on its own feet',[22] as if it would be strengthened by its association with or derivation from some non-moral fact. On the contrary, for this theological interpretation, moral obligation stands aside decisively from all the contingencies and positive facts, from all the uniformities and continuities, which make up the created order of things. In a sense it breaks through that order and, with all the unique quality of what is normative for human life, it makes contact with, it is itself the impact of, what is beyond the creation. For the theological interpretation of morality, that is to say, the moral continues to stand upon its own feet, to shine by its own light, the mystery of its uniqueness is not denied; but it is seen as a pervasive aspect of an even larger mystery, the mystery of God the Creator.

It is further to be noticed that when Professor Maclagan extends his discussion to take account, not only of the formal side of the moral demand, its authoritativeness, but also of the material side, what he calls the order of values, which provides the content of the demand, his contention that this too cannot be grounded in God is likewise supported by acute ethical analysis bedevilled by questionable theological presuppositions. Thus whether the order of values is thought of as grounded in the purpose of God or in the character of God, Maclagan's criticism in the end requires that God be considered as an individual existent. Thus, so far as grounding in the purpose of God is concerned, the argument is that this is no more and no better than a theological version of Sartre's treatment of the individual as the creator of values, and, by implication, the fact that it is a *theological* version is not held to make any essential difference. So far as grounding in the character of God is concerned, the criticism is that in the end on this hypothesis God becomes at most the Great Exemplar of an independent order of values. Indeed at this point Maclagan discloses the assumption that lies behind his discussion, namely, that God as person is an individual, for 'persons are individual existents'.[23]

For Christian thought, on the other hand, God and his will or command are *not* extra items within the created world but lie behind the whole creation. Accordingly the theologian or Christian moralist who affirms that God's will is the source of moral distinctions is really saying that moral obligation *is* the impact of the divine will upon human life, the impact of the will and claim of God from whom human life itself derives, not by a logical progression, but by his creative act, and that man's moral consciousness is already an apprehension of God's will, though, it may be, an apprehension which divorces what is willed from God who wills it and which shrouds its ontological status in obscurity and ambiguity.

The question may be raised, with a reference back to Maclagan's discussion, whether this account of duty is a definition or not; and the answer is, I think, that for faith it is a definition but for natural reason it is an interpretation. In either case it seems a legitimate account which comprehends the objectivity of moral distinctions without either reducing them to the non-moral and non-normative or making them contingent and accidental. It does not place a substitute for morality of one kind or another *alongside* morality, but it does affirm the divine will *behind* and *in* the moral sphere.

It is of course open to anyone to say that this is not what he means by morality, but in the first place that must be taken to mean that he for his part does not find God in the moral sphere. Then it should be observed that the account proposed does not come forward on the basis of an examination of morality by itself, and that it does not presuppose the conviction that 'moral obligation cannot be left to stand on its own feet'. It rests rather upon the basis of an examination of morality in relation to a certain context constituted by the claim which God lays upon human life in Jesus Christ, and therefore explicitly upon the basis of an examination of morality in the light of Christian faith.

Moreover, it is worth noting that there is nothing in morality considered by itself which is violated by this account. The permanent and non-contingent character of morality remains as strong as ever, since the God of Christian faith is the same yesterday, today and for ever, and its reality as a norm is not affected, it commands us none the less. If it should be said that the basic factor in morality considered by itself is a quality and not, as on the present view, a relation, it must be insisted – and it cannot be too much emphasized – that this so-called quality is exceedingly odd and difficult. The linguistic prescriptive form, however, on which some contemporary moralists prefer to lean their weight is in no better case and does not clarify the fact that our human moral prescriptions seek to echo some kind of ideal prescription. In the end it is very far from clear, as indeed we have already seen, that in fact the basic element in morality, even considered by itself, is not after all a relation, a rather complicated relation involving an agent, several possible actions, and perhaps other agents or patients (I ought to do act A rather than act B in such and such a situation involving X, Y and Z, as well as myself). In that case the present account may properly be interpreted as underlining the fact that the relation in question is more complex than at first appeared.

There are indeed points at which Professor Maclagan comes close to the position I am upholding. He admits, for example, that as the moral agent continues to pursue his moral course 'a conviction of the friendliness of the universe, that in a sense its ways are as our ways, that it is not simply our place but our home, may then take possession of him'.[24] 'It will not come to him', he adds, 'as the conclusion of an argument, but rather as an integral part of the very experience of demand and attempted response ... a man's moral experience can take on a sort of religious quality; for it seems not improper to speak so of the vital sense that one is at once challenged and sustained by "ultimate reality".' Thus moral experience 'may reveal itself as more than it is ordinarily acknowledged to be, as having a character such that in, and not by any transcendence of, its nature as moral it is also religious, and could perhaps itself be called experience of God'.[25] In this way it is clear that Maclagan does not understand his own argument as leading him to the out-and-out rejection of theism and that it is not with theism as such that he is quarrelling.

Into the bargain, he does not seem to favour any view which regards the moral law as wholly independent of God and even as itself commanding God. 'For', he asks,[26] 'is this view consistent with the dignity of God? Are we not now suggesting that an "order of values" or a "moral law" ... has its being not merely apart from but above God, in that to its authority God Himself must bow? God, it would seem, is in relation to it much like the Platonic demiurge in relation to the eternal and immutable Forms. And the Platonic demiurge is not the God of theism.' Consequently there is for Maclagan something of a dilemma in connection with the relationship between God and the moral law. 'It is unsatisfactory', he says,[27] 'to view the moral law as something independent of God, and it is also unsatisfactory to view it as dependent upon Him.'

The solution which Maclagan proposes has as its nerve the identification of God and the moral law, in the sense that 'the moral experience in its very character as moral is ... an *index* to what we mean by "God",'[28] but not in the sense that it is thereby denied that the word 'God' stands for more than moral law. On the contrary, the word 'God', it may be taken, does stand for something more than moral law as well as for moral law itself; and this something more must be held 'to be somehow ontologically one with the moral law, one that is to say with the very same Being to which we also refer under the name of "moral law".'[29] Even so, however, the doctrine of an independent and self-contained ethics is not thought to have been infringed by this development in Maclagan's thought, and he does not retract his contention that 'the moral philosopher as such, starting with no theological presuppositions, is competent to tell us what morality is'.

It is legitimate apparently to identify moral law with God but it is not legitimate for theology to attempt to modify the findings of moral philosophy. 'It seems proper to claim', says Maclagan,[30] 'that in a sense the moral law would be illuminated if it were rightly seen as an aspect of this richer totality of Divine Being and were not considered simply in and by itself. And a theologian might perhaps say that illumination in this sense, by lateral enrichment, so to call it, and not by vertical grounding, is all that he ever looked for. It may be so: but if it is so, the fact is certainly not faithfully reflected in the theological interpretations of morality that are commonly put forward. These seem to me at best to waver between identifying the moral law with God and deriving it from Him; to waver in a way that would not be possible if the point I have been endeavouring to make had really been grasped. We must altogether repudiate the language of derivation. And theology as well as ethics has, I believe, an interest in this.' It may not be easy to see what is involved in the lateral enrichment to which Maclagan refers, but at any rate he is clear that it does not jeopardize the theological frontier of ethics whereas a vertical grounding would apparently do so.

Professor Maclagan has given a very careful and valuable defence of the integrity and sovereignty of the moral; and it is important for theology and for Christian ethics that this ethical case should be put as clearly and as forcibly as possible, especially by a thinker who is not averse to a theistic outlook. Yet it remains a question whether Professor Maclagan has not been driven by the exigencies of his own argument to overstate the case and to occupy an indefensible position. Certainly, from the theological standpoint, two serious questions arise, one concerning his concept of God and the other regarding his view of the moral in relation to God.

As for his concept of God it is clear that for Maclagan God is not the Author of moral law but *is* moral law itself along with undefined lateral extensions; and on this side of his thought Maclagan appears to be moved chiefly by a compelling horror of anthropomorphism. 'Mere anthropomorphism', he rightly says,[31] 'must be held in with bit and bridle'; but if accordingly it is necessary to be on constant guard in applying the concept of personality to God it is surely much more than an excess of caution to take flight from the personal altogether and to identify God with impersonal, inanimate law. Indeed, curiously enough, with the substitution of a mere abstraction for the concrete reality of God the result may be both a more insidious and a more dangerous form of anthropomorphism, or even of idolatry.

Thus it has been a fairly characteristic contention of present-day neo-Protestant thought that the traditional theological conception of God as pure Being erred in two ways, by constructing God out of the created world, and by proceeding on this path by a method of abstraction. Accordingly Emil Brunner argued that 'the development of the doctrine of God has been determined, not only by medieval theology but also in post-Reformation theology – and thence to a large extent even in modern Protestant theology – by the ontology of neo-Platonism: God as Being, the *Summum Bonum*, the *One* who cannot be named'.[32] 'Measured', he said,[33] 'by this ideal of the "pure" Idea of God, certainly all that in any way reminds us that God is Subject or that He is Person, must look like anthropomorphism ... From the standpoint of speculative thought about the Absolute every Christian statement about God must inevitably end in an *"in humanum transire"*, it must seem an unfitting "anthropomorphism", something which is *"non digne loqui"*.'

But here of course, as Brunner saw perfectly well, the governing idea is not based upon revelation, it is a speculative idea reached by abstraction; and moreover, since it is reached by abstraction, it never really leaves the creation behind, it simply leaves more and more of it out. In much the same way Professor Maclagan's thesis that God *is* moral law seems to deify a human ideal or a human apprehension of the ideal, and since ideals and human concepts of them are many it might well tend, perhaps in Maclagan's discussion it is already tending, towards the deification of the abstract element of commandingness, authoritativeness, and at the same time of an abstract order of values which, according to Maclagan, lies behind our power to create ideals. If that is so Maclagan's account sets out what may fairly be regarded as a practical and moral, and so in a sense as a modern, version of the ontological error of medieval theology against which Brunner amongst others was so forcefully in revolt.

Moreover, it should be noticed that if Maclagan regards the category of the personal applied to God as anthropomorphic he does so very largely because he thinks of the personal as the individual; and, as we have already seen, his criticisms of the theological interpretation of morality mainly stem from this view. Further, this view is almost inevitable if we begin our thinking from the side of the creation without making adequate allowance for the gulf between the Creator and his creation. Beginning thus, if we think of God at all, we are bound to think of him either pantheistically as identical with the whole or theistically as an individual within it; and then in the latter event polytheism is one possibility and monotheism is another. On the basis of speculation it may not be possible to make any more adequate allowance for the gulf between the Creator and the creation; but for Christian theology, relying upon the revelation of God the Creator, God is certainly One but not another one, he is the One who is behind and beyond all that is, in the hollow of whose hands lies everything that can be counted whether it be one or many. Thus Brunner was right when he said that monotheism is not a characteristically Christian belief, for while it is right in what it denies it may be wrong or misleading in what it affirms.

Thus too there is an inescapable dilemma in Maclagan's own position. For if it is the case that to say that God is personal is to say that he is an individual then it is perhaps nearer the truth to identify God with moral law and the order of values than it is to think of him as personal. On the other hand, if God, as moral law and the order of values, is abstract, inanimate, static, impotent, impersonal, a drive is necessarily set up to return to the category of the personal. Short of the recognition of God as the Creator of everything else there seems no escape from this dilemma. On the contrary, it opens the door on to an even more radical one which posits the rejection either of theism itself or of the ontological ultimacy of the impersonal. These tensions are inevitable in Maclagan's position because they are inherent in his presuppositions and in the project which he sets himself, namely, to maintain a theistic outlook which has no real room for revelation.

This design, however, manifests itself in the light of the Christian revelation as that of upholding an idea of the Creator which is yet bound on every side by the creation. Rightly in the course of his discussion Professor Maclagan rejects the argument which proceeds from moral law to moral lawgiver, but if the argument is unsound it does not follow that the conclusion is false. The argument does not set out the grounds of Christian belief in God; but to say that God is the Author of the law is to come nearer to that belief than to say that the law is God, and it is to come nearer to the revelation in the light of which the belief takes its rise and maintains itself.

As for the relationship between the moral and God, Professor Maclagan's view is dominated by two principal factors. On the one side, positively, there is his sense of the absolute supremacy, the unquestionable authority and commandingness of the moral, so that the moment of moral confrontation in human experience has a quite unique importance of its own, so that too Maclagan can speak of the moral as remaining 'its own master'.[34] On the other side, negatively, Maclagan's position is governed by his outright rejection of the arbitrary and the contingent in connection with the moral. It is for this reason that he regards himself compelled to put aside any view which finds the origin of moral distinctions in the will of God. Yet, as we have already argued, the view which finds in the divine will the constitutive reality of the moral sphere is by no means committed to the substitution of arbitrary and contingent connections for the intrinsic ones of morality as ordinarily understood, nor does it involve the destruction of the normative character of the moral. To say that the view is so committed is itself anthropomorphism with a vengeance, unchecked and without correctives.

## (d) Moral insight and faith in God the Creator

On the other hand, Professor Maclagan's emphasis upon the 'autonomy of the moral life', upon the self-mastery of the moral, is valuable, his warning that even the works of morality can be threatened by man's fanaticisms is salutary, and his insistence that against many corruptions of religion 'the only competent preventive or cure (all else being at best palliative) is a constantly renewed realization of the true character and quality of the moral life'[35] is most important. It would be unwise to fall behind him in his impressive and convincing recognition of the unique authority of the moral, and for my part I would wish to go with him all the way. None the less there is a danger, even in this direction, for if we do not distinguish between the ontological reality of the moral in all its fullness and our human and fallible apprehension of it, we run the risk of defying the moral in the name of what is only an imperfect idea of the moral, and that would be to commit an error similar to that of the scribes and Pharisees in the lifetime of Jesus, who had a zeal for God but not according to knowledge. Consequently, where Maclagan says that moral law *is* God, I should prefer to say that our apprehension of the moral is already an apprehension of the divine; and it should be noted that it is not only in respect of detailed content that our apprehension of the moral may be defective but even, it may be, in respect of our articulation of it in the form of *law*.

If, however, we say that our apprehension of the moral is already an apprehension of the divine, and if, further, realizing that idolatry is an error just as much as anthropomorphism, we allow that of God it is nearer the truth to say that he is personal than that he (or it) is impersonal, and, in particular, that he is a God who reveals himself, who has in fact already revealed himself in the moral consciousness of mankind – if we say all that it seems perfectly permissible to recognize the possibility that a further revelation might exhibit the 'natural' moral consciousness or apprehension as not only imperfect and inadequate, as we might in any case have expected, but as in a peculiar way distorted so that it is bound to come under a specifically *theological* judg-

ment. In fact this is precisely what Christian theology affirms in
the light of the revelation it finds through the Scriptures in Jesus
Christ, using the word 'sin' to signify the peculiar distortion
diagnosed.

This distortion consists of a man-centred twist, an anthropocentric distortion from the theocentricity of the full moral order,
wherein men in recognizing the claim of morality centre it in man
rather than the Creator, subtly alter the whole atmosphere of the
moral life as seen against its total or ontological context, and
taking the knowledge of good and evil into their own hands pose
as gods. Thus if in their 'natural' outlook there is any place for
God it must be on the circumference of a predominantly human
order; it is in other words a place for some pale reflection of
themselves or their interests or some part of their created environment, not for God as God, the Supreme Being, morally as well as
metaphysically, that is to say, absolutely.

How very different was the outlook of Jesus in this respect!
'If ye then, being evil', he said[36] – and he did not mean that his
hearers were child-haters or wife-beaters, he had in mind, not
any of their specific moral defects, but the fact that they were
alienated from God – 'if ye then, being evil, know how to
give good gifts unto your children, how much more shall your
Father which is in heaven give good things to them that
ask him?' Further, this radical theocentricity – and it cannot
be genuine theocentricity if it is not radical – he not only taught,
he also lived it in all the varied circumstances of his career and
not least in his death. 'Father, into thy hands I commend my
spirit.'[37]

The fact that the moral consciousness can suffer a pervasive
distortion, can be a sinful consciousness, is the reality which lies
behind Brunner's dictum that 'in the last resort it is precisely
morality which *is* evil';[38] but while this way of expressing the
matter is arresting and therefore may have some pedagogic value,
it is none the less inaccurate and misleading. In fact it is the proud
and rebellious spirit over against *God*, which may permeate our
moral apprehension as well as our moral practice, which is seen
as sin in the light of the Christian revelation, not specifically the
legalistic and self-righteous spirit which Brunner seems here to
have had in mind. This is only one form that the sinful outlook

of natural morality may assume,[39] and, as it happens, it is a form which may readily come under the judgment of natural morality itself.

Moreover, there is no reason for supposing that in its impact upon the human world the biblical revelation stands apart from the moral consciousness as a sheerly heteronomous, arbitrary and contingent factor. On the contrary, it evokes its characteristic response of faith (which without works is dead), and faith, although it has been variously described – by John Baillie alone as a moral trust in reality and, years later, as the characteristic disturbance set up in the soul by its confrontation by God[40] – faith shows itself as a radical reorientation of the moral judgment which is yet also its height, climax and fulfilment, so that Job could say, 'I have heard of thee by the hearing of the ear: but now mine eye seeth thee. Wherefore I abhor myself, and repent in dust and ashes.'[41]

### (e) A theological cross-roads: Either the deification of moral law or the ethical interpretation of divine revelation

From the discussion several conclusions are emerging. The first is that while Professor Maclagan's warning against anthropomorphism must certainly be heeded, it must also be matched by a warning against idolatry. Accordingly, Christian theology must rightly decline to be governed by a philosophical or speculative idea of God, not based upon revelation but reached by the deification of an abstraction from the created world.

Secondly, the interpretation of moral law as the command or will of God, if it is guided by an adequate conception of divine revelation, does not involve the substitution either of arbitrary and contingent connections for the intrinsic ones of morality as ordinarily understood or of fact for norm as Maclagan has contended. On the contrary, the interpretation carries with it the representation of moral distinctions as no less authentic, intrinsic, necessary and compelling than they normally are.

Thirdly, if the moral is an aspect of a larger whole which is identical with the living God who reveals himself, or, more accurately, if morality is the will of such a God, or the human apprehension of that will, then revelation, one would think, may quite properly exhibit that apprehension as not only inadequate but as radically distorted, that is, as sinful in a strict theological sense of that word. Further it may quite properly correct it, and in correcting it, so far from destroying its character as moral, it may actually fulfil and complete it. It is true that not all theological writers have been careful enough to make this quite clear. In particular, it may well be thought that Emil Brunner fell into error when he said that 'if I feel I *ought* to do right, it is a sign that I cannot do it . . . the sense of "ought" shows me the Good at an infinite, impassable distance from my will'.[42] In this Brunner seems to have made the mistake of accepting too readily and of conceding too much to a rigoristic understanding of obligation; and consequently, having jettisoned the important category of obligation, he was compelled to give a one-sided account of the Christian life, defining the Good, not only as 'simply and solely the will of God',[43] but as 'that which God does in us and through us',[44] and Christian ethics as 'the science of human conduct as it is determined by Divine conduct'.[45]

In the fourth place, if the Christian revelation lays a claim upon human life – and it would not be the Christian revelation if it did not, for in it absolute claim and absolute promise inextricably interpenetrate each other – then either this claim of the Christian revelation and the claim of morality must coalesce and be seen as ultimately one claim, or else we are compelled to entertain the intolerable supposition that there are two diverse but absolute claims upon the same life. This supposition simply cannot be defended; but then it is no more defensible to seek to make the situation tolerable by ignoring, by passing by in silence, one or other of these two claims, in the manner either of Kant or of Barth.

Thus the argument moves on inevitably to a further and fifth conclusion, that involved in the situation is a dilemma, for either the Christian revelation must be rejected altogether or else the thesis that there is a natural and independent doctrine of ethics which theology must simply accept requires to be surrendered. Christian theology, as I understand it, cannot accept Professor Maclagan's contention that 'the moral philosopher as such, starting with no theological presuppositions, is competent to tell us what morality is', and that therefore theology has no alternative but to accept what the moral philosopher says, supplementing it perhaps but not modifying it in any way. There seems to me to be no escape from this verdict. At stake here is the existence of theology as a science which reckons seriously with the reality of God as One who is certainly hidden beyond the boundaries of creation but who also reveals himself, and as a science therefore which may not treat that revelation as an illusion or as a static, immobilized revelation which lays no claim upon human life and is indeed at the disposal of the human will.

Consequently theology may not accept the judgment of the moralist when he dismisses the command of God as arbitrary fiat; but, on the other hand, since the revelation addresses men as moral beings, *it is no less objectionable* when the theologian dismisses ordinary morality as in its place arbitrary[46] and so as beneath his notice. Nor may moralist and theologian consent to go their several ways, practising a policy of 'live and let live', turning a blind eye to each other's existence, acting as if each alone were in sole possession of the field, but knowing perfectly well that this is not so. Almost to be preferred, in point of intellectual honesty at any rate, is the Barthian policy of annihilation and annexation.

It might seem of course that the two moralities can simply be added together, but, apart altogether from the question whether conflict between them is impossible or not and therefore mere addition a possibility or not, this representation of the matter is ethically unsatisfactory since it allows two diverse origins of different parts of the total moral sphere and fails therefore to do justice to the integrity of the moral life. For in morality as well as religion no man can serve two masters. Likewise from the theological standpoint it is no more defensible since it regards the moral law as both different from, and yet as ultimate and authoritative as, the divine will. Along the suggested path, it seems clear, there is no real line of escape, and Professor Maclagan's contention is sound that 'if theism is true then certainly, by definition as I suppose, nothing, be it the "moral law" or what you will, can be more ultimate than God, or even co-ultimate with God'.[47]

Mutual recognition as between the claim of morality and the

claim of divine revelation and mutual integration in a manner consonant with the remedial character of the revelation, these together appear to define the way forward for Christian ethics. Yet perhaps what the history of Christian ethics proves more than anything else is that this is indeed a straight and narrow path which it has been extremely difficult to find.

## Chapter 5

# IMITATIO CHRISTI

*(a) Supreme authority and great example*

So far as the discussion has yet gone two conclusions have been emerging regarding natural morality. The first is that Christian ethics cannot afford to sit loosely to it, still less to ignore it completely, although this has not always been clear from the writings of Christian moralists. Christian ethics as a distinct study takes its stand in some sense upon the Christian revelation; and if the revelation of God in Christ addresses men as moral beings, as it seems unquestionably to do, then this revelation itself holds us firmly to natural morality. The other conclusion is that none the less this natural morality suffers from an all-pervading defect, its sinfulness. This is the fact that as it stands it is divorced from its origin in God, is withdrawn within a purely human world, so that its centre of gravity is now to be found, not as it ought to be in God, but in man, not indeed in this man rather than that but in man at large. It is this man-centredness – not self-centredness, it is important to notice, but man-centredness – it is this anthropocentricity that is the essence of sin, and this is the fundamental, all-pervading defect of natural morality.

This does not mean of course that man-centredness is the only deficiency in natural morality and that if only this could be corrected morality would stand forth perfect and sublime. On the contrary, the Christian life too is marked by struggle and conflict and by the possibility of a growing apprehension of what is required. What is suggested, however, is that anthropocentricity is the fundamental and universal defect of natural morality; and the implication is that Christian ethics, taking its stand upon the Christian revelation which is a remedial revelation in respect of sin, ought to portray a morality in which this distortion has been in principle corrected and overcome. This is what is meant when it is said that the Christian ethic is an ethic of redemption.

What must now first of all be considered is whether this defect, the sinfulness of natural morality, is effectively transcended in that representation of the Christian ethic which fundamentally accepts Jesus Christ as the ultimate pattern in the moral sphere and which thus concentrates attention upon him as a unique authority in the realm of morals and religion. 'Christian morality', said Bishop Henson,[1] 'is the morality inculcated by Jesus Christ, and illustrated by His example.' It is, in the words of John Stuart Mill which Henson quoted with approval,[2] 'to endeavour so to live that Christ would approve our lives'.

This is certainly one possible account of the Christian ethic and it represents a distinct type of Christian moral theory; but the question inevitably arises whether this representation of Jesus Christ as example and moral authority is such that it comprehends or can comprehend that distinctive correction of the all-pervading defect of natural morality which belongs to the Christian revelation and which is inalienably associated with the work of Christ. On the face of it this is an account of Christian morality which finds room for the idea of revelation and for the claim it imposes upon human life, but it is an account which in doing so treats revelation as indistinguishable from human discovery and its claim as a smooth extension of the claim of ordinary morality. The question then is whether on these terms the Christian ethic can genuinely be represented as an ethic of redemption.

It is plain that at this point the discussion is bound to impinge upon other topics of Christian theology and, in particular, upon the problem of Christological dogma, and that there is therefore a danger that the argument may become side-tracked into a consideration of questions which clearly do not belong to ethics but to dogmatics. Even if this danger is deliberately avoided so far as the explicit discussion is concerned there are bound to be presuppositions and implications which transgress the barrier thus erected; but even so the erection of such a barrier is a firm prerequisite of any systematic investigation of the Christian ethic. To this end accordingly, in this part of the discussion, and so far as possible, the name 'Christ' will be used to signify the revelation of God, that is, God in the act of revealing himself, the name 'Jesus' or 'Jesus of Nazareth' will indicate the historical *locus* of that revelation, and it will, quite properly, be left to dogmatics to articulate what is intended by the name 'Jesus Christ' and to explain how the self-revelation of God is linked to the Jesus of history.

It may not be easy to carry through such an arrangement consistently since what may be regarded as minimizing views in ethics may well carry with them implications for dogmatics which are also of a minimizing character; but plainly it is important that an ethical view should be assessed on its merits as an ethical view, and that it should not suffer prejudice because of its non-ethical implications. This does not mean, however, that Christian ethics has no distinctive standpoint of its own and must therefore be swallowed up in general or philosophical ethics. Rather, as we have already argued in the first chapter, if the proper perspective of Christian ethics is to be maintained the discussion cannot acquiesce in any ultimate divorce between ethics and dogmatics. The doctrine of God, Barth maintained, is at every point ethics; and, we may add, in the background of every Christian ethical judgment there is or ought to be the Christian doctrine of God. On the other hand, if the articulation of Christian ethics measures up to the unique and final place assigned to Jesus Christ in the Christian religion, that articulation can proceed without attempting to determine whether this unique and final place of Jesus Christ is to be expressed and safeguarded by Christology, let us say, in epistemological terms or in metaphysical terms. At the moment then it is not this latter question, or any similar one, which is to engage our attention, but rather whether the moral instruction and example of Jesus provide the necessary and sufficient condition of that life and ethic which are properly denominated Christian.

There is no doubt that this is a view which has commanded the assent of many who are not professional theologians, as the earlier reference to John Stuart Mill indicates; and whatever be the final verdict on it it is not designedly reductionist in character. It is not without zeal and enthusiasm that many have recognized in Jesus a moral genius who contrived to confront the human world with a new and unsurpassable ideal. At the present time, sometimes with the emphasis on his teaching, sometimes on his example, he is widely commended as 'the man for others'. Whether, however, as teacher he is hailed as genius, or as example is acknowledged as leader, the fundamental affirmation seems to be that he is our final moral authority; and the question is whether a Christian ethic erected on this foundation is both adequate and defensible.

Fortunately the affirmative view on this basic issue was well brought out in an admirably clear and careful discussion which came from the pen of Hastings Rashdall more than fifty years ago under the title *Conscience and Christ* and in which the author concentrated attention upon Jesus of Nazareth as the supreme moral authority. Even after the lapse of half a century Rashdall's argument is of the highest value because, while accepting in principle this representation of the Christian ethic, he did not attempt to wrap up its implications in obscurity but was prepared to draw them out quite unambiguously. His book may very well be placed alongside Professor Maclagan's *The Theological Frontier of Ethics* because, although written specifically from the standpoint of the Christian ethic, it is likewise concerned to maintain the strict autonomy of the moral sphere. The supposition is that this can be achieved in explicitly Christian terms if Jesus is represented as a moral authority. Thus the infringement of the autonomy of the moral sphere is kept to a minimum if indeed it exists at all; but Rashdall was eminently clear-headed in recognizing what was involved in this proposal. Indeed one could wish that the questions discussed by Rashdall were likewise raised and answered by those of our contemporaries who in the name of the Christian ethic proclaim Jesus exclusively as the man for others.

'An ideal', said Rashdall,[3] 'must be thought of before it can be approved, and to think of a new ideal of life requires genius no less than to think of a new tune or a new scientific hypothesis.' In these words, by implication, Rashdall identified divine revelation with human discovery and concentrated attention upon the figure of Jesus within the normal dimensions of humanity. Along these lines it does not seem possible to pitch the case any higher than has been done when Jesus is set before the different generations of men as their supreme authority in the matter of living. Other terms than that of 'authority' may of course be used. Jesus may be described as the supreme pioneer or pathfinder, as our 'elder brother', or by means of any one of a whole host of terms; but the essence of the matter, along this line of approach, is indicated most clearly and unambiguously by the word 'authority'. Unwittingly some terms may be designed to obscure the situation, to enable those who use them to run with the hare and hunt with the hounds, to suggest that they mean more than actually they do or can mean, or, more charitably and perhaps more accurately, to remain in communication with those from whom in fact they have parted company. Again, these other terms may quite legitimately emphasize one aspect or another of the authority assigned to Jesus, the example at the expense of the teaching perhaps or the teaching at the expense of the example. Yet the core and essence of what is affirmed seems to be grasped most unambiguously by the word 'authority'.

Even so a critical question remains, which can be seen from two opposite sides. Although it may not commonly deal with such a matter there seems no reason why general ethics should not recognize moral authorities, but can it make sense of a supreme or final authority around whose work there has grown up an elaborate system of ecclesiastical structure and ritual and theological dogma? From the standpoint of Christian ethics, on the other hand, can even a supreme and final authority accomplish the reorientation of the moral realm which lies at the heart of the Christian ethic as an ethic of redemption? Can Jesus so represented continue to be 'the way, the truth and the life'?

*(b) The threefold relativity involved in the concept of an authority*

The crucial problem here is easy enough to conceive but more difficult to solve. On the one hand the very name 'Christian ethics' assigns to Jesus Christ a position of permanence and finality which is kept in view when the Christian ethic is described as an ethic of redemption. By the very nature of the case a discussion of Christian ethics makes claims which are not made by an essay on Socratic or Platonic ethics. On the other hand, there can be no doubt that the simplest and most obvious way for Christian ethics to accommodate the person of Jesus is to designate him a moral authority or teacher, even the supreme moral authority; and the question then is whether this characterization is compatible with, whether it can possibly embrace, that permanence and finality which by its very name Christian ethics attributes to Jesus Christ, that is, to the revelation of God in and through Jesus of Nazareth.

To classify Jesus as a moral authority is clearly to bring him close to ordinary men and to make him readily comprehensible to them. Rashdall saw something of this for he held that 'when the truth of a moral rule is not actually seen, it is quite justifiable to accept the decisions of a moral authority whom we judge to be more likely to be right than ourselves'.[4] The implication is that we ourselves see something of what our authority sees, and it is only because we do so that we have any right to regard him as an authority. In other words, he is on the same road as we are, although ahead of us. If we had no knowledge of right and wrong we should have no reason and no grounds for accepting him as our authority. It is, however, precisely this fairly ready comprehensibility, this inescapable proximity and shared reality, which are the source of uneasy self-questioning at this point, for in the last resort it is impossible to avoid asking whether in these terms and along these lines Christian ethics is any longer possible except in precisely the same sense as that in which there can be a Socratic ethics, a Platonic ethics and a Kantian ethics.

Sooner or later therefore this whole approach to the subject of Christian ethics must confront the issue whether, having caught sight of the historical figure of Jesus, it has not lost sight of the fact that God was in Christ reconciling the world to himself. Is not the concept of an authority too mundane to comprehend that reality to which Christian ethics bears witness by its very existence as a distinctive discipline, occupying the same ground as general ethics but claiming to enunciate the way, the truth and the life?

In the end, as it seems to me, the criticism implicit in this last question must be pronounced valid. This is not to say that men may not legitimately find in the record of the earthly career of Jesus of Nazareth morally authoritative elements. It is certain that they have done so in the past and it is highly probable that they will continue to do so. Yet it must be stressed that what confronts us is not the career itself, the actual words and deeds of Jesus, but the record of the career; and the record does not always agree with itself, as on the question of marriage and divorce.[5] It is therefore a record that must constantly be subjected to literary and historical criticism and does not provide an unchanging yard-stick. Ethical fundamentalism, even when restricted to the Gospels, is no longer a live possibility. On the other hand, the general pattern or framework of the career and the spiritual outlook and character expressed in it are much firmer realities than the detailed contents which fill them out; and yet it is more than a little doubtful whether they relate themselves to the moral life of the individual Christian or of the Christian society as would a moral authority. The difficulty here lies with the very concept of such an authority, and in fact it appears to suffer from a threefold defect.

In the first place it is clear that a moral authority must not go too far ahead of those to whom he is an authority and must not try their blind allegiance too greatly, or else, quite properly, they may find themselves unable to follow him with a good conscience. Their loyalty is based upon something which they know and see for themselves; and what the authority does is really, on the basis of that knowledge and experience, to extend the range of their consent beyond the point at which they can see clearly for themselves. Obviously, however, if this is the way of it, the authority must keep in touch with this common range of knowledge and experience if he is to remain an authority.

Rashdall saw this with admirable clarity. 'We defer to him', he said,[6] 'beyond the limits within which we can see clearly because we have tested his insight, and seen it to be superior to our own, within the limits within which we can judge for ourselves. But there must be a point beyond which such blind submission cannot go. . . .' Accordingly, if it were now to be found on the evidence of some ancient but newly discovered document that Jesus had really said, 'Thou shalt not put away thy wife in case of adultery but thou mayest take two others', 'can we suppose', asked Rashdall,[7] 'that any one of those Anglican ecclesiastics who are so irreconcilably opposed to the remarriage of the innocent divorcee on the strength of a saying of Christ would be prepared to act upon the recommendation?'

The point is that an authority, one who is an authority and only an authority, ceases to be even that when he gets beyond those to whom he is an authority, when in other words he tries them too far. Consequently our deference to any authority is by the nature of the case a relative deference, a deference which remains only so long as our authority stays within striking distance, as it were, of what we see and know and experience for ourselves without his help. The description of the authority as supreme cannot alter this and cannot justify the judgment that the due deference of his followers is not relative in the way indicated but absolute. Indeed, in the case of Jesus, if it is said that his authority is relative for all in this way it must then be allowed that his authority is relative to each in a different way, since each man's moral experience and insight are apt to differ from those of his neighbour. But then doubt is cast on the original statement so far as it implies that Jesus is a moral authority for all men.

Secondly, even if the authority does remain within striking distance of his followers' own experience, his dominance over them is limited in another way, for it can properly be only for the time being. Once again Rashdall saw the point quite clearly for he argued that 'when we come to fundamental principles of conduct, to act in obedience to authority must be regarded as a lower kind of morality – one only to be recommended as a step towards the cultivation of an independent ethical judgment'.[8] This means that the function of a moral authority is to guide those to whom he is an authority until they can at last guide themselves, coming to see for themselves what their authority has for long seen for himself. St Paul held that the law was our schoolmaster to lead us to Christ, but the present representation of the matter implies that Jesus is our schoolmaster to lead us to an independent moral judgment of our own.

No doubt on this view Jesus would still fall to be honoured for the ethical genius which, first of all men, thought of the way of life which he advocated and exemplified; but, on this reading of the situation, there must or there ought to come a time when his authority is at an end, simply because it has succeeded in its inherent aim and is no longer necessary, a time, that is to say, when Jesus can step aside and allow his followers to stand upon their own feet.

There is a third way in which the idea of a supreme moral authority is limited and relative, for it is difficult to see that we can ever say more than that he is the highest authority so far to appear. He may be so high an authority that his coming has shed a totally unexpected light upon the dark places of man's moral experience; but if that sort of thing has happened once there seems no good reason why it should not happen again. Presumably those who preceded him in time and lived their lives without him did not bargain for his coming nor for what it involved; and consequently there are no real grounds for excluding the possibility of another and higher authority of the future whose shoes the earlier authority would not be worthy to bear. It may be unlikely, but that follows in any case from the nature of the hypothesis. If Jesus is regarded as neither more nor less than a moral authority there can be no escape from the possibility of his being superseded in this way, and certainly the word 'supreme' used in this connection affords no such escape.

Not only, then, must a moral authority keep in touch with what his followers can already see for themselves, not only must he aim that they can see all for themselves and so dispense with his authority, but both he and those who follow him must bargain for the possibility that a greater than he will arise. It is interesting to watch Bishop Henson struggling against the recognition of this very point. He had quoted Martin Dibelius to the effect that to say 'hitherto without analogy' is one thing and to say 'unique' is quite another; but Henson was content to overrule the point without ever meeting it. He simply added that 'on this point of the final and plenary authority of the Founder's teaching and example there has never been any difference among Christian folk'.[9] This is simply to use authority to bolster up the concept of authority; and the conclusion is quite irresistible that if in the Christian life and the Christian ethic Jesus Christ occupies a place marked by finality some other concept than that of a moral authority is required to characterize it.

There are then three distinguishable respects in which the very concept of a moral authority is a limited and relative one; and these three features of the idea serve to underline the seriousness of the question whether, while accommodating Jesus of Nazareth as an authority, Christian ethics can properly claim to survive as a distinctive discipline in continuity with the traditional interpretation of the subject and in line with the biblical claim that Jesus Christ is in some sense the way, the truth and the life. Indeed not only do these three characteristics essential to the very idea of an authority underscore the gravity of this question, but they even suggest in outline the indispensable marks of a more adequate concept or characterization, namely, transcendence, sovereignty or lordship, and finality. These are, moreover, the marks which again and again Christian faith has found itself affirming of Jesus Christ. It has seen in him both a transcendent figure and a final revelation, and it has acclaimed him as Lord and Master.

Accordingly, Christian ethics can hardly avoid the task of exploring these affirmations more closely; and yet in so doing, because in the vicinity of these affirmations there are many difficult questions of dogmatics rather than ethics, Christian ethics must remind itself that the word 'Christ' is to stand for the revelation of God, God in his reconciling act, and the name 'Jesus' for the historical *locus* of this act. Thus for Christian ethics the name 'Jesus Christ' is a perfectly permissible combination even if for Christian thought it is still a highly problematical one.

### (c) Ethical transcendence

So far as the first limitation or deficiency is concerned, the conception of a supreme moral authority falls short of what may be called the transcendence of Jesus Christ. Rashdall said, quite rightly, that a moral authority must not go too far ahead of his followers and try their allegiance too severely, or else for the sake of conscience they will cease to regard him as an authority; and consequently there is and must be a limit to blind obedience. But can Christian ethics contemplate and accept such a limit in respect of the Christian's obedience to Christ? Surely not, the logic of the situation is quite against the suggestion. The Christian must obey Christ with all that he is and has. What he demands of his followers is not the observance of some manageable code of behaviour but the complete surrender of their wills to him in obedience and love; and this they acknowledge even when they know that what he requires overwhelmingly exceeds anything that they have yet given, any degree of single-minded obedience they have yet achieved. They may have forgiven their brother seven times, but he requires – and they themselves are ready to admit it – that they forgive him seventy times seven, and even that is by no means the end of it.

The limit to what is required of men in love over against their neighbour is precisely the same as the limit of Christ's love towards their neighbour. He requires what actually offends their ordinary moral common sense. Did he not say that unless a man hates his father and mother and wife and children and his own life also, he could not be a disciple of his? Not that he willed to inculcate hate but rather to destroy utterly the restrictive practices of love which seem so eminently sensible to natural man and are embodied in his moral codes. There is no limit to Christ's moral transcendence or to the obedience which he requires.

If Rashdall's hypothetical case of the lost document and the wife who committed adultery was both plausible and yet misleading, it was so because Rashdall drew from it the wrong conclusion. What explains it is not that Christ is merely an authority and therefore morally not too far ahead of other men, but rather that by the grace of God there is a sense in which they are not too far behind him, that God has made them in his own image and has given them some knowledge of his will, writing his law upon their hearts. Thus, although in its fullness Christ's demand may greatly exceed anything that they might think to offer or do of themselves and their consciences can never set a limit to his demand, yet in another sense they can, for what he demands is never in a direction which makes utter nonsense of what they already see for themselves and are perhaps prepared to do. When a stranger asks for their coat and ordinary morality is almost prepared to accede to the request, Christ may urge them to give their cloak also or indeed anything else that is theirs; but he will not say, we may be sure, 'Nay, rather, take you his shirt instead'.

Indeed, so far is it from being the case that his ethical transcendence is conditioned by the requirement that he should not go too far ahead of us, that, as a mere matter of historical fact, he, as the historical *locus* of the revelation, can fall far behind us, he can pass from the scene of earthly life, and the social conditions which contained him can recede into the mists of history; and yet he, as the revelation itself and the reconciliation, can remain at the centre of human life, laying an incomparable claim and promise upon it in all its varied ramifications and diversifications down the centuries.

It is as if God were saying to man through Christ, as one writer puts it: 'Let Me have your tools, the little stage of your workshop, surround Me with your identical temptations, add the malice and suspicions of man, narrow the stage to the dimensions of a dirty Eastern village, handicap Me with poverty, weigh the scales, crib and cabin Me in a little Eastern land, and there, at the point where you have failed in the flesh, I will produce the fairest thing earth has seen; I will give the world the dream come true.'[10]

### (d) Moral sovereignty

In the second place, the representation of Jesus as a moral authority fails to do justice to what may be called the moral sovereignty of Christ. If he were merely a moral authority, even the supreme moral authority, he would require to aim at the time when he could stand aside, for his followers would then be able to see for themselves just as deeply into moral reality as he ever did. The relentless pursuit, however, of this implication of the very idea of a moral authority serves only to underline its inadequacy. From the outset, so far as this aspect of the matter is concerned, this representation of the Christian life is at odds with that which it seeks to represent. The biblical description of this development is that men grow in grace and in the knowledge of God; and it seems quite beyond dispute that the grace in which they do grow is what Scripture calls 'the grace of the Lord Jesus Christ', and that the knowledge of God is the knowledge of God in his revelation – in Jesus Christ. He himself is not a mere instrument or servant of men's growth in a reality quite other than, and external to, himself. He is the central content of that in which they grow. He is not leader only but Lord.

St Paul could say that whereas now we see through a glass darkly one day we shall see face to face; but by that he did *not* mean that whereas we now lean upon Jesus as our authority then we shall see for ourselves without his help. Rather for St Paul to live at all, now or then, was Christ – 'I live; yet not I, but Christ liveth in me'.[11] Then, says the writer of the First Epistle of St John, 'we shall be like him' – not because we shall have risen to equality of insight and practice – 'we shall be like him; for we shall see him as he is'.[12] In the final consummation, as the Christian understands it, when all things shall have achieved their destiny and come to fruition and perfection, Christ will remain King and Lord; and neither St Paul nor St John can bargain for a day, no matter how distant, when he shall have passed from the moral centre of Christian lives.

The truth is – when we follow out the moral implications of the Christian faith – the truth is that the relation of Christ as the revelation of God to moral reality is quite different from ours. We do not stand alongside him, over against moral reality, looking over his shoulder as it were and perhaps following the movement of his pointing fingers, as if he were saying, 'Do you not see that a man ought to behave like this or that and not thus?' Rather for him moral reality is no abstract impersonal order like that of Euclidean space, so that men can understand its axioms and its laws. It is a personal order – and only in a personal order can it be said that love is the fulfilment of the law – it is a personal order, not just in the sense that it is inhabited by human persons who owe duties one to another and ought to live according to its principles, but, more than that, it has a divine Person at its head, it is a kingdom, not a republic, and the will of the King is the law of the kingdom. More even than that, Christ is King. He is sovereign of the moral universe. His relationship to moral reality is quite different from ours. He is sovereign, we are subjects; and that remains the truth of the matter although for us and for our salvation he who is sovereign took upon himself the form of a subject, the form of a servant, and became obedient, though remaining King in his obedience.

In all this, admittedly, the necessary restraint upon anthropomorphism, mentioned at an earlier stage of the argument, is by no means obvious. In determining the precise sense in which these various statements have to be understood full weight must certainly be given to the fact that they are statements, not about an individual person, but about God the Creator in his revelation, who envelops the whole creation both by his creative act and by his redemption of the world. From one point of view therefore, the simple statement, without epistemological qualification, that

Christ is King is an uncomfortable and indeed intolerable anthropomorphism; but from another point of view it is clear that,
whatever the necessary epistemological qualifications and correctives, such affirmations must be made, and that unless they are
made the Christian life is radically misrepresented. So much so
that if there were no other alternative it would have to be said
that the truth lies with anthropomorphism rather than humanism.

Thus for the Christian, however mature, there is no end to
Christ's sovereignty and dominion, as there would be and would
have to be if he were only a moral authority, even the supreme
one. When all is said and done a moral authority and his position
of dominance are only a means to an end beyond themselves, but
for Christian faith the sovereignty of Christ is an end and not a
means, *the* end and goal of human life and history. It was because
he was sovereign that he could say, a Jew to the children of Israel,
something which no real Jew would ever have expected his ears
to hear, 'Ye have heard that it was said by them of old time . . .
but I say unto you . . .'[13] It is easy enough to imagine a mere man
using these words, 'but I say unto you', either as a piece of moral
bravado or as a pedagogic device to drive home his message to
unwilling ears; but in this case they flow, not from a passing
mood nor from the pressures of a particular environment, but
spontaneously from the nature and vocation of Christ himself.

It is not to be wondered at that the people said that he spoke
with authority, and not as the scribes who were mere authorities.
It was because he was sovereign and had the inalienable right
that he summoned men to himself, 'Come unto me . . .'[14] It was
because he was sovereign that he dared to question them concerning himself, 'Whom say ye that I am?'[15] And it was because he
was sovereign that in his own picture of the final judgment a
man's relationship to him is represented as decisive. 'When the
Son of man shall come in his glory . . . and before him shall be
gathered all nations . . . then shall the King say unto them on his
right hand, Come, ye blessed of my Father, inherit the kingdom . . .
for I was an hungred, and ye gave me meat . . . naked, and ye
clothed me.'[16]

This passage is frequently misunderstood as if it simply meant
that men obey Christ and the law of his kingdom by feeding the
hungry and clothing the naked; but whether they feed the hungry

or not is clearly not the primary question, still less can it be the only question. The primary question concerns their relationship to Christ, and their attitude to the thirsty and the poor is a test of their attitude to him. Thus *he* said even to good men, 'Love your enemies, bless them that curse you, do good to them that hate you, and pray for them that despitefully use you, and persecute you'.[17] As the New Testament understands his message and the kind of human life to which it leads, we love him because he first loved us and we are to love others as part of our love toward him who first of all loved both them and us. To take Christ away from the sovereign centre of the Christian life and to represent it as something self-contained and self-complete is to make nonsense of the Christian life and the Christian ethic.

It is of course possible to speak grandly, glibly and sentiment-ally of all men loving each other; but in the world, in point of fact, they do not and by themselves never will. Such speech does not belong to the hard practical world where ethics ought to be at home, but to a dream-world to which it may be pleasant to escape but in which there is no Bethlehem, Gethsemane and Calvary. Christ, on the other hand, came to the real world and lived in it, and he did not simply say, 'Let all men love each other, let there be love', but rather, 'Love your enemies' – for enmity is a fact – 'love your enemies and love them without stint and without end'. So radical and so revolutionary is the Christian ethic.

Even that, however, does not exhaust the matter, for what moral justification can there be for such a course of unrequited, one might almost say, irresponsible love? The answer is that there is none apart from Christ. If, moreover, he were at the most a moral authority this would be the point at which men might well begin to distrust his judgment. Would it not be better to concentrate their goodwill upon other men of goodwill and follow the way of the world with the transgressor? Would it not be wiser, in other words, to follow a way of moral salvage rather than the way of Christ's salvation? There is indeed, so far as I can see, no moral logic which will really justify unrestricted and unlimited love in this imperfect world, except the moral logic of Christian faith which bids men love their enemies because God's love actively embraces all men in an incredible brotherhood, the good and the bad, the just and the unjust, and has established in the midst of things gone wrong a kingdom of peace and goodwill, a kingdom of life and love.

Thus when we work out the moral implications of the Christian faith we see – and there is in the last resort no escape from the insight – we see the divine initiative of grace as the sovereign centre in the sphere of morality, affording an inexhaustible authority in moral matters because it provides very much more than that, and remaining inalienably at this centre because from it it has transformed the entire moral universe. And this all the more so because, in the mystery of the Incarnation, he who is sovereign became subject and was obedient, and because in the same mystery he who summoned men to himself and exercised an absolute authority and autonomy ('I say unto you') none the less practised a complete heteronomy ('My meat is to do the will of him that sent me'; 'There is none good but one, that is, God').[18]

## (e) Final goodness

Moreover, when attention is turned to the third deficiency already noted in the characterization of Christ as the supreme moral authority, it is evident that because he is thus sovereign in the moral sphere his supremacy is not just an empirical supremacy, a supremacy so far as has yet appeared, but an inherent inalienable supremacy, a genuinely final supremacy, in relation to which we may not bargain for the outside possibility of its supersession by another and a higher. If Christ were only an authority, the greatest of all authorities, his supremacy would relate only to the past, and there would be no good reason for supposing that a greater might not appear in the future; but if Christ is sovereign his sovereignty embraces the future as well as the present and the past. His sovereignty is not just for the time being, nor simply so far as has yet appeared; it is for all time, it is for time and eternity.

Such a contention is clearly a contention of faith that cannot be legitimately made apart from divine revelation; but the argument is that it does represent the moral meaning of that revelation. Moreover, if the whole argument and analysis are sound the conclusion is inescapable that the conception of a moral authority falls short of the reality of the Christ of faith, in respect of the transcendence, sovereignty and finality which are included in his moral significance. It would probably be a mistake, however, to regard these as if they were three separable aspects of his moral reality. Rather his transcendence and his finality seem to derive from his sovereignty. He is transcendent and final precisely because he is sovereign of the moral universe; and in this connection it is thus above all that he must be described.

If, however, he is more than a moral authority, if in fact he is Lord, that is, moral sovereign, it is no longer possible to separate his significance for Christian ethics from his significance for Christian dogmatics. Accordingly the oft reiterated claim that Christian morality is just natural morality at its best can no longer be sustained, and in spite of Kant's emphatic rejection of it the possibility of a theological ethics must be investigated.

### (f) Lord and Saviour – and an ethic of redemption

First of all, however, since Christ's significance for Christian ethics cannot in the end be divorced from his significance for Christian dogmatics, it is necessary to supplement what has been said about the moral status of Christ by considering briefly his religious status.

On this side of his being too he has been described as a religious genius who deserves to be reckoned as the supreme religious authority. It is sufficient to recall the opening sentences of a book which was published anonymously but written at the beginning of the present century by Lily Dougall, *Pro Christo et Ecclesia*. 'All of us', she said,[19]

> who are called by the name of Jesus, whatever our form of creed, acknowledge him to be the supreme religious genius. We admit that all the broken lights that flickered before him gather in his light, and that all force of development since has this for its condition – that it should occur in nations that have accepted him as Master. We see all the reasonings of the race about life and death, God and duty, enter the heart of the Christ as the rays of light focus in the burning glass, passing thence to set fire to the world.

There can be no question that this is a possible characterization of Christ and that it carries with it a high estimate of him; but once again the crucial question is whether it is really viable. There is no need to repeat the earlier analysis of the conception of an authority, and it can hardly be doubted that the limitations and so the deficiencies found in the idea of Christ as a *moral* authority are likewise present in the idea of him as a *religious* authority. That is to say, as neither more nor less than a religious authority, he must not go too far ahead of his followers, he must deliberately prepare for the day when they can dispense with him, and they if they are wise must acknowledge the possibility that a greater than he may appear. If these limitations proved themselves deficiencies in the characterization of Christ as a moral authority, they are no less deficiencies in the representation of him as a religious authority, even the supreme religious authority.

So far from being on the same road as we are, ahead but not too far and for the time being only, Christ is the object of Christian worship and transcends the religious experience of all his followers. In face of this Christian estimate of him a mere religious genius might well be expected to use the words of Paul and Barnabas when the people of Lystra called the one Jupiter and the other Mercurius, 'Sirs, why do ye these things? We also are men of like passions with you . . .';[20] but Christ in transcending the religious experience of all his followers transcends also the category of religious genius. He is not just a pioneer of faith but the object and content of faith, even if this object of faith is given to men through a human career which is a veritable pattern of faith. Once again there is apparent a transcendence and a finality which only a failure or a faltering of faith can deny, which leave behind them the category of a mere religious authority, and which are themselves aspects of something which in the religious sphere corresponds to what I have called sovereignty in the moral sphere. This fundamental religious characterization is that Christ is also Mediator and Redeemer, not only the sovereign but the saviour of men.

This has been so well brought out by D. M. Baillie that I can do no better than quote a significant passage from his book, *God Was in Christ*. 'It is perfectly true', he there says,[21]

from the historical point of view that in mankind's agelong enterprise of the quest of God, Jesus is the climax. He is the greatest of all believers, 'the pioneer and the perfection of faith', the supreme spiritual pathfinder, mankind's supreme discoverer of God. He is all these things, and if He were not, He could not be more. But is that the whole truth? If Jesus was the supreme discoverer of God, I should wish to carry the high argument yet further by asking: What kind of God did He discover? . . . It is a God who takes the initiative, a God who is always beforehand with men, a 'prevenient' God who seeks His creatures before they seek Him. Nowhere does this appear more unmistakably than in . . . His message about human sin and the divine forgiveness. It is well known how the Jewish scholar Claude Montefiore, when he set himself to see whether there was anything quite new in Jesus' teaching . . . singled out this one thing as quite distinctive: the picture of the Divine Shepherd going out into the wilderness to seek a lost sheep, the picture of God as not merely receiving those who turn to Him, but as taking the initiative in seeking those who have not turned to Him . . . Now that does not consort well with a theology which speaks only of the human quest of the Divine, and which will say no more even about the climax of the quest than that it is the supreme discovery by the supreme human pathfinder. Such language makes one wish to ask: What was God doing during the long ages when man was seeking Him? Did He leave man to do all the seeking? . . . The whole story in the Bible suggests not so much phrases like 'human quest' as phrases like 'divine revelation', 'divine vocation', 'divine visitation'. And if that long story represents reality, and if Jesus truly was the climax of it, leaving nothing more to be desired or waited for, then there must be something further to be said about Jesus than that He was the supreme discoverer of God. If Jesus was right in what He reported, if God is really such as Jesus said, then we are involved in saying something more about Jesus Himself and His relation to God, and we must pass beyond words like 'discovery' and even 'revelation' to words like 'incarnation'.

All that is well said and reflects accurately the insight of faith and its logic. Thus, if Jesus was indeed right as a religious authority in his representation of God, then either he himself was much more than an authority or else we must look some other way, we must look to some piece of history other than that which contained him, for the saving activity of such a God. But to what other piece of history can we go in such a search? And what need to go to any piece of history save that which has already apprehended us and given its name to our faith? 'Lord, to whom shall we go? thou hast the words of eternal life'.[22]

Thus it follows that the Christian life is not simply a life lived by the light of natural man's moral understanding, which for all its validity is yet a sinful understanding or misunderstanding, and, further, that it is not even to be identified *simpliciter* with a life lived according to the pattern of the teaching and example of Jesus. He is for the Christian much more than merely a moral authority, for that category cannot comprehend his unique place in the Christian faith and the Christian life, as the analysis and discussion have attempted to exhibit it. He is, as we have argued, sovereign of the moral universe, and this means that his place in the Christian life is more central and more secure than that of any authority. In other words, he is Christ the Lord, and only by an arbitrary stroke can we separate that from the further fact that he is Christ the Saviour. As Lord and Saviour he is characterized by a transcendence and a finality which by the nature of the case one who was merely a moral and religious authority could not possibly possess. Consequently, if the account of it is to be adequate, the Christian life must be represented as both Christocentric and redeemed, and its ethic as not only, quite properly, a theological ethic, but also as an ethic of redemption.

Thus Christian ethics must be seen as a distinctive discipline which has an understanding of the moral life characteristically different from, and, one may perhaps claim, more profound than, that available to philosophical ethics in at least two important respects. For one thing, it regards the *summum bonum* as fellowship, it sees love as the fulfilment of law, and the good life as essentially something like a partnership in which we human beings are caught up into purposes in relation to which we can certainly have a sympathetic insight, namely, conscience, but which all the time immensely transcend our highest comprehension of them. Then in the second place, because it sees the moral realm as thoroughly and ultimately personal, it knows something of the power of the moral, something of its resources to re-establish itself in the midst of things gone wrong, at the centre of a world and a history in which 'truth is fallen in the street, and equity cannot enter',[23] in which indeed violence has gained the upper hand.

## Chapter 6

# PROLEGOMENA TO
# THEOLOGICAL ETHICS

## (a) The Christian ethic of redemption and general ethics

The recognition that the Christian ethic is an ethic of redemption does not of itself contain the solution to every problem nor does it bring the inquiry to a final conclusion; but it does provide a life-line or a truth-line amid the perplexities and obscurities that remain. To say that the Christian ethic is an ethic of redemption is to say that the Christian life is one which is built upon the foundation laid once for all in the remedial work of Jesus Christ whereby his followers acclaim him Lord and Master. 'Other foundation', said St Paul,[1] 'can no man lay than that is laid, which is Jesus Christ'; and he went on to speak of the possibility that men might build upon this foundation 'gold, silver, precious stones, wood, hay, stubble'. In like manner the student of Christian ethics may go forward from the present point well or ill, into truth or error.

None the less, to recognize that the Christian ethic is an ethic of redemption is at least to take a step along the road which leads to an adequate account of the Christian life; and it would be misguided at this point to try to drive a wedge between the teaching of Jesus and the witness of St Paul.

Professor George F. Thomas has made a similar point which, if it does not carry the argument any further, may yet confirm it at the stage it has reached. He insists that 'Paul makes it absolutely clear that the Christian ethic is an ethic of redemption',[2] and he holds that 'those who contrast sharply Paul's "religion *about* Christ" with the "religion *of* Jesus" are oversimplifying the latter'.[3] Quite rightly he reminds his readers that 'Jesus always assumes that repentance for sin is necessary for membership in the Kingdom, a clear indication of his realism about man'.[4] This judgment seems eminently sound for where St Paul said, 'Believe on the Lord Jesus Christ', Jesus demanded repentance and a radical reorientation of spirit. Indeed St John put into his mouth the words, 'This is the work of God, that ye believe on him whom he hath sent'.[5] The first and fundamental 'duty' of a Christian, that is to say, is not that he should do this or that but that he should believe, that he should believe on him whom God hath sent, that he should believe on the Lord Jesus Christ – in other words, that he should take his stand upon a given foundation laid in human history.

To say this, however, may be to give the impression that Christian morality is something quite different and apart from natural morality, so that between them there is not a single line of connection nor a single point of contact. Yet this impression, if it does arise, involves a serious misunderstanding of what it is to believe in the lordship of Christ. To believe in him is not just to feed the hungry, to clothe the naked, to succour the distressed; but no less certainly it includes all these things and many more, and it would be inconceivable without them. Christian morality may be a radical reorientation of natural morality, but no less it is of natural morality that it is both the fulfilment and the reorientation.

In the same way the recognition that the Christian ethic is, not only a theological ethic but, within that classification, an ethic of redemption is in line with our earlier rejection of the thesis that there is a natural, self-contained and self-complete doctrine of ethics which theology is bound simply to accept. Equally, however, this insight does not require, and indeed when properly understood it is incompatible with, the dismissal of general ethics as 'necessarily a perversion of the truth'.[6] The insistence upon this point is the first clarification of the problem of theological ethics; and it raises the question of what properly ought to be said about general ethics from the point of view of Christian ethics.

Just as the claim of morality is a genuine claim upon human life and the neglect of it unanswerably reprehensible, just as, in other words, 'the law is holy, and the commandment holy, and just, and good',[7] so too the ethical inquiry is a legitimate inquiry within which there is a real possibility of valid and invalid argument and the discussion may or may not succeed in making sense. This does not mean of course that everything that every moralist has to say must be accepted as true! Even moralists themselves would demur from such a high pretension of infallibility; and it sometimes happens that ethical opinions which the theologian finds himself compelled to question are no less questionable from a severely ethical point of view. Indeed the theologian's question may often be, strictly speaking, an ethical question on the lips of one who is also a theologian. Thus it has been argued, by Professor H. D. Lewis for example,[8] that moral responsibility properly belongs to the individual and that therefore the idea of collective responsibility is virtually a self-contradiction; but, while theology may well have an interest in disputing this contention, it seems arguable within ethics itself, and on the basis of strictly ethical considerations, that the thesis is open to serious doubt.

There is, however, a further point which affects general ethics more incisively, for although the ethical inquiry is a legitimate and genuine one in which there is a real possibility of valid and invalid argument, it is at the same time an inquiry which is concerned with an abstraction, natural morality, from the total 'moral' sphere. Its conclusions therefore are liable to modification when the abstraction is made good. It is not indeed ethics which makes the abstraction, but rather the sinful spirit of natural man; and we have already taken pains to reject Brunner's thesis that ethics is specifically a work of human pride and rebellion, the function of which is to erect and secure a rational standard over human life in place of the divine will.[9] This, we have held, is an error on Brunner's part. Ethics is a work of human reason, and it is not ethics which produces the sinfulness of natural morality; but it is a work of human reason which takes as its subject-matter this natural morality and which thus presupposes this sinfulness.

Consequently the conclusions of ethics are liable to correction from the standpoint of an ethic of redemption; but to say this is to hold a position far removed from that which dismisses general ethics as necessarily a perversion of the truth. An abstraction from reality is clearly not a figment of the imagination alternative to reality, and it can provide the subject-matter of a legitimate and genuine inquiry. On the other hand, since it is an abstraction, the investigation which deals with it cannot yield a final conclusion. It is only when the abstraction is made good and 'morality' is 'seen whole' that the possibility in principle of a finally adequate treatment comes into view. Thus the account of general ethics to be given from the standpoint of Christian ethics is a finely balanced one which includes both positive and negative elements; and in this respect it is in contrast to what in the history of theological thought have been the two main solutions of the problem, for of these one has been predominantly positive and the other predominantly negative.

## (b) The medieval solution

The first of these, the predominantly positive solution, is characteristic of the Middle Ages and is the product of medieval scholasticism and a part of the medieval synthesis, which St Thomas Aquinas elaborated in its definitive form. There has already been occasion to refer to St Thomas as one of the first moralists to take account of *both* the moral end *and* the moral law, of *both* goodness *and* rightness; and it was noted at the time that St Thomas deserved the greatest credit for his early attempt to achieve an integrated view of morality which could find an appropriate place in the articulation of the Christian faith. It was noted further that, although subsequently his name has been closely associated with the idea of natural law, in fact he achieved this integration by subordinating law to end or good. It was also suggested at that stage in the discussion what cannot be too much emphasized, that the result is a theory of morals which falls under the rubric of naturalism. Indeed one might say that the theory of natural law which developed on scholastic ground doubly deserved to be so described, for, not only was it a theory of natural law because this law could be perceived by the natural light of reason and was not therefore dependent on a special act of revelation by which it was imposed, but into the bargain it was a theory of natural law because this law was read off by reason from the concept of human *nature*, which carried with it the idea of the *good* of a rational being. It is here indeed that the ultimate justification is to be found for Etienne Gilson's verdict that 'Thomist morality is unquestionably autonomous'.[10]

It is of course not to be forgotten that in Greek thought too there had been an attempt to grasp and express the unity of the moral life. For Aristotle all virtues were exemplifications of the one principle of the mean, for virtue, he held, is always a mean between two opposite and contrary vices; while Plato arrived at the conclusion that there are four moral virtues on the ground that there are three principal parts of the soul and that the four virtues represent the three excellences of the three separate parts and the excellence of all three in their proper relation one to another. Even so, in St Thomas there is to be found an impressive reaffirmation and reinterpretation of the integrity of morality within the larger context of the Christian religion, although it is marked by the naturalism which also pervaded Greek thought.

Not only, however, is the treatment of natural morality autonomous and naturalistic, but, as the discussion has already noted, it is also highly abstract. The concept of human nature, we have suggested, operative in the thought of St Thomas, was much less concrete than that to be found both in Thomas Hobbes and in his far less cynical successors, not to mention the characteristic discussions of the present day. That being so, it is more than a little doubtful whether the entire system of moral law could ever be plausibly inferred from the abstract concept of human nature, even if in principle and in theory it was persistently affirmed that this was the way of it. Perhaps at this point already in St Thomas there is an element of integration by force. Perhaps at this point too there is already a tendency, or the possibility of one, for law to break loose and set up on its own, as something standing in its own right and not to be derived from something else such as the inherent good of human nature.

If this is so, however, the integration achieved is gravely threatened, for the very category of law itself is deceptive. No doubt the idea of law in connection with morality has something to be said in its favour, for if, for example, moral judgments are to be understood as similar either to the necessary connections of mathematics or to the contingent associations of experience it is arguable that they must throw in their lot with the former; and this is what is accomplished by the concept of natural *law*. On the other hand, the theory deceives by giving at first sight an appearance of unity which a second and more critical glance will not sustain. The theory speaks of itself in the singular as a theory of natural *law*, but clearly it consists, not of one law only, but of many. It suggests an extravagant idea of its own unity which the facts themselves cannot support.

Yet as a final statement of the case a theory of natural *laws* represents a grave misconception of morality, for if the claim of morality is not one claim but many it ceases to be what we mean by morality. Morality can never contradict itself nor come into conflict with itself, but laws may and do collide. In getting to understand any moral system it is at least as significant to grasp how such collisions are to be dealt with as it is to know what are the different laws which may collide. Thus Christ, we must suppose, demands both loyalty to himself and loyalty to the members of one's own family; but either (or both) of these demands is not more significant than his own declaration that if any man hate not his father and mother, his wife and children, he cannot be his disciple. Yet to this area or dimension of the moral life, to this depth and tension, the medieval theory of natural law is oblivious. In the end it can do no other than acquiesce in the breaking up of the claim of the good life into a number of particular, discrete claims, and in doing so it lends itself to what is very far from being a profound view of natural morality, practically as well as theoretically.

From saying that the demand of morality is exhausted in a number of specific particularizations it is only a short step to the thought of that demand as easily met and satisfied; and, as Jesus well saw, it was the desire of his disciples for a manageable ethic which led them on one occasion to confront him with a morally naïve inquiry, 'How oft shall my brother sin against me, and I forgive him? till seven times?'[11] Indeed, the ever-recurring controversy of Jesus with the scribes and Pharisees over the law, and in particular over the distinction between obeying the letter and obeying the spirit of the law, is largely concerned with this very point, for the letter is manifold and the spirit is one.

Moreover, even as a theory of natural laws, this account of morality oversimplifies the situation and works with a deceptive unanimity as well as a deceptive unity. It exaggerates the extent of the moral agreement between different races, different periods, and, indeed, different individuals. It suggests that these quite fixed, natural laws are known, or are at least in principle knowable, by human reason as such. Even if it were granted that the knowledge of natural law is corrupted to some extent by sin and is not therefore to be found perfect and complete in all men, this concession would not exactly meet the criticism.

On the question of the moral agreement of different peoples and periods two diverse points have frequently been made, that it is all too easy to underestimate the extent of that agreement and that it is all too easy to exaggerate it! What is much more important than either contention, however, is the more fundamental point, that within whatever common area of moral opinion there is, whether it be large or small, there is to be found not a universal code, as the medieval theory implied, but something like an abstraction, the greatest common denominator of different moral codes, perhaps only a series of points of contact between them. A moral code is not just a number of different precepts in the same way as a wall may consist of a number of bricks. A moral code has an elusive, but no less real, unity, an *esprit de corps*, which expresses itself in the different precepts, and which consequently makes it impossible to separate off some of these as universally agreed and as constituting another code, a universal one. For the same precept means different things in different codes, and this is not altered by the fact that these different codes may be varying approximations to, or aberrations from, the one ideal code.

Thus the medieval theory in thinking of natural morality as a corpus of laws is guilty of an oversimplification in two directions. It misses the elusive unity that is characteristic of a moral code, and it fails to understand the complex relationship between one moral code and another. If, however, its mechanical method of *addition* is inadequate to the sphere of natural morality, it is no less inadequate – to say the least – to the sphere of total morality. To represent the moral component of the Christian revelation and the Christian religion as simply added to natural morality, divine law to natural law, is to misrepresent the real situation in not one respect but several.

For one thing, it is to add dissimilar things that cannot properly be added. No doubt the intention is to regard the divine law as in every way superior to the natural; but in representing it as falling quite beyond the furthest range of human insight it inevitably implies that the obedience it commands is of a different kind and is of a lower order. In truth, on the other hand, the revealed will of God should not be conceived, in its impact upon the human will, as a sheerly heteronomous, arbitrary and contingent factor and the faithful response as other than the height, climax and fulfilment of the moral judgment.

If Christ is our law he is not a purely external law, over and above and in spite of our consciences, he does not ride roughshod over them, he commends himself to us through our consciences; and if we do not see this we do not appreciate to the full the condescension of God in Christ which is the very core of the Christian revelation. 'God commendeth his love toward us, in that, while we were yet sinners, Christ died for us';[12] and as he commends his love so also he commends his law. He does not turn our consciences aside but raises them up, until our wills are finally brought into obedient and worshipful harmony with his. These things, doubtless, the medieval theory was not at pains to deny. At its best medieval thought conceived of faith as more than blind assent and of the life of faith as more than blind obedience; but – this is the point – in the last resort these insights are not available to an outlook dominated and determined by a rigid dichotomy between reason and revelation, nature and supernature, natural law and divine law.

More than that, since it is to natural morality unscathed that the divine law is added, on this understanding of the situation, there is simply no room for the recognition of the pervasive sinfulness of natural morality, in respect both of its apprehension and of its achievement. If God was indeed in Christ reconciling the world to himself he was doing much more than supplement the world's life. Moreover, although on the medieval interpretation the law of Christ seems simply to be added to natural law, it is by no means certain that the overlordship of Christ leaves ordinary duties thus unchanged. It is not simply erected upon the moral outlook of ordinary men but itself produces a total and integrated moral outlook within which ordinary duties are comprehended, coloured and transformed. The Christian moral life can hardly be reached by the simple method of addition, supplementing an old motive by a new or adding a new duty to an old one. The duty of the Christian towards his neighbour is not equal to the duty of the non-Christian but no more is it that plus something else – as if of the two miles one ought to go with another[13] one can be assigned to natural law and the second to divine law. The duty of the Christian towards his neighbour is plainly and simply love; but he does not know what love is except in the context of God's love. Thus in doing it unto his neighbour, even unto the least of all his brethren, he is doing it unto Christ the Lord; and that Christo-reference of the act is not something added to an act of natural man for rather it pervades and transforms the whole act.

Even if, however, the concept of natural law is not thus allowed to break free, even if it is kept in subordination to the idea of good as St Thomas in principle certainly affirmed, and even when every effort is made to keep in view Gilson's verdict that 'Thomist morality is unquestionably autonomous', it must be held that in the last resort, in bringing into union not just natural law and divine law but also, more fundamentally, man's natural *good* and his supernatural *end*, St Thomas had no method at his disposal save that of simple addition. It is no less clear that this method was quite inadequate to the task of exhibiting the unity and integrity of the total moral claim as understood from the standpoint of Christian faith. It is ultimately in relation to man's natural good and his supernatural end that the distinctions respectively between natural law and divine law and between the cardinal virtues of justice, temperance, fortitude and prudence and the theological virtues of faith, hope and charity are to be understood. By the nature of the case, however, St Thomas had no way of bringing the two together into a unity except by a process of dogmatic addition and affirmation. This is so because the supernatural end is by definition beyond nature, the sheer gift of grace, a *donum superadditum*, whereas the conception of man's natural good is by its nature self-contained and self-sufficient.

It is true that Gilson maintains that for Aquinas 'charity never leaves a moral virtue as it finds it';[14] and it may therefore be thought that the separation between the spheres of nature and of grace is not complete. Probably, however, no such inference is justified. For St Thomas the fall of man consisted essentially in the loss of an original gift or *grace* which yet disturbed the balance of *nature*; and it is a question whether in this he was more consistent than those other medieval theologians who denied any such indirect disturbance. At any rate, having taken this view, Aquinas consistently believed that the restoration of the lost gift or grace brought with it a renewal of the natural balance which had been disturbed. Thus *in a sense* 'charity never leaves a moral virtue as it finds it'; but plainly such effects were indirect and did not bridge the gap between nature and grace, which was assumed both by those who denied these indirect effects and by those who affirmed them.

How could it be otherwise in an age which assumed the primacy of the intellect and had not yet caught sight of the possibility that man is basically an agent, a being involved in action? So long as man was thought of as primarily a rational being whose fundamental function is to know and understand (so that Socrates could describe even virtue as knowledge), nature and grace could not be brought into a closer unity than such as is possible for rational insight and supernatural knowledge; and that is a 'plus sum', $x + y$, to which no simpler answer is possible.

## (c) The Protestant solution

In this way inevitably the medieval theory, with its predominantly positive conception of the relation between general ethics and Christian ethics, failed to establish itself. The ultimate causes of this failure were its reliance upon a mechanical and artificial process of addition to bring into view the unity and integrity of the moral life in its fully Christian form, and its failure to grasp either the sinfulness of natural morality or the all-pervasive reorientation involved in the Christian ethic. Moreover, it was precisely in the attempt of Protestantism to comprehend both the sinfulness of natural morality or, more broadly, of natural man and that all-pervasive Christian reorientation that the predominantly negative view of the relation between general ethics and Christian ethics had its rise.

For far and away the most part, however, this solution has been presupposed rather than stated. Protestant theology has usually chosen to ignore, simply to turn its back upon, both natural morality and general ethics, treating them in effect as of no account. If Karl Barth's explicit classification of morality with chance as an arbitrary factor in human life strikes the reader as a startling aberration it is important to realize that, no matter if, and to what extent, Barth himself may be thought to have corrected this ill-considered judgment, the judgment itself is in line with a long-standing assumption integral to the influential evangelical tradition in Protestant thought.

The silent dismissal of natural morality and general ethics in the thorough-going doctrine of total depravity may be exceedingly difficult either to accept or to understand, especially in view of the fact that the very terms in which the total depravity is described are, many of them, clearly borrowed from that natural morality and would be quite unintelligible without it. The fact remains that in practice much Protestant thought has treated natural morality and, with it, general ethics as if these were indeed arbitrary factors in human life, things of no account. And certainly if the only alternative to this doctrine of total depravity were the positive account of human nature in scholasticism then it would have to be said that in the end there is no alternative. On the other hand, the revelation attested in Scripture firmly holds us to our reality as moral beings and permits no flight into self-deception. Moreover, it is arguable that the silent dismissal of natural morality, when it has been allowed to go uncorrected, has helped to provoke more superficial interpretations of Christianity which have been content to affirm that natural morality almost without question and without qualification, and so to sit loosely to the Christian foundation itself.

The situation at this point is obviously complex and confusing; and yet if Christian faith is not exclusively an intellectual phenomenon, if it takes its rise as much from a situation in life as from a situation in thought, if in other words Christian faith properly considered cannot be separated from Christian life, it is difficult to think of any other point than this one at which it is more important, for the sake of theological truth at large, to be clear and precise.

Accordingly it is refreshing to find the matter explicitly discussed in some important contributions to modern Protestant thought, and the negative view of natural morality not only assumed but defended. This view is certainly to be found in Karl Barth; and yet, although Barth clearly saw that theological ethics enters a field already occupied, he was content to declare that for theological ethics in this situation the only possible course was one of aggression and annexation. Thus he was content to leave his readers in a cleft stick, uncomfortably held fast by two irreconcilable theses, that man is from the outset exposed to the moral question and yet that 'ethics ... has its basis in the knowledge of Jesus Christ'[15] and nowhere else, that 'it is within this circle, within the doctrine of God, that the question arises'.[16] No doubt this is an advance upon the largely silent dismissal of natural morality and general ethics associated with the traditional adumbrations of the doctrine of total depravity; but it is an advance which seems to reach no stable resting-place and which therefore demands to be carried further.

It is very doubtful indeed whether it can be fairly claimed that this further advance did take place in the ethical thought of Barth's close contemporary, Emil Brunner. On the contrary, Barth's main contentions can be almost exactly matched by Brunner's, for, in particular, where Barth said that man was exposed from the outset to the moral question, Brunner held that the flight from morality was a flight from one's own reality and a form of self-deception, and where Barth found the sole basis of morality in the knowledge of Jesus Christ, Brunner identified the good with what God does. None the less for two main reasons Brunner deserves a separate and even more extensive consideration. For one thing, he was prepared, as we have already noted, to come to grips much more closely than Barth with the 'give and take' of the ethical debate in philosophy, and so he was able to relate his findings in theological ethics to the movements in that other discussion. In the second place, accepting as he did what Barth rejected, the idea of general revelation in creation and conscience, he had in his hands, one would think, the very instrument whereby some further advance might be achieved.

In fact, however, Brunner did not achieve it, and his predominantly negative account of the relation between general ethics and Christian ethics is in the end no more tenable than either the implicit and contemptuous rejection of both natural morality and general ethics or Barth's more considered and explicit expulsion of them. The reason is that Brunner's negative account followed inevitably from his peculiar view of general ethics as a defiant attempt of natural reason to erect its own standard in place of the divine command and, into the bargain, as an attempt doomed to end in the dilemma, either law without content or else life without law.

None the less, in comparison with the medieval view, there is some merit and some point in both the implicitly and the explicitly negative conception of the relationship between general ethics and Christian ethics, and this, naturally enough, comes out most clearly in Brunner's explicit and more elaborate treatment. Having argued that general ethics is an attempt by sinful man to erect and secure his own standard over human life rather than God's and that the attempt is bound to end in a dilemma that cannot be resolved, Brunner went on to maintain that this contradiction is overcome in the Christian ethic; and in the course of this further discussion he had many important things to say.

The Christian message, according to Brunner, is essentially a Christian ethic, it is the revelation of the Good, the one really and truly Good; and in it the inescapable contradiction of natural morality is effectively transcended. Moreover, it is clear that even if Brunner's treatment of general ethics and natural morality is deemed unsatisfactory, and the conclusion in which it issues, that there is here an inescapable contradiction, is likewise rejected, it is still possible to recognize that what he had to say positively about the Christian ethic is true. If the Christian revelation is accepted it seems quite incontrovertible that there is some sense in which it is the case that here is revealed the one true Good. The only way to avoid this conclusion is by interpreting the Christian revelation non-morally and by forcing it into an alien mould so that it appears as, let us say, a predominantly intellectual phenomenon or a predominantly aesthetic one.

Even so, however, there is still a question whether it is the case that here is revealed the one true Good in precisely the same sense as Brunner himself gave to that statement, and it is therefore necessary to understand clearly what exactly he meant when he said that the Christian message is the revelation of *the* Good. In this connection the important point is to realize that Brunner meant what he said in a very radical sense. He meant that 'what God does and wills is good; all that opposes the will of God is bad. The Good has its basis and its existence solely in the will of God'.[17] He explicitly rejected 'the idea of a law which is even higher than God Himself' to which God might be thought perfectly to conform.[18] 'No one has a claim on a man, or on a people, save God alone, and this claim permeates all the relationships of life. It is the only valid norm.'[19]

Once again what Brunner had to say is true in some sense, and everything depends upon the precise sense in which he intended it. He was in line with the argument of the present discussion and so he was, I think, right in rejecting the possibility of a law independent of God to which God himself may or may not conform. In that sense goodness, the only true goodness, is dependent on God's will. To suppose otherwise would be to run counter to the revelation of God in Christ, wherein, in spite of all the manifest humility and condescension of that revelation, God retains supremely an unqualified sovereignty incompatible with his subordination to anything outside himself, such as an independent moral law. On the other hand, to say that the only true goodness is dependent on God's will and has its rise there is not in itself to say that our *knowledge of* that goodness is wholly and completely dependent upon the *remedial* revelation of God's will in Jesus Christ.

It is at the very least conceivable that, while goodness is entirely dependent on God's will, we should have a general knowledge of that goodness and of its immediate requirement, and that we should have this through a general and universal revelation of God's will which is constitutive of human nature as such. It is at least conceivable that the doctrine that man is made in the image of God means that, whether he likes it or not and whether he recognizes it or not, man stands in the presence of his Creator and that the symptom of this condition is the elusive challenge of his moral consciousness. It is thus conceivable – to say the least – that there should be this general knowledge of goodness, of right and wrong apart from Christ, which is the moral consciousness of natural morality and which can survive without any explicitly religious conviction or profession. That is to say, it is at least conceivable that in this way men should have some knowledge of *what* is willed by God without suspecting *that* it is willed by him.

This possibility, however, Brunner does not seem to have considered. He preferred to say that our knowledge of genuine goodness is entirely dependent upon the revelation of God in Jesus Christ and that any knowledge of goodness we may have apart from that is not a knowledge of goodness at all but only of a pseudo-goodness, a rational substitute for the real standard, a human yardstick in place of the divine. This is involved in Brunner's contention that 'nothing is good save obedience to the command of God, just because it is obedience. No reasons of determination from content here come under consideration. The "form" of the will, obedience, is all.'[20] What he was here saying is that the Christian ethic, the command of God in Christ, makes no contact in men with a prior knowledge of goodness, even though it be general, incomplete and confused; there is no such knowledge of goodness with which it could make contact. When men are confronted by the command of God in Christ it is the commanding that compels them and not in the least what is commanded. Obedience to God is their one duty, obedience and only obedience, no matter what God happens to command, although as it happens he commands love. 'Nothing is good save obedience to the command of God, just because it is obedience. No reasons of determination from content here come under consideration. The "form" of the will, obedience, is all. But to be obedient to the will of God means: "love your neighbour!"'

I cannot think, however, that this account of the matter answers accurately to the revelation itself, and, in particular, it seems to me that the word 'but' in this quotation – obedience is everything *but* (as it happens, as it were) what is commanded is love – this word 'but' is altogether out of place. The God whom we acknowledge in Jesus Christ could do no else than command love; certainly, if that seem too strong a statement, he could not command hate and remain God, or, more accurately, he could not command hate and remain the Lord *our* God; and the confidence of that conviction is based in part upon *what we already know of the difference between right and wrong.*

In saying this, it should be noted, we are not bringing with us some abstract moral idea by which we seek to limit and even define God. It is not an independent and abstract moral idea that lies behind the conviction I have just expressed and gives it its force, but rather a prior acquaintance with God's ways in the ordinary moral consciousness such as it is. We may not of course allow our ordinary moral consciences to dictate to God, we may not allow them to say to him our Creator, 'Keep off the grass!' Our consciences cannot properly be allowed to limit God's action, but that is very far from meaning that they cannot be a pointer and a guide in our understanding of his saving deeds. While our consciences may not limit God there is no reason why their law should not be *fulfilled* in his; and we may have every confidence that he being God, the ultimate source of moral distinctions and of whatever knowledge of them we may possess as men, will not turn them completely round about to face in the opposite direction, with their white denounced as black and their black exalted as white.

It does appear quite probable that it was because he did not wish to portray our consciences dictating to God that Brunner flew to the opposite extreme and represented God as dictating to our consciences, dictating to them the first and only knowledge of genuine goodness. But the truth is more complex than Brunner ever allowed; and it is very difficult to believe that his view coincides with that of the Bible. There are certainly passages which momentarily lay the stress upon blind obedience, but there are many others which it would be difficult to harmonize with Brunner's account simply because they seem to presuppose a prior, though doubtless a confused and incomplete knowledge of the genuine goodness which God wills.

It was so when Abraham argued in his prayers with God on behalf of the cities of Sodom and Gomorrah, 'Shall not the Judge of all the earth do right?'[21] It was so when Jesus declined a straight answer to the question, 'Art thou he that should come? or look we for another?',[22] but sent the disciples of John back to their master with an account of the good things that were being done. It was so again in most of the parables which would totally have failed to make sense if spoken to men without consciences; and indeed it was so pervasively throughout the divine action of Incarnation and Atonement so that it constituted a Gospel and not simply a second instalment of the Book of Genesis.

There is an old theological puzzle to which no simple solution is possible: Is a thing right because God commands it or does God command it because it is right? It is a cleverly difficult question but its difficulty is not logical but psychological. It is apt to put the person facing it into a frame of mind which assumes that one or other of the proffered alternatives must be chosen; and yet that is really not the case. Thus the religion of Zarathustra chooses one alternative, that a thing is ordained by God because independently it is right, in accordance with some law or principle higher, presumably, than God; while Brunner seems to embrace the other possibility in saying that a thing is right because God commands it, apart altogether from reasons of determination drawn from content. There seems little to choose between the alternatives offered in this puzzle, the one is as unacceptable and indefensible as the other, and both lead to equally absurd conclusions. The truth appears to be more complex than either alternative has grasped, and perhaps it may best be understood in terms of a general knowledge of goodness through a universal revelation of God which is exactly as universal as the natural knowledge of right and wrong, the natural awareness of moral distinctions, and which is the source both of that knowledge and of the humanity of man.

In the order of being goodness is entirely dependent upon and derivative from the will of God; but in the order of knowledge goodness may come before the will of God, in the sense that men may have some knowledge of goodness before they know that it is the content of God's will, and certainly apart from the remedial revelation of that will which is denoted by the name 'Jesus Christ'. Moreover, it is precisely this prior knowledge which makes it intolerable for us to suppose that by God's fiat the deepest black may become the purest white. It is precisely this prior knowledge of goodness, too, incomplete, confused and impure as it may be, that firmly places a question-mark against Brunner's use of the word 'but' – 'the Good is simply and solely the will of God. *But* the will of God is the will of God for the Kingdom'.[23] Finally, it is this prior moral knowledge which, without any theological presuppositions, general ethics seeks to investigate.

*(d)  A third solution: Christian morality the radical but reconstructive criticism of natural morality*

It can now be seen that even if natural morality is a sinful abstraction from the total 'moral' realm, the investigation of it which is to be found in general ethics is a legitimate and genuine investigation which may proceed by valid or invalid argument and which may conclude in truth or error. On the other hand, its final conclusions, if it may be said to have final conclusions, may require to be modified when its subject-matter, natural morality, is at length set and seen in its proper context, the context of divine will, love and grace. The thesis cannot stand that the ethical inquiry by itself leads to an adequate account of morality which theology in its turn is bound simply to accept.

In this respect the situation of general ethics is not unlike that of the natural morality with which it deals. When the sinfulness of that morality is seen and acknowledged it is not at all implied that the moral life of natural man is totally depraved. On the contrary it is capable of almost unlimited moral progress; but it is subject in the end to moral frustration because it does not know that it is God's will to give us his Kingdom and that only by his hand can the Kingdom be achieved. Similarly, it is not in the least implied that the ethical inquiry is null and void from the beginning and is a total perversion of the truth. Rather it is a legitimate and genuine inquiry; but it is also one for which the final and complete truth of the matter is never more than a mirage, since the natural morality with which it is concerned is itself essentially incomplete and, in a sense, self-contradictory, being both in accordance with God's will and in defiance of it. It is important, however, to emphasize that of course it is not ethics as such which makes the sinful abstraction lying at the root of natural morality, nor is it the purpose and function of ethics to maintain and safeguard this abstraction once it is made. Ethics presupposes it; and although it does indeed accept it, it wrestles none the less in its investigation with genuine reality.

On the other hand, something more has to be said, for there are other abstractions which ethics makes; and although these are not identical with the sinful abstraction already mentioned which sets morality at odds with its own true nature, yet they do hinder ethics from recognizing this other abstraction which lies at the root of natural morality and which along with the divine will is constitutive of it. Indeed so far is it from the case that philosophical ethics can in principle produce a final account of morality which theology in turn must accept, that in fact ethics itself requires to be supplemented by a doctrine of history and by a doctrine of the divine remedial activity in history. But what is here intended may best be approached in several stages.

In the first place, although on the face of it this does not seem to be a necessary characteristic of general ethics but merely an empirical fact about it, ethics concentrates attention upon the individual moral agent, and accordingly it seems to the moralist simply a matter of good sense when it is affirmed that moral responsibility attaches to the individual. Yet the human situation to which morality belongs is a social situation; and it is difficult to believe that this situation is not over-simplified when it is treated as if it were nothing more than the sum-total of atomic situations in which individual agents may by their actions affect other individual agents. What I am suggesting is not of course that ethics ought to turn back the clock and attend to the group rather than the individual. The point is rather that it is a precarious *assumption* for ethics to accept the isolated or separate individual as the ultimate unit, so that any larger unit is but an aggregate of such smaller separate units.

Indeed, even in Christian ethics this mistake has been made. Thus E. F. Scott maintained that Jesus 'no longer made the *group* the governing factor in human action';[24] and he inferred that for him 'men have value in the sight of God not merely as units in a society but as personal beings' and that 'in this individualism his social teaching had its roots'.[25] Yet another and later interpreter, H. R. Mackintosh, who was plainly not turning back the clock, held that 'living Christianity . . . is by nature social and corporate and cannot really exist in any other form',[26] that 'the place of the social character of Christian religion is not in a footnote, but right in the text',[27] and that 'the New Testament . . . takes for granted that Christ's followers will hold together, that they share each other's life, and that apart from the mutual giving and receiving of the brethren they would not be what they are, but something quite different'.[28] To the contemporary understanding of the Christian faith Mackintosh's statements are doubtless more congenial than Scott's; and yet if they were so understood that they completely opposed the latter they would for the most part substitute one error for another.

The truth at this point seems to have two sides which it is

equally important to grasp; and the Roman Catholic writer, Jacques Maritain, saw this clearly when he rejected a unilateral answer to the dilemma, either society or the individual. 'Among the truths of which contemporary thought stands in particular need', he argued,[29]

and from which it could draw substantial profit, is the doctrine of the distinction between individuality and personality. . . . The Nineteenth Century experienced the errors of individualism. We have witnessed the development of a totalitarian or exclusively communal conception of society which took place by way of reaction. It was natural, then, that in a simultaneous reaction against both totalitarian and individualistic errors the concept of the human person, incorporated as such into society, be opposed to both the idea of the totalitarian state and that of the sovereignty of the individual.

If this is true it suggests that if there is such a thing as racial evil and if, further, there is an ethical goal of fellowship, perhaps *the* ethical goal, the net which general ethics casts, is ill-adapted to contain them; and this may be said without any suggestion that it catches nothing at all. On the contrary, in spite of its limitations, what it does catch is of the first importance to theology, unless we are prepared to say that the Christian revelation is non-moral in character and is designed to satisfy our intellectual curiosity or to excite our aesthetic interest. For my part, if anything is clear in theology it is that to be properly understood the Christian faith and the Christian revelation must, in P. T. Forsyth's words, be 'morally construed', and that, for example, Professor Roger L. Shinn is abundantly right when he says that 'theology exists for the Gospel, not the Gospel for theology. And the Gospel – the good news of God's kingdom and of His gracious deed in Christ – is social', and that consequently 'ethics is basic to theology. Just as there can be no Christian ethics without theological foundations, so there can be no theology without ethical foundations'.[30]

On the other hand, general ethics has its limitations; and if the account just given of one of these limitations is correct, it suggests that there is a moral area of common will, purpose and action which is likely to escape an ethical approach and inquiry that concentrate upon the individual moral agent. It is more difficult to be sure whether this individualistic bias belongs inherently to general ethics or has its root in some temporary, though perhaps longstanding, assumption. Such an assumption might well be that of the egocentric predicament which, it has been argued, has bedevilled much philosophical thought at large in the modern period, and which consists in taking it for granted that the proper starting-point for the philosophical inquiry is to be found in the isolated individual and his ideas.[31] In any case it is clear that, although the individualistic bias does not create the situation of natural morality, it may well arise out of that situation, and it certainly provides a hindrance to the recognition of that situation in its fragmentariness and defectiveness as but a sinful abstraction from the total 'moral' sphere.

By virtue of its individualism then, whether inherent or merely persistent, general ethics unwittingly removes itself to a degree from the reality of the concrete historical process. It tends, however, to make another abstraction which removes it still further, for it abstracts the moral moment from the complex of human experience and historical process. It thus tends to treat it as unchanging and invulnerable, in a way as self-sufficient, not necessarily as self-complete (for it may point backwards and forwards to other situations), but *qua* moral as self-sustaining. It is almost as if, in choosing to investigate morality, general ethics understood itself as having abstracted an element of the eternal from the temporal flux.

Into the bargain, significantly, when ethics does take account of movement and change in history it seems to move irresistibly towards a doctrine of moral progress, and indeed in some moral theories the idea of moral progress is an integral and indispensable part of the whole. Thus it is so in the ethical philosophy of T. H. Green where the moral life of the individual is understood as the work of the eternal consciousness incessantly and progressively seeking complete satisfaction. Certainly, the thesis could not be sustained that some such doctrine of moral progress is integral to ethics as such; and doubtless it was easier for Green to propound his particular theory when he did than it would have been today. It seems, however, that ethics does not understand seriously enough the fact and the effect of evil. Where it sees in morality more than a mere by-product of the historical process, without ontological or ultimate significance, it does seem to do one or other of two things both of which are marked by undue optimism, one positively and the other in a negative or neutral fashion. Either it finds the substance of morality within and at the root of the historical process and then, as in T. H. Green, it inevitably enunciates a positive doctrine of moral progress, or else it takes what may, curiously enough, be described as an other-worldly view of the moral ultimate, thinking of it as hovering over the historical scene, inviolate, invulnerable and always available, in some timeless habitation of its own.

I have said that the positively optimistic doctrine is to be found in T. H. Green, and it is of course not far away from the minds of moralists who find the idea of evolution congenial and relevant. The neutral optimism on the other hand may be illustrated from Professor W. G. Maclagan's book *The Theological Frontier of Ethics*, for there he distinguishes between ideals, which are but the human apprehension of values in relation to particular situations, and the order of values itself. Of the latter he holds that 'it may quite intelligibly be said that they do have a substantial being which ideals lack . . . this "substantiality" of values is, I should hold, intrinsic to them; they can quite properly be thought of as "self-supporting" . . .'[32] 'If there really are to be values at all', he says,[33] 'we must represent them as independent of all actual purposes, though implied as the objective control and standard for those purposes.'

Whether, however, the optimism of general ethics takes a positive or a neutral form it offers a striking contrast to the biblical outlook and the Christian understanding of the situation, which in comparison reveal a greater realism and a closer approach to history itself. Christian faith neither places the moral ultimate within and at the root of historical process, nor does it see it or set it exalted, aloof, far above the historical process, as an impersonal standard and control. The truth is more complex than either of these interpretations of it; and the Christian faith acknowledges the moral ultimate as both in and beyond the historical process. It finds that ultimate in the divine will and word which is understood as neither contained wholly within history, since it has its transcendent source in God, nor yet static, abstract, remote, somewhere above history, but which is explicitly the divine will and word *for the creation, for history*, not the will and word of God in itself, in some secret heaven, but his will and word for the world, his will and word cast as bread upon the waters of history, the *revelation* of his will and word.

It is one important aspect of this situation that the moral ultimate is not permanently available – except by grace. 'The secret of the Lord', says the Psalmist, 'is with them that fear him';[34] and the fate of moral knowledge is closely linked with that of moral practice. Even with regard to the moral realm there is a truth contained in the parable of the talents, that 'unto every one that hath shall be given' whereas 'from him that hath not shall be taken away even that which he hath'.[35] It is moral insight, as well as moral realization and achievement, that is at the mercy of history; and accordingly there is for the biblical and Christian view a depth of sombre realism which is in the plainest contrast to the optimism, positive or neutral, of ethics.

For the biblical and Christian view, however, there is also an ultimate resource of divine grace and mercy so that if in man there is nothing to prevent his self-destruction as a moral being there is beyond him a power of goodness which he can neither exhaust nor frustrate. 'None calleth for justice,' cried Isaiah the prophet,[36] 'nor any pleadeth for truth: they trust in vanity, and speak lies; they conceive mischief, and bring forth iniquity . . . And judgment is turned away backward, and justice standeth afar off: for truth is fallen in the street, and equity cannot enter. Yea, truth faileth; and he that departeth from evil maketh himself a prey: and the Lord saw it, and it displeased him that there was no judgment.' The concept of such a cosmic displeasure, of a cosmic concern and grace, may not be congenial to philosophical ethics; but these things belong to the total moral sphere as seen through the eye of faith. The will and word of God are cast as bread upon the waters of history, but when the enemy comes in like a flood it is the Spirit of the Lord that lifts up a standard against him.

Thus by virtue both of its individualism and of its optimism general ethics removes itself from the actual historical process, abstracts as it were from it, and so far hinders itself from the recognition of its limitations as concerned with natural morality.

It is in this way that ethics, so far from being self-sufficient and acceptable without modification by theology, needs instead to be supplemented by a doctrine of history, and not by that only but by a doctrine too of the divine remedial activity whereby the total 'moral' sphere is restored in its integrity. 'I am come', said Jesus, 'that they might have life, and that they might have it more abundantly';[37] and the Christian claim is that he is the way, the truth and the life.

To make these strictures, however, upon general ethics is by no means to imply that it is necessarily a perversion of the truth. On the contrary, it remains a legitimate, genuine and necessary inquiry, and its insight a valid one within the limitations to which the argument has directed attention. Viewing the moral within the larger context of divine grace, what we have called the total 'moral' sphere, theology may well have to modify some of the findings of ethics and may come into collision with others, especially where ethics passes into an articulated philosophy of morals. In this way theology bridges the gulf between ethics and reality, between ethics and the historical process. In this way it drives a passage through the dilemma, either subjectivism or undue optimism; but in doing all this it does not, or it ought not to, lose touch with ethics.

Professor Shinn in the article from which I have already quoted refers to the three stages recognized by Kierkegaard, the aesthetic, the moral and the religious, and he holds that for the great Danish theologian the moral was not only a necessary step towards the religious, but was reinstated in the latter. On his own account Professor Shinn declares that 'Christian faith can never be contained within ethics', but he notes in contemporary theology a reluctance to reinstate the ethical within the religious and wonders whether when that happens theology has not in fact stopped short at Kierkegaard's first stage, mistaking it for the third. The question is an important and critical one; and it seems to me that if, comparatively speaking, ethics is an abstract science and theology a concrete one, the former remains something like the mathematics of the latter.

*(e) The Christian ethic and Christian ethics: description and logical analysis*

If the foregoing analysis is correct it follows that Christian ethics cannot afford to ignore general ethics and that the problem of their relationship is one of outstanding importance which must be faced fairly and squarely in the interests of clarity of thought. Thus failure to consider this problem is perhaps the main weakness of what is otherwise a notable contribution to Christian ethics, Professor Paul Ramsey's *Basic Christian Ethics*. In this book the author's dominant thesis is that 'love for neighbor comprises the full meaning of absolute, unhesitating obedience to God',[38] and that by this ethic 'men may know themselves, their customary morality, their institutions and cultures to be subjected to an ultimate criticism and found wanting in terms of an absolute standard which was never drawn from the customary morality of any people and can never be identified with the structures of any particular civilization'.[39] 'Strictly speaking', Ramsey says,[40] 'this is a new "principle" for morality only in the sense that here all morality governed by principles, rules, customs, and laws goes to pieces and is given another sovereign test.'

From this basic contention the author proceeds to discuss such questions as the identity of one's neighbour, distinguishing him in his concreteness from man in general, and the relationship of Christian love to Christian salvation and the possible thought of reward. He finds a place in this ethic of neighbour-love for duties to oneself and speaks of 'an *enlightened* unselfishness',[41] holding that a man '*ought* to love himself for the purpose of loving his neighbor as he naturally loves himself'.[42] He discusses Christian virtue in the light of his basic thesis and the relationship of Christian love to the creation and preservation of community amongst men. 'For Christian ethics', he says here,[43] '. . . love is always the primary notion, justice derivative, since justice may be defined as what Christian love does when confronted by two or more neighbors.' He gives extended consideration to such theological topics as the image of God, sin, idolatry and original sin; and he then turns his attention to 'Christian Love in Search of a Social Policy'.

The result is a remarkably comprehensive survey of different aspects of the Christian ethic and the Christian life. Within its own scope the argument may certainly suggest critical questions at one point or another. For example, it may well be doubted whether the concept of a neighbour's *needs* will bear all the weight that is placed upon it, and there seems no answer to the point made by H. J. Paton and quoted by Ramsey himself, that 'if Joseph had acceded to the desires of Potiphar's wife, his action would have been altruistic, but it would not therefore have been moral'.[44] Certainly, to emphasize in reply '*enlightened* unselfishness' is simply to beg the question. Again, it may be queried whether the so-called duties to oneself are properly represented as instrumental duties which are justified by the ultimate service of a neighbour's needs; and it is by no means clear that the most substantial ethical reality involved in the institution of permanence in marriage can be brought under the rubric of restraint of sin, as is suggested when Ramsey says that 'to promise permanence means, in part, to acknowledge that at his best man remains sinful and that sin may invade his very best emotions . . .'[45] Indeed pervasively, within the scope of Ramsey's treatment of his subject, there may be detected an unconvincing atomism which begins with me and my neighbour, adds a few more neighbours, and ends with a complex society and all its institutions.

What is important for the present discussion, however, is none of these things. Even if Ramsey's positive treatment of the Christian life were at every point entirely beyond question, there would remain the limited scope of his inquiry and his failure to face the question of the relationship between Christian and general ethics.

For the most part Ramsey is concerned to underline the contrast between these two and the fact that in Christian ethics 'the standard is a supernatural measure';[46] and by and large he represents the Christian ethic as a *rival* to all other ethics, even if with some of them it may enter into a coalition for the time being but never a concordat.[47] This is, so far as I can judge, Professor Ramsey's last word on the question in this book; but logically it cannot be the last word. 'Yes' does not say 'no' to 'no', 'yes' does not contradict 'no', except within the same universe of discourse. If you say 'yes' to one man and I say 'no' to another, you and I are not contradicting each other unless we are answering the same question. If it is, however, *the same question*, it defines or indicates an area to be investigated. The systematic inquiry into the nature of the Christian life cannot rest content with the pragmatic outlook which holds that the Christian way is an alternative or rival to other possible ways of life. It must rather pursue the 'ought' which overflows Christian morality precisely in so far as the latter enters upon a ground already occupied; and it must seek to understand the ethical dimension of human life common to believer and unbeliever alike. Christian ethics, accordingly, is (in the singular) a science which cannot possibly rest in a descriptive account of the contrasting features of different ethics (in the plural). Contrariwise, to add one ethic to another, in terms of similarities or of dissimilarities, is still to fall short of ethics as a science; and the student of Christian ethics must be prepared to rise above the pragmatic level to the reflective and to wrestle with what I have called the mathematics of his subject.

## Chapter 7

# THE PROBLEM OF
# THEOLOGICAL ETHICS

*(a) The problem of autonomy and heteronomy*

The insights of general ethics are not left behind as either invalid or irrelevant as the discussion moves on to take account of the Christian life and to enter the field of Christian ethics; but no more can these insights be allowed to assume a status of inviolable sovereignty, so that anything inconsistent with them is by that very fact ruled out of court and their own survival, completely unscathed, guaranteed as a foregone conclusion. Into the bargain there is no possibility that tension and conflict may be avoided by extracting the sting from the Christian faith and the Christian ethic, so that it is no longer foolishness to the Greeks and a stumbling-block to the Jews. It has already been judged an ethic of redemption, and to portray it in any other light is to misrepresent it.

Accordingly, collision there must be and that very soon. As essentially an ethic of redemption, the Christian ethic is necessarily related in a quite explicit manner to God's remedial activity in Jesus Christ, to the saving Word of God in Christ and so to the revelation of the divine grace. If, however, the Christian ethic is an ethic necessarily and explicitly related to the self-revelation of God that fact in itself is the immediate occasion of questions and difficulties which are largely concerned with the problem of autonomy and heteronomy.

This problem, it is worth observing, does not arise only for Christian ethics. Even in general ethics there is a difficulty in this connection. It is certainly possible to by-pass the problem by representing the ultimate factor in morality as the agent's own desires. In this way, by some form of naturalism, the fact that one ought to behave in a certain way becomes in the last resort subordinate to, and derivative from, the fact that one wishes for this rather than that. Such a treatment, however, is tantamount to the elimination of morality altogether. The problem of autonomy and heteronomy is evaded only because in fact the *nomos*, the law or standard, is in effect denied; and many moralists would hold, and rightly so, that this kind of theory misses the mark completely so far as morality is concerned.

Morality by its very nature involves a law or a standard or a norm which is independent of the desires of the individual agent; and the problem of autonomy and heteronomy arises in connection with this standard, for it may be conceived as self-imposed or as imposed from without by another. Thus by autonomy is meant a conception of the moral life as one lived in accordance with a law which proceeds from within and is imposed by the self upon itself, whereas by heteronomy is meant a conception of that life according to which the law or standard comes completely from without and is imposed by some independent reality such as the will of another.

If this were all that had to be said it would perhaps present no difficulty, for then an ethic of redemption and revelation would, almost by definition, be a heteronomous ethic, whereas Kant's conception of the moral life would stand forth as the supreme representation of the case for autonomy. It might then seem that the individual ethical thinker had to choose for himself between these two types of ethical theory just as he has to make up his mind between, let us say, utilitarianism and intuitionism. But the matter is not nearly as simple as this would suggest. On the one hand, it is the case, as indeed we have already seen, that if Kant does provide a thoroughly autonomous conception of the moral law and the moral life, it is at the same time one which is entirely empty, for reason does not bring with it any concrete practical principles of its own. Morality is not simply a matter of self-consistency and universalizability in practice; rather, moral distinctions and principles arise for moral agents in the act of living.

On the other hand, there is a large and impressive consensus of moral opinion to the effect that a heteronomous conception of the moral life, as in the end a life of blind obedience to arbitrary law, is plainly an inferior conception. Almost by definition it is a life totally lacking in moral insight and totally unable to give a reason for itself. The question of autonomy and heteronomy is then not nearly as simple as at first sight it may appear; and in fact it seems to present something of a dilemma, for on the face of it either the moral life is empty or it is arbitrary. Moreover, it is important to notice, with this dilemma even general ethics has to reckon, it does not arise first of all for the Christian moralist.

Indeed some moralists have sought to modify the principle of autonomy so that it no longer strictly means what Kant meant by it, that is 'the principle that a rational will makes, or gives itself, the laws which it obeys'.[1] Thus Professor H. D. Lewis has distinguished three different but related interpretations of the principle, namely, that 'the moral law is not to be derived in any way from a natural impulse or tendency',[2] that 'duty . . . must be accepted because of its obligatory character and, therefore, independently of any natural urge to act as it requires',[3] and that it must 'be "self-imposed" in the sense that I accept or recognize it'.[4] While, however, these are all elements in the Kantian conception of autonomous action and while no doubt the word is sometimes used as if it meant no more than some or all of these, it remains the case that there is a problem here which a change in the meaning of the word may help to obscure but which it certainly does not solve.

So long as men are regarded, necessarily and sufficiently, as rational beings, and so long as reason is deemed productive of practical laws out of its own resources, that is as pure practical reason, there seems to be no difficulty about the suggestion that a rational being should act in accordance with these laws. To do otherwise would be to flee from his own reality as a rational being, and the obligatoriness of morality might then be understood as just the pressure of his true or rational nature upon his actual or empirical nature. On this representation of the matter reason as pure and practical is the ultimate and all-sufficient factor; and although the question may still be asked, 'Why should I act morally?', the question really means 'Why should I act rationally?' and is itself irrational.

If, however, reason is *not* productive from its own resources of practical laws in the sense of quite categorical imperatives, a difficulty does arise concerning moral behaviour. It immediately becomes a question whether it is now possible to avoid a sheerly heteronomous representation of morality according to which moral action is inescapably action in blind obedience to a wholly external law. On this hypothesis, even where one moral agent is prepared to act on the advice of another as an authority on moral matters, it is in a real sense a case of the blind leading the blind; and in the last resort no moral agent is in better case than any other. It is worth noting, moreover, that the three statements already quoted in which Professor Lewis seeks to discriminate three meanings of the principle of autonomy might, without violence but contrary to their author's design, be applied to sheerly heteronomous action.

Consequently some moralists look for a way which will carry them between pure autonomy and sheer heteronomy. The general principle of this type of solution is affirmed by Professor W. G. Maclagan when, having referred to what he calls the 'vital element of autonomy', he goes on to insist that this element 'is not exclusive of, but complementary to, a sort of heteronomy that is every whit as important. The man who "gives the law to himself",' he continues, 'certainly does not regard himself as inventing it, or as free to do so. It is what he, more or less adequately, discovers. ... And ... he necessarily takes what he regards as the discovered *content* of the law to be authoritative for him in virtue of its being that content ... and it is because of this authoritativeness of the content that the formula of autonomy fails us.'[5]

This is a very important statement because, in spite of his indebtedness to Kant, it reveals Maclagan departing decisively from him in his own emphasis upon the authoritativeness of *content*. This is professedly an element of heteronomy which Kant could never have accepted, although it is consistent with the three, alternative or mutually supplementary, criteria of autonomy put forward by H. D. Lewis, namely that the law is not derived from natural impulse, that the inclination to obey is distinguishable from the natural urge to perform the act in question in any case, and that there is free recognition without compulsion. Moreover it does seem more accurate to acknowledge here an element of heteronomy than to describe it as a variant of the principle of autonomy. This way the difficulty is not obscured; and the difficulty is that, once the Kantian emphasis on the *form* of reason is lost, it is not easy to distinguish in principle between this element of heteronomy, with its recognized authoritativeness of content, and thorough-going heteronomy and blind obedience. Nor does the solution adumbrated by the school of linguistic analysis afford any real help in this difficulty, for, as we have seen, it proceeds by confusing the coerciveness of duty and the conservatism of the moral consciousness.

None the less, even if difficulties remain, Professor Maclagan's statement offers the outline of a solution to the problem of autonomy and heteronomy which seeks to hold together the truths to be found on either side and to avoid the different errors of pure autonomy and of sheer heteronomy. Consequently, even by itself it expresses an important insight which is relevant when it arises in connection with specifically Christian ethics and its task of giving an account of what is explicitly an ethic of redemption, an ethic inherently related to the divine self-revelation.

### (b) Heteronomy and ethical fundamentalism

Perhaps the simplest and the earliest attempt within Protestantism to give an account of the Christian ethic as an ethic of redemption and revelation is to be found in a tendency or trend already mentioned as one of the main types of Protestant ethics. This is the account which seems to meet the expectation of Calvin when he said that 'it will be useful to collect from various places of Scripture a rule for the reformation of the life',[6] and which proceeds along these very lines by bringing together the different practical injunctions and exhortations to be found in Scripture and by presenting them in as systematic a fashion as possible. This was doubtless the earliest form that a specifically Protestant account of morality assumed, but although it is mainly characteristic of the first century or so of the post-Reformation period it is possible to find examples of the same kind of treatment at much later dates.

Indeed, although this method of approach is now largely outdated, it is perhaps not too much to say that so far as Protestantism has an official view of the moral life this is it. It still lies behind much of the *ad hoc* treatment afforded within Protestantism to particular problems of the Christian life; and as late as the middle of the nineteenth century it appeared in deliberate and systematic form in a popular textbook, *The Outlines of Theology* by A. A. Hodge. In the argument of this book the author first of all distinguished what he called 'the three grand departments of Christian theology',[7] the exegetical, the dogmatic or systematic, and the practical; and then he described the practical as having as its object 'to deduce, from the doctrines and precepts of the Bible, rules for the organisation and administration of the Christian Church in all her functions, and for the guidance of the individual Christian in all the relations of life'. The word 'all', used twice in this statement, is significant, and it is clear that for Hodge the word of Scripture was the supreme and sufficient rule of life for all who profess to be Christian.

There are, however, two serious objections to this account of the matter. The first of these is that it presupposes a superficial view of divine revelation as primarily concerned to convey correct information and, it ought to be added, authoritative commands. This is what has come to be known as the propositional view of revelation as consisting of the various propositions contained in the Scriptures, and it implies that Scripture is uniformly and without qualification the word of God to men. It is not too much to say, however, that although this view can claim something like official status it has never really answered to the faith of the Church, or even to the faith of those who propounded and upheld it. Yet it has taken the Church a long time to visualize an alternative to it.

None the less when the theory is critically considered it becomes very difficult to defend. It represents revelation as if it consisted of objective, external, and, so far as its recipients are concerned, arbitrary truth which is simply set there to be blindly accepted, and of objective, external and similarly arbitrary commands which are likewise set there to be blindly obeyed. Revelation itself, however, both as it appears to Christian faith and as it is portrayed in Scripture, is personal, not propositional. When God reveals himself it is he himself whom he reveals, divine reality, not just divine truths or divine commands, and his revelation is the reconciliation of the world and the establishment of fellowship between man and God. In this context there is room for the work of the Holy Spirit, for when man speaks seriously of the revelation of God he is already positing that work. Scripture too is indispensable; but the question is whether Scripture is the instrument of the Holy Spirit or the foregone conclusion of the Spirit's work, and the present contention is that it is the former conception that measures up more adequately to the reality of revelation.

The other defect in the theory is that it misrepresents the human response to the divine work. On the one side faith is much more than a merely intellectual assent, which a bare nod of the head might convey, to certain divinely presented propositions; and on the other side life for the Christian is much more than a blind obedience to commands with which a man is arbitrarily but, it is thought, divinely confronted. If God's will is depicted in this way it remains wholly external to man's will and something totally alien and arbitrary, and in turn human obedience to it is likewise wholly external because completely blind and totally void of thought and understanding.

This, however, is not at all as Scripture itself represents the matter. 'Create in me a clean heart, O God,' cried the Psalmist, 'and renew a right spirit within me.'[8] 'Master,' said the lawyer to Jesus, 'which is the great commandment in the law?' And Jesus said to him, 'Thou shalt love the Lord thy God with all thy heart, and with all thy soul, and with all thy mind. This is the first and great commandment. And the second is like unto it, Thou shalt love thy neighbour as thyself.'[9] 'I live,' wrote St Paul, 'yet not I, but Christ liveth in me.'[10] These statements are representative of the Bible, coming as they do from the Old Testament, the Gospels and the Epistles; and it is impossible to think that they could ever be regarded as incidental aberrations from the central message of Scripture. On the contrary, that message speaks as clearly in them as anywhere else; and they in turn no less clearly exclude any interpretation of the religious life which basically represents it as one of merely blind and external obedience to external and apparently arbitrary demands. Accordingly the type of Christian ethics presently under review must be set aside, and that because, although it did try to portray the Christian ethic as one of redemption and revelation, it did so along the lines, and within the framework, of a sheerly heteronomous theory.[11]

*(c)  Autonomy and the ethical implications of (the ethico-logical
appendix to) theology*

Thus, as the discussion has proceeded, another of the four main
types of Protestant ethics already distinguished has fallen by the
wayside. At an earlier stage in the argument two principal kinds
of Protestant theory were rejected on a more elementary issue,
namely, that they failed to measure up to the reality of the Christian ethic as an ethic of redemption and revelation. Now a
Protestant account of morality which has tried to portray the Christian life as a redeemed life, as one dominated by divine revelation,
has failed, and has done so at the hurdle presented by the problem
of autonomy and heteronomy, in particular by falling on the side
of sheer heteronomy. It now remains to be seen that an ethic of
redemption may stumble at the same hurdle and fall into something like the error of pure autonomy, for that in a sense must be
the verdict on the remaining type of Protestant ethical theory so
far mentioned.

At the time[12] I described this theory as one in which the Christian life is ultimately and basically conceived as a life lived deliberately within the theological framework of all human existence.
That seems a fair description of a type of Christian ethical theory
which has flourished for something like a century, from the time
of Schleiermacher until very nearly the present day, although, as
is only to be expected, different expressions of it vary considerably in respect of their adequacy to the Christian life with which
they are all professing to deal in a systematic manner.

So far as the distinction between autonomous and heteronomous theories is concerned it is fairly clear that this type of theory
falls within the former category. Negatively at least, it does not
depict the Christian life as one lived in relation to a quite external
and apparently arbitrary standard to which by will, without insight and understanding, men ought ever to try to conform themselves. Rather the moral life on this view proceeds from within a
man; and yet if in thus being autonomous this interpretation
necessarily associates itself with the ethical outlook of Immanuel
Kant, it does not accept his view that a man himself and by
himself can produce, from his reason or from any other part of

himself, the practical principles and the guiding stars by which he should live. Instead it contemplates man as one to whom God has spoken in revelation through the Scriptures, and therefore as one who has absorbed into himself the whole teaching of revelation or at any rate its central ideas. If on this view man is a morally autonomous being he is so, not just as a rational being, but as an instructed or enlightened being – instructed by divine revelation. So far from being excluded revelation is clearly posited on this view; but it operates, one might say, only indirectly through various ideas which the moral person has been able to absorb from revelation and which together constitute the theological framework of all human existence.

That is why in describing this type of theory as autonomous it is necessary at the same time to attach some qualification to the adjective and to say, for example, that it is *in a sense* autonomous. What is clear is that Christian moralists who expound this kind of theory, such as Theodor Haering and A. B. D. Alexander, although they have learned much from Immanuel Kant, do not accept even in its broad outline the Kantian conception of the moral life as by itself adequate. On the other hand, it is no less clear that they neither favour a position of sheer heteronomy nor do they seek some other alternative in the middle way between the errors of pure autonomy and sheer heteronomy. On the contrary they are sufficiently close to Kant to believe that the truth lies and must lie with some form of autonomous theory; but unlike Kant they posit at the outset of their ethical inquiry, not just man, a rational being, a being who exercises pure reason, practical as well as theoretical, but explicitly Christian man, man whose mind is no *tabula rasa* but who has been instructed in, and has accepted, the truths and tenets of the Christian faith.

These truths and ideas are not of course innate, they do not belong to pure reason; but since they are *presuppositions* of the Christian moral life it remains true that for these writers that life proceeds from within a man. Accordingly it is necessary, for the sake of precision, to say that the type of theory adumbrated is *in a sense* autonomous, where the qualification does *not* mean that it is in any degree heteronomous or that on the whole it seeks some middle way between autonomy and heteronomy. Rather, so far as autonomy, heteronomy and any middle way between them are concerned, this type of theory is clearly autonomous, but it is autonomous in a way which is in certain important respects in contrast to the pure autonomy of Immanuel Kant.

That this analysis and classification are correct is borne out by the fact that it suggests another characteristic which in fact theories of this type are accustomed to reveal. If dogmatics deals with the content of revelation and ethics with the life which a man must seek to live who has been apprehended by this revelation, then it is possible to see how, along the lines which are characteristic of this type of treatment, there can be combined a recognition of the necessary connection between dogmatics and ethics on the one hand and, on the other, the affirmation of a relative independence on the part of ethics which has the effect of stabilizing and immobilizing the insights and ideas derived from revelation.

Indeed, some such combination is necessary for this point of view. The affirmation of a close connection between dogmatics and ethics corresponds to the interpretation of the Christian ethic as an ethic of redemption and revelation, while the affirmation of a relative independence on the part of ethics corresponds to the contention that none the less the Christian life must be conceived in terms of moral autonomy. Thus Theodor Haering maintained of dogmatics and ethics that 'on external grounds of convenience they are separately treated, but they form one whole. . . . Ethics rests entirely on Dogmatics';[13] while A. B. D. Alexander was able to list Haering himself as one of those who accentuated the difference between ethics and dogmatics.[14] To what extent there is justice behind this judgment it would be beside the present point to stop to inquire, although it is worth noting that in propounding the maxim that 'Christ is the principle of Christian Ethics'[15] Haering may well have pointed forward more clearly to subsequent developments in Christian ethical thought, and so may have approached more closely the perspective from which the limitations of the present type of ethical theory can be transcended than most other thinkers of the time. What is perhaps even more certain is that Alexander himself appears to have offered an account of Christian morality in which both the essential characteristics and the serious deficiencies of the present approach are plainly to be seen.

Like Haering, Alexander could speak of the necessary connection between dogmatics and ethics, but quite explicitly he represented the contribution of the former, so far as ethics was concerned, as consisting of certain postulates, that is to say, of certain *ideas*, which ethics must simply take for granted and treat as its indispensable presuppositions. 'Ethics', he maintained,[16] 'assumes the Christian idea of God.' 'On the one hand', he said,[17]

Ethics saves Dogmatics from evaporating into unsubstantial speculation, and by affording the test of workableness, keeps it upon the solid foundation of fact. On the other hand, Dogmatics supplies to Ethics its formative principles and normative standards, and preserves the moral life from degenerating into the vagaries of fanaticism or the apathy of fatalism. But while both sciences form complementary sides of theology and stand in relations of mutual service, each deals with the human consciousness in a different way. Dogmatics regards the Christian life from the standpoint of divine dependence: Ethics regards it from the standpoint of human determination.

This statement suggests fairly clearly the kind of view to which Alexander was committed. On the one side his reference to 'human determination', so far as it goes, is an indication that for him the Christian life must be understood in autonomous rather than heteronomous terms, while, on the other side, his description of the contribution of dogmatics to ethics as principles and standards justifies what has already been said concerning this outlook, namely that it deals with man as one who has absorbed certain *ideas* from revelation.

Moreover, when Alexander subsequently came to closer grips with the problem of the Christian life, it is noticeable that his emphasis was different from that of Haering. Where the latter, in dealing with the nature of the Christian good, laid it down as his first maxim that 'Christ is the principle of Christian Ethics' and further contended that 'all the moral action of Christian men is referred to Christ as the personal source of the highest "Good",'[18] Alexander had something else to say. 'The highest good', he argued,[19] 'is not uniformly described in the New Testament, and modern ethical teachers have not always been in agreement as to the chief end of life. While some,' he continued, have found in the teaching of Jesus the idea of social redemption alone, and have seen in Christ nothing more than a political reformer, others have contended that the Gospel is solely a message of personal salvation. An impartial study shows that both views are one-sided. ... While the writers of the New Testament vary in their mode of presenting the ultimate goal of man, they are at one in regarding it as an exalted form of *life*. What they all seek to commend is a condition of being involving a gradual assimilation to, and communion with, God. The distinctive gift of the Gospel is the gift of life. 'I am the Life', says Christ. And the apostle's confession is in harmony with his Master's claim – 'For me to live is Christ.' Salvation is nothing else than the restoration, preservation, and exaltation of life.

And the culmination of Alexander's argument was in line with this important stage in its development, for in the end his contention was that 'life is nothing but the growing realisation of God',[20] and that in the Christian life a man 'lives in an ever-expanding life in the life of others, manifesting more and more that spiritual principle which is the life of God, who lives and loves in all things'.[21]

This is by no means an unimpressive account of the Christian life and it may well have considerable merit; but its relevance to the present discussion lies, not in the details of Alexander's presentation, but in the light it throws upon a trend and a type in Christian ethical thought. From what has been said it seems quite clear that Alexander regarded the correct conception of the Christian life as one which did justice to its total autonomy, and accordingly represented it as proceeding from within the man himself. On the other hand, without qualifying or minimizing in any way this fact about it, it is also clear that Alexander tried to deal seriously with its Christian character and so with its dependence upon revelation. As he outlined his conception of the Christian life he held these sides together and indeed held them together without any suspicion of tension. It is important to notice, however, that this was possible only because for him the contribution of revelation was assumed to consist of certain postulates or presuppositions, of certain *ideas* about God, drawn certainly from revelation but operating on their own account and separated off from their origin in the living reality of God himself, and so, inevitably, in some sense immobilized in the ethical sphere.

In some respects it may be unfair to Alexander, and in particular to his specifically Christian intention, to say that for him the autonomy of the moral self is uppermost and provides the first principle of his Christian ethics. But at any rate it cannot plausibly be denied that if for him the autonomy of the moral self is no more the first principle of his Christian ethics than his other main principle, the recognition of the theological postulates, the former principle is in his system entirely uninfringed by the latter and the two live happily and easily side by side.

*(d) Tension between an autonomous ethic and an ethic of redemption*

In spite of this verdict there is some sense in which the fundamental factor in this type of ethical thought is after all a belief in autonomy. It has already been said that this kind of ethical theory is one which has flourished from the time of Schleiermacher; but it has to be admitted that if the student were to look to others who stand in this line of development for precisely the two ideas which seem to be definitive of Alexander's position he might well look in vain. What has to be remembered is that the line of development from Schleiermacher was not primarily, still less exclusively, a development in Christian ethical thought. It was rather a development in theology as a whole. Moreover it was a development in which those who produced it turned their backs upon the rationalism which had prevailed for centuries and concentrated attention upon the concrete reality of religion. No longer was theology primarily and directly concerned with an area of objective truth to be discerned either by the unaided exercise of reason or with the assistance of revelation. Its immediate concern was rather to recognize the concrete reality of religion as a human activity or phenomenon to be acknowledged and understood. Consequently from the very beginning of this development an autonomy wider than the purely moral was firmly posited, since religion was recognized as a genuinely human phenomenon.

It is true that the great originator of this approach, Friedrich Schleiermacher, in his zeal and under the influence of his fundamental conviction that piety is neither a knowing nor a doing but a feeling, was constantly in danger of leading theology into sheer subjectivism, and it has been an oft-repeated criticism of him that he substituted human discovery for divine revelation and religious psychology for theology. On the other hand, where he comes near to the recognition of revelation it is never in the shape of general metaphysical ideas nor of impersonal truths, but in that of a personal and concrete approach, in the sense of an embodiment if not of an encounter. A system of propositions, he said, can be involved in revelation only 'as a moment of the life of a thinking being who works upon us directly as a distinctive existence by means of his total impression on us'. And, he added,[22] 'the original fact will always be the appearing of such a being'.

Because in theology at large Schleiermacher was ambiguous on the matter of divine revelation and a genuinely divine reconciliation he was bound to be ambiguous with regard to the character of the Christian ethic as an ethic of redemption, and he was bound to be clearer about the subjective realization of this redemption than about its objective conditions and source. None the less too much weight should not be placed upon Schleiermacher's minimizing aberrations, upon his tendency towards subjectivism or upon his leaning towards some form of theological liberalism – certainly not to the extent of allowing these characteristics of his thought to blot out everything else.

What is important here and historically influential is his concentration upon religion as a concrete human phenomenon and his insistence upon looking at it from the inside. It is this which justifies the impressive verdicts that have been passed upon him. 'Next to the *Institutes* of Calvin', wrote H. R. Mackintosh of *The Christian Faith*, 'it is the most influential dogmatic work to which evangelical Protestantism can point, and it has helped to teach theology to more than three generations. One could no more understand present-day systematic thought without this book – its faults equally with its virtues – than one could understand modern biology without Darwin.'[23] 'He may have no disciples in the strict sense of the term', said W. B. Selbie in an article in *The Encyclopaedia of Religion and Ethics*,[24] 'but every theologian is his debtor.' 'Away back in the beginning of last century', declared Professor H. H. Farmer, 'the great thinker Schleiermacher began a new era of thought on these matters by insisting that "piety" is not theological or philosophical theorizing about ultimate things, nor is it the seeking to achieve certain standards of behaviour and self-discipline, but is just piety.'[25]

What Schleiermacher pre-eminently contributed was a theological approach and method which concerned itself, not immediately with some objective realm of ideas, but with the concrete human phenomenon or reality of religion, to be examined and understood from within. Accordingly what he impressed upon the line of theological development which stemmed from him was an indelible sense of what might be called the humanity of religion,[26] its non-alien character, in a word, its autonomy in a wider sense than the purely moral. Henceforth, without going back upon Schleiermacher, there could be no place for the sheerly heteronomous; and although Schleiermacher's concern was with autonomy in a wider sense than the purely moral it was bound to determine the understanding of the moral too, and of the specifically Christian ethic. Henceforth they too would be looked at primarily as human phenomena, possibilities and indeed realities of human existence, to be investigated from within.

Indeed Professor Paul Lehmann has suggested that Schleiermacher's posthumously published work on Christian ethics 'in significance for the history of theological ethics paralleled the influence of the *Glaubenslehre* upon dogmatics'.[27] 'Schleiermacher', he says,[28] 'had painstakingly faced the problem of the relation between Christian and philosophical ethics'; and Professor Lehmann uses the term 'dia-parallelism' to describe the kind of position which Schleiermacher contrived to work out. He affirmed both the parallel enterprises of Christian ethics and of philosophical ethics in such a way that in the last resort no contradiction was possible between them. On the contrary, if Schleiermacher was right, each involved an intrinsic thrust towards the other, both being 'identical to this extent . . . that each must include within its own concern what is central to the ethical reality and integrity of the other'.[29]

Thus, on Lehmann's analysis, Schleiermacher in his dia-parallelism made a significant advance upon what Lehmann calls the revisionism of St Augustine and the synthesis of St Thomas Aquinas. 'Schleiermacher', he says,[30] 'has proposed the most forthright interpretation of the relation between Christian and philosophical ethics since the Thomistic synthesis. Here is, however, no logical and hierarchical subordination of philosophical to Christian ethics. Instead, there is an inner and organic dynamic intrinsic to the full elaboration of Christian and of philosophical ethics which presupposes and drives toward what is ethically real and central to the other.' 'Yet,' he concludes,[31] 'the question whether the methodological parallelism between philosophy and theology can be sustained without an ultimate capitulation of one of these disciplines to the other still remains.'

Professor Lehmann's whole discussion of Schleiermacher's contribution to Christian ethics is valuable and penetrating; but the main, or the most interesting, element of his analysis, so far as the present argument is concerned, is undoubtedly his recognition of what he calls a 'middle term'. 'The fact is', he says,[32] 'that Schleiermacher had found what was for him a satisfactory middle term between rationality and Christian faith. The religious consciousness is the hidden ground of meeting between reason and faith.' The religious consciousness, however, which thus occupies a key position in the system of Schleiermacher's ethical thought, both philosophical and Christian, and renders possible his solution of dia-parallelism, was for him something that could not be understood except from within itself. Thus the lines were laid down for an account which, whatever else it might be, would certainly be autonomous, and this not for Schleiermacher alone but for his successors.

It is indeed possible to set Albrecht Ritschl, perhaps the greatest of these successors, in almost unrelieved contrast to Schleiermacher. It is possible, for example, to hold that 'Schleiermacher had been the great subjectivist; broadly speaking, he had found the starting-point of theology in what happens within the believing soul, not in historic fact', whereas it was left to Ritschl to follow the latter course, finding 'the needed foothold . . . in the Person of Jesus Christ, the revealer of the Father, as set forth in the New Testament'.[33] It is possible, moreover, to fix on 'this newness of approach' as the decisive factor in any attempt 'to "place" Ritschl in this historical succession'.[34] There are, however, two things in Schleiermacher which ought to be carefully distinguished, namely, his insistence, in the first place, that religion is a concrete human phenomenon to be investigated from within, and then what has been called his immanentism or psychologism which is the particular line he followed in pursuing this investigation and which has given rise to the charge that he was much too ambiguous on the question of divine revelation.

It is the former emphasis which has already been singled out in the present argument as Schleiermacher's definitive contribution; and Ritschl himself stands squarely in the line of development which it opened up. As much as anyone he too finds his starting-point, not outside in some immediately neutral realm of general ideas, but inside 'personal Christianity'.[35] It is a further fact about him that starting there he proceeds, rightly, not by directing his gaze inwardly to the believing soul, but by turning it outwardly to the remedial action of God. In this, without a doubt, Ritschl was right and was in fact correcting one of Schleiermacher's most peculiar and most distinctive aberrations. It is important, however, to see that none the less he shared Schleiermacher's starting-point and accepted no less the autonomous conception of religion, whatever modifications he might find himself compelled to make as he proceeded.

In fact he did not find himself compelled to introduce any drastic modification, and it is the mark of his weakness that he did not. Certainly, starting from within the reality of personal Christianity he directed his gaze not inwards but outwards, towards the revelation of God. Certainly, he thus brought morality even more closely to the centre of the stage; but understanding morality in autonomous terms he allowed it to achieve a position of dominance in relation to the whole field of religious truth.

Indeed one of his fundamental convictions was that religious judgments are what he called judgments of value; and although this contention has been the subject of considerable controversy, especially over the question whether in concentrating in this way upon value Ritschl had lost his hold upon objective reality, substituting what *ought to be* for what *is*, H. R. Mackintosh's comment seems eminently sound. 'As to the objective intention of religious value-judgments', he wrote,[36] '. . . no question ought to have been raised. The vital issue emerges at quite another point. It is whether the standard of value we apply in thus affirming our recognition of God in Christ is merely moral or also transcendent; or, to put it otherwise, whether in confronting Christ and forming the judgment of faith upon Him and His work we bring with us, as it were ready-made, the standards by which He is to be estimated, or have them new-created in us, through specific revelation, by the Spirit of God.'

This is indeed the crucial point, and Mackintosh's comment hits the nail squarely on the head. In Ritschl's hands the moral, conceived in autonomous terms, was certainly allowed to gain control and to exercise it unbrokenly over revelation, so that only so much of the latter could appear as was acceptable to the unredeemed moral consciousness of humankind. If, however, natural morality is permitted this ascendancy over revelation, the autonomy of the Christian life may be secured but its character as a redeemed life is left in obscurity and ambiguity. Once again the judgment seems vindicated that the fundamental idea along this line of development is that of autonomy.

Perhaps, however, the most significant evidence is to be found in the work of Theodor Haering, a follower of Ritschl but one who sought to correct Ritschl's overriding defect, his subordination of the grace and truth of the Christian revelation to the natural unredeemed conscience of humankind. In fact, in making this correction Haering came as near as anyone to transcending the limitations of the ethical trend or type presently under consideration; and although Alexander listed him as one of those who 'accentuate the difference' between dogmatics and ethics, he made not a few important points of which any adequate theory of the Christian ethic as an ethic of redemption would have to take account.

For one thing, Haering retained the moral in a central place in the total theological picture, as indeed any Christian moralist or theologian must do who, in spite of prevailing fashions, is prepared to allow that the revelation in Christ addresses itself, not to the intellectually curious nor to the aesthetically susceptible, but to men as such, to men as moral beings. Furthermore, Haering saw that on this account the relationship between what he called philosophical and theological ethics cannot be totally negative. It was, he argued,[37] 'a matter of prime consequence for the friends of the latter to remember that it damages its own cause if it allows the fruits of philosophical investigation to remain unused; as, for example, what human reflection has worked out on the basal relations of ethics in regard to Rule, Motive, Purpose of moral action. Theological Ethics does thereby damage its own clearness as well as its capability of being intelligible to others.'

Nothing could be clearer and nothing perhaps could be more important, and yet there are few lessons which Christian ethics has been slower to learn. For Haering the moral was unique[38] and, in relation to religion, uniquely important, for in the moral life 'we really reach our destiny, the deepest characteristic of our spiritual life – the impulse to unity and freedom'.[39] Yet for the Christian nothing less than 'Christ is the principle of Christian Ethics' and 'the highest Good is the Kingdom of God'.[40]

Thus Haering could both regard the moral as uniquely important and yet see in the Christian ethic an ethic of redemption and revelation. So far as the contrast between autonomy and heteronomy is concerned he could even raise the question 'whether this antithesis is not comprehended in a higher unity' and could suggest that 'the Christian conception of morals plainly points to this'.[41] Far more than in Ritschl the revelation was on the verge of controlling, dominating and transforming the moral, not cancelling and destroying it indeed, but controlling, dominating and transforming, so that the question is bound to be posed whether Haering has not in effect burst through the ethical trend and type in which he has been placed.

To this question, however, a negative answer must be given in view of one all-governing factor in the system of Haering's thought, and that factor was his apologetics which Haering still understood as a 'proof of the truth'. This, as a *rational* proof, was of course the traditional concept of apologetics; and although Schleiermacher's work had by implication undermined this concept, Haering had been unable to shake himself sufficiently free of it to re-think the question of apologetics and to break quite new ground. Although for him the traditional rational proof was no longer either a feasible or a relevant project, apologetics was still a 'proof of the truth'. It was, he held, the quite necessary 'foundation of Dogmatics and Ethics', so that even 'if ... Ethics is separately treated, it is still impossible to dispense with the Apologetic foundation'.[42] As the indispensable prerequisite both of theology and of ethics, apologetics provided a proof of the truth, but for Haering that meant not a rational proof but a *moral* proof.

Thus at the very foundation of his system, both on the theological side and on the ethical, there was posited an ultimate and autonomous moral sphere; and consequently the verdict is once again vindicated that along the present line of thought moral autonomy is indeed the first principle. If with Schleiermacher who, though disowned and discredited by many of his successors, gave the impetus to this line of thought, the moral was left apart, to one side of religion as it were, it rapidly assumed a position of importance and dominance within the realm of theology itself and imposed a far-reaching principle of autonomy upon Christian ethics. Further, if Haering did not so readily as Ritschl leave the impression that revelation must be reduced to what was morally acceptable, he did none the less contend that only as it was morally provable could it legitimately lay its claim upon human life.

*(e) Pointers towards the future: beyond autonomy and heteronomy*

No doubt if the choice before the Christian moralist were a very simple and straightforward one, either heteronomy or autonomy, he would be bound to agree so far with this development in Christian ethical thinking. Even an obedience which is complete and perfect, though totally blind, is morally inferior to a life lived for the most part in accordance with principles embraced with some measure of conviction and understanding. The difficulty is that in the light of contemporary theological insight there is an even more important side of the truth which this account of the matter fails to comprehend. In making the autonomy of the moral self the first principle and the dominating consideration it is bound to give the appearance of error, and to raise questions concerning its ability to reckon seriously with the reality of revelation and so to make a genuine claim to be, not just ethics, but *Christian* ethics.

No doubt, within this account of the matter, the attempt was made, as we have seen, to represent the Christian ethic as an ethic of redemption and revelation; but whether revelation was compelled to submit to moral scrutiny or at least to moral proof, or was simply recognized in the shape of theological postulates, absorbed Christian teaching, the result was that the autonomy of the moral self was uninfringed and in effect the revelation of God was subordinated to, was placed at the disposal of, the mind and the will of man. No doubt it happened again and again, as we have also noted, that along this line of thought the connection between dogmatics and ethics was insistently affirmed, in refreshing contrast to some earlier outlooks; but at the same time a relative independence was accorded to ethics, whereas, if Karl Barth may be allowed to speak for contemporary theology, 'ethics so-called I regard as the doctrine of God's command and do not consider it right to treat it otherwise than as an integral part of dogmatics, or to produce a dogmatics which does not include it'.[43]

It is not that for Barth ethics and dogmatics are necessarily connected. Rather ethics is a *part* of dogmatics and is included within it; and with this insight the road is opened up for a more adequate account of the Christian ethic as an ethic of revelation and reconciliation. There remains, it is worth repeating, the first side of the truth, that if there were a straightforward choice between heteronomy and autonomy it would be necessary to choose the latter. This side of the truth is not to be surrendered to the other nor lost completely, and it may be that Karl Barth did not sufficiently appreciate the necessity of this choice; but while the problem has still to be faced of holding *both* sides together in effective relationship, it is important at the present juncture to emphasize that there is a second side of the truth which it has been the peculiar merit of modern theology to comprehend. For if man is represented as a completely autonomous moral being and if the divine revelation is thought to influence his conduct only through certain theological postulates or ideas, or only as morally acceptable or morally provable, then there seems to be no question left, in that case man is sovereign and God is but a human idea, man has God pocketed as it were, subordinated to his will, immobilized.

Once both sides of the truth have been recognized the problem is to hold the two together. The discussion has shown that Christian ethical theory of the type favoured by men like Haering and Alexander is one-sided and fails to do justice to the Christian ethic as an ethic of revelation and redemption. Although its intention was doubtless to represent the Christian ethic in this way, yet by subordinating everything to the autonomous moral being, by making autonomy in the final analysis the first principle, it immobilized the divine self-revelation and so made it no revelation at all. This means that the choice between autonomy and heteronomy is not as simple as has often been supposed, and that there must be some third and more complex possibility, no matter how difficult it may be to discern.

Pure autonomy of the Kantian type, that is the concept of a law which is completely self-imposed in that its content is determined wholly and exclusively by the inherent demand of practical reason that it should be capable of universalization without contradiction, has largely proved itself, even to philosophical ethics, formal, empty and unsatisfactory. Professor Maclagan, for example, quite apart from any thought of an ethic of redemption and in full appreciation of the necessary element of autonomy, finds himself compelled to admit that 'this vital element of autonomy is not exclusive of, but complementary to, a sort of heteronomy that is every whit as important'. The self-imposed law is not invented by the moral agent but is discovered by him, and 'it is only as and because it is something discovered and not something invented that he can then *authoritatively* impose it on himself, not by creation but by adoption'.[44]

Clearly this statement leaves the Kantian concept of autonomy behind and contemplates a third and more complex possibility. No less clearly, however, it is not a possibility that meets the needs of the present discussion at the stage so far reached. Something even more complex is required, for so long as the objective heteronomous element is conceived as static and impersonal it cannot be properly identified with divine revelation. On the contrary, while the move from the purely Kantian type of autonomy to Maclagan's combination of autonomous and heteronomous elements is a move in the right direction, it does not carry the matter outwith the egocentric situation or predicament in which so much modern philosophical thought has been held to be imprisoned.[45]

It may be difficult to hit on a single word and category which would be adequate to meet the situation, but the difficulty itself is one that can be understood. It is the general difficulty of finding categories adequate to the interpersonal situation which is the human situation, adequate to what some existentialists have called the condition of intersubjectivity. What is required is a conception which will correspond in ethics to Emil Brunner's idea of dialogical truth as distinguished from monological truth,[46] a conception, that is to say, of what may be called a bi-polar autonomy within which there is room for passing, temporary elements of heteronomy, but within which, more characteristically, deep calleth unto deep, spirit witnesseth with spirit, and obedience to the very highest law may well be identical with perfect freedom.

This is an element in the Christian truth about man which is, not that he *is* in the image of God, but that he is *made* in the image of God, finite, a creature, and yet in the image of God the infinite Creator. Somewhat more precisely, man stands in the presence of God and, whether he knows it or not, God's Spirit witnesses with his spirit. In other words, where medieval thought assimilated human nature to nature in a wider sense, and then contrasted the realm of nature with that of grace, I would rather say that there is no *human* nature apart from grace.[47] The distinctive feature of man's being is, not only his peculiar endowment, but also the peculiar and fateful relationship in which he stands to his Creator. Thus autonomy is part of the truth about man but not the whole truth, for his autonomy is a responsive autonomy or a secondary autonomy, responsive to God his Creator of whom alone may be predicated complete autonomy. Within the human sphere the distinction and the dilemma between absolute autonomy and absolute heteronomy arise only when abstraction is made from what is none the less the fully human situation.

In this way the limitations of the important trend in Christian ethical thought which has been under review are effectively transcended. It is no longer possible to speak simply of a necessary connection between dogmatics and ethics. It becomes appropriate to regard Christian ethics as a part of dogmatics.

### (f) Christian ethics and general ethics

This means too that although general or philosophical ethics is relevant to Christian ethics it is no longer possible to think of Christian ethics as totally dependent upon general ethics as did Haering, nor even more explicitly to say with Alexander that

'Christian Ethics is a branch of general Ethics'.[48] In such contentions autonomy was firmly posited as the first principle, and even
the theological postulates were brought within the self-contained
human enterprise of the general ethical inquiry. When, however,
the assertion is critically examined that Christian ethics is a branch
of general ethics it becomes very difficult indeed to understand
what this can possibly mean. It can hardly be intended that Christian ethics should concern itself with the duties of Christians as
some other branch might concern itself with the duties of doctors
or of bachelors or of some other group, or that it should deal
with the ethical teaching of Jesus while some other branch is
allowed to deal with the teaching of Socrates or of Bishop Butler.

Strictly speaking, however, what Alexander maintained was
that Christian ethics is a branch, not of applied ethics nor of the
history of ethics, but of *general* ethics; and yet this is even more
difficult to understand. If Christian ethics is taken to be one
branch of general ethics then perhaps utilitarian ethics might be
regarded as another; but utilitarianism is not a branch of general
ethics; it is one possible solution to the problem of general ethics,
whereas Christian ethics is not even such a solution although it
may imply one. Christian ethics claims to occupy the same ground
as general ethics after general ethics has done its work in terms of
this moral theory or that. In other words, Christian ethics arises
because there is a Christian life which claims to be the fulfilment
of all life. 'I am come', said Jesus, 'that they might have life, and
that they might have it more abundantly.'[49]

The truth seems to be that Christian ethics is not a branch of
general ethics at all. Christian ethics and general ethics occupy
the same ground. This is so because of the high claim which God
in Christ makes, not simply upon those who acknowledge the
claim but upon men of every colour, class and creed, the claim
that here are the way, the truth and the life. On this account
Christian ethics demands to be seen as occupying the same ground
as general ethics and consequently as being a separate study over
and above general ethics, never to be confused with the latter nor
assimilated to it, but never able to be entirely dissociated from it
as if it had never been or as if it contained nothing but a distortion
of the truth.

The logic of this situation seems plain and inescapable. The claim of Christ transcends any conceivable claim by the world's moral teachers and reformers. He claims nothing less than to master man's conscience, in the words of P. T. Forsyth, to 'master man's inner master'. He claims, not to take the place of conscience, as an external authority intruding and expelling the inherent authority of a man's own insight, but rather to centre conscience in himself as the very truth of life to which conscience itself is only a poor witness. Thus it happened that, while Christ did issue commandments and in general did enter the field of moral teaching, he did something significantly beyond all that, for he summoned all men to himself. 'Come unto me, all ye that labour and are heavy laden, and I will give you rest. Take my yoke upon you, and learn of me; for I am meek and lowly in heart; and ye shall find rest unto your souls. For my yoke is easy, and my burden is light'.[50] Thus it happened too that the fellowship of believers, not only hearing his successive words in this situation and in that, but witnessing in the end his completed work, faithfully answered this claim and acknowledged him to be Lord and Master.

It is precisely because Christ claims to be Lord and Master, it is because he claims to master man's inner master and to centre the human conscience in himself, that Christian ethics can be and must be a separate study outside, over and above, general ethics. This is so because Christian ethics occupies the same ground as general ethics but in doing so introduces a radically different conception of the moral life. Its conception, unlike that of general ethics, does not appeal in the last resort to the autonomous ordinary moral consciousness, but regards that autonomy, so far as it is self-contained, as surrendered, without loss of personal dignity or moral responsibility, rather in fulfilment of the highest freedom, as surrendered and given over in faith, obedience and love to the Lord of all life and the Master of man's conscience, God who was in Christ reconciling the world to himself. Thus Christian ethics occupies the very same ground as general ethics but in doing so introduces a radically different conception of the moral life, and accordingly it must rank as a distinct study and not as a mere branch of general ethics. Christian ethics is indeed the systematic study of human life and conduct as given over in faith to the rule and overlordship of Christ as containing within himself the whole duty of man.

## Chapter 8

# THE ETHICS OF NEO-PROTESTANTISM

*(a) The way forward and the dilemma between formalism and naturalism*

Up to this point the discussion has served to underline several aspects of what seems to be the truth concerning Christian ethics. For one thing, it is not a part or a branch of general or philosophical ethics but covers the same ground as the latter. Secondly, it is a part of Christian dogmatics, a substantial part and the appropriate subject of systematic investigation, but a part which, though distinguishable, is not separable, which cannot be adequately treated in relative independence of dogmatics, and which must therefore remain an integral part of the latter. No doubt, with regard to any given treatment, it might be difficult to say whether it assigned a relative independence to the subject or retained it as an inseparable part of dogmatics; and clearly the question cannot be settled by referring to some external criterion, such as the author's expressed intention or the order and method of presentation which he favours for his work.

The truth is that by themselves the denial of relative independence and the insistence instead that Christian ethics is essentially a part of dogmatics are only pointers which direct attention to a more fundamental consideration, that the Christian ethic is an ethic of redemption. More decisively, this is the recognition that, beyond the problem of autonomy and heteronomy as it arises in general ethics, Christian ethics relates to a situation and a sphere which resists even more radically the dichotomy of autonomy and heteronomy and in which moral truth appears in the form of a dialogue. 'Lord, I believe; help thou mine unbelief.'[1] We are unprofitable servants; we have done that which was our duty to do.'[2] 'I live; yet not I, but Christ liveth in me.'[3]

The major and the decisive point, in a nutshell, is that Christian ethics discloses and demands for its articulation a context, a situation, a sphere, large enough to contain the divine grace, not as an idea of the human mind of which account must be taken in practical decisions, not as the printed injunctions in a book which must be blindly obeyed, not as a completed example to be assiduously copied, nor as at most a general spirit, an *esprit de corps*, imprisoned and embodied in a way of life, but as the sovereign grace of the living God, as the concrete and decisive factor, the perennial source of spiritual renewal, and always the first voice in a difficult dialogue, a dialogue out of which it is fatally easy to fall – to fall indeed and not to know it, for the ground on which we land may be holy ground, ostensibly and empirically Christian ground. To this situation neither the principle of autonomy nor that of heteronomy is entirely adequate; but, if it is remembered that even in self-contained general ethics the principle of autonomy requires to be supplemented by an heteronomous element, it may not be misleading to describe this situation in terms of bi-polar autonomy, wherein deep calleth unto deep and spirit witnesseth with spirit, that is, the autonomy characteristic of the creature made in the image of his Creator, whose very nature it is to stand in the presence of God.

None of the earlier views considered has comprehended this situation; but it is the strength of the vigorous theological movement of Protestantism in the twentieth century that it has come within sight of this situation and has helped to impose it upon contemporary thinking in this field. On the other hand, operating on this deeper and more fundamental level, seeking to outline explicitly an ethic of redemption and revelation, working openly and confessedly within the field of dogmatics, and claiming no relative independence, seeking rather to echo in its systematic teaching the dialogue of grace and faith, this neo-Protestantism has on the whole failed to resolve the problem of autonomy and heteronomy or even to keep both sides in view. Having failed to do this, moreover, it has split into two one-sided and opposing accounts of the same ethic and has confronted the Christian mind with a dilemma similar to that which Brunner held to be the foregone conclusion of the general ethical discussion, either law without content or life without law, either formalism or some type of actualism or naturalism.

## (b) Emil Brunner's ethical thought: the Good is what God does

Of one wing of the movement no better spokesman could be found than Brunner himself, for he more than most gave the Christian ethical problem a close and prolonged examination; and his book, *The Divine Imperative*, must remain for a long time one of the most important publications on this subject. Already isolated elements of his view have intruded themselves into the present discussion. One of these is his interpretation of general ethics as dominated by the search for a human rational standard of conduct in opposition to God's standard and as issuing inevitably in the dilemma, either life without law or law without content. Another is his conception of the Christian life as essentially one of obedience, of obedience first and last whatever the content of the command that is to be obeyed, although as a matter of fact, he admitted, the content of that command is always love.

These are in themselves distinctive features of Brunner's view of Christian ethics; but there is another side to the account he gave which deserves attention, for Brunner emphasized that in the Christian message and gospel there is given, not only the revelation, but also the reality, of the Good. 'This revelation of God's will for humanity', he said,[4] 'is more than this: it is a gift, and therefore a reality.' 'The true Good lies only in the power of God and not in that of man.'[5] This is another way of saying that Jesus Christ is not just a moral teacher but also a Saviour, that the Christian ethic is indeed an ethic of redemption; but a great deal depends on the particular meaning and peculiar slant which Brunner here gave to these truths. He held that 'the Good is that which God does; the goodness of man can be no other than letting himself be placed within the activity of God. This is what "believing" means in the New Testament. And this *faith* is the principle of "ethics".'[6]

This statement of the case does of course portray explicitly an ethic of redemption, but in it at the same time Brunner gave a one-sided version of the truth. He represented faith as if it were entirely a matter of standing, or rather of being placed, in the sun; but, although it is right, and for any ethic of redemption altogether necessary, to emphasize the activity of God, it is a mistake to overlook that of man in response. Both are indispensable to faith, otherwise there would be no fellowship in faith. The human activity of faith is certainly a response to the work of divine grace, and it is certainly such a response in every way, from beginning to end; but because it is a response it is also a reality. Although it is secondary in the sense of being responsive and derivative it is an obvious error to treat it as if it were secondary in the sense of being insignificant. So to emphasize the objective basis of the Christian life, so to emphasize that it is all along the line a life justified by God's grace, that its character as a life of faith is obscured and left in doubt, is to invite and provoke a reaction in which the original truth will be swallowed up and lost.

It is because Brunner's view is in this way seriously one-sided that it yields the curious definition of Christian ethics as 'the science of human conduct as it is determined by Divine conduct';[7] but when he had offered this definition it seems preposterous that Brunner should have claimed that 'here the antithesis between freedom and necessity is removed'.[8] It is removed only in the sense that one side, freedom, has been totally overshadowed and destroyed. It is certainly true, as Brunner claimed, that the Gospel is 'concerned with the release of man from bondage';[9] but while it is important to preserve the sense that the state from which man is rescued by divine grace is one in which he cannot possibly help himself nor contribute in any way to his own salvation, it is no less important to safeguard the insight that the being thus released from bondage is man, a self-determining being who is responsible for his plight, and that this is no merely interesting additional fact about him but stands in the closest possible relation to the affirmation of his redemption. In other words, while it is true that the idea of divine redemption is violated if any notion of man's contribution to that redemption is permitted to intrude, it is no less true that it is also violated if sight is lost of the fact that, while lumps of lead may be salvaged, only men can be redeemed.

Certainly it is the case that, more than Karl Barth for example, Brunner did try to keep this truth in view. In his celebrated controversy with Barth in the thirties he held out for the recognition that sin had not wholly destroyed the *imago dei* in which man had been made but had left intact, not indeed any of its proper content, but its form of rationality and responsibility. Yet, as has often been argued, this rather academic refinement was insufficient to restore to the theological picture the object of God's grace, which should never be eliminated from either preaching or theology. It was indeed insufficient to secure Brunner's triumph in the debate with Barth or to check Brunner's own tendency to lapse into a position which he knew to be unsound.

Beyond question there are points at which Brunner seems on the verge of transcending his own position; but the conclusion can scarcely be avoided that in the end he did not do so but provided rather, on one wing of the neo-Protestant movement, an account of the Christian ethic which is fundamentally onesided.

In particular, Brunner's account of natural morality and general ethics (despite his manifest and refreshing interest in them) is finally a predominantly negative one. Although he entered with sympathy and interest into their reality, he ended by bringing them under a Christian judgment which is, so far as one can judge, thoroughly negative, and thoroughly negative on every side and in every respect. The new knowledge of God and of the Good which comes with the Christian Gospel 'does not merely constitute a positive answer to man's question; it is also a polemical, radically critical denial of man's natural view of his own nature'.[10] 'Natural ethics', he said, 'is dominated by the principle of self-seeking and self-reference',[11] and as for natural morality this 'can be distinguished from rational ethics by the fact that it is more naïve and therefore less self-conscious'.[12] For Brunner, in the light of the Christian revelation, there is nothing positive to be said of natural man, save that in spite of everything there survives in him the bare form of the *imago dei* in which he was made, the formal ability to respond to the revelation and the reality of the Good when by divine grace it comes upon him.

Brunner's account of the Christian ethic is also marked, as we have already noticed, by a pervading and fundamental quality of formalism. For him in the last analysis it is exclusively obedience that is important, obedience to God's will, although, as it happens and as he was perfectly ready to admit, the content of that will is in fact love. This is no caricature of Brunner's position, for he himself said[13] that 'nothing is good save obedience to the command of God, just because it is obedience. No reasons of determination from content here come under consideration. The "form" of the will, obedience, is all. But to be obedient means: "love your neighbour!"' If, however, this is no caricature, it is a confession of one-sidedness. Moreover, as the discussion has also disclosed, this pervasive element of formalism is matched by a no less pervasive element of determinism, which fits in well both with the formalism and with the negative attitude to natural morality, but which obscures the freedom and responsibility essential to man's being as man. The result, it is clear, is a one-sided theory which errs on the side of heteronomy.

A substantially similar judgment must be made of Karl Barth's work in this field. It is true that in the early disclosure of what was to become Barth's characteristic theological position there seemed to many to be a strange streak of indifference and even contempt towards morality. It is difficult to forget that in his Gifford Lectures he allowed himself to classify morality with chance, good luck, as an arbitrary factor in human life. Moreover, in what was doubtless a more considered judgment, he had from the beginning of his dogmatics defined faith as the *determination* of our nature by the Word of God. In the later development of his dogmatics, however, Barth was led to give an extended, and much more balanced, account of ethical reality, and one of very great merit and interest. It is difficult to believe that this did not represent a considerable development of, or at least a clarification in, Barth's theological thought; and yet, like so many developments in his thinking, it did not really infringe the basic structure of his theology. For him, it is plain, faith was still first and last the determination of our nature by the Word of God. Consequently, at one point after another, Barth is to be found affirming ethical theses closely akin to those propounded by Brunner years before.

It has already been pointed out that, just as Brunner insisted that 'the moment that human consciousness exists the problem of ethics is raised',[14] so Barth declared that 'man . . . is exposed from the very outset to this question'.[15] Further, just as Brunner held that 'the Good has its basis and its existence solely in the will of God',[16] so Barth maintained that 'ethics . . . has its basis in the knowledge of Jesus Christ'[17] and nowhere else. Moreover, both adopted a thoroughly negative account of natural morality, and where Brunner could say that 'in the last resort it is precisely morality which *is* evil',[18] Barth could insist that, strange as it might seem, the 'general conception of ethics coincides exactly with the conception of sin'.[19] It is true that Brunner defended and Barth resisted the idea of a general revelation in the creation and in conscience; but this divergence made remarkably little effective difference to their final judgments.

Indeed the parallelism between these two spokesmen of neo-Protestantism is impressively more extensive than the argument has yet seen; and, in particular, it must be allowed that in his own way Barth committed himself to pervasive elements of formalism and of determinism corresponding to those already detected in Brunner. The latter has already been quoted as holding that what is exclusively important in the Christian ethic is obedience, although as it happens what obedience involves is love. For his part Barth, who held that 'the grace of God protests against all man-made ethics as such' and gives 'its own answer to the ethical problem' in Jesus Christ, declared:

The good is done here ... But it is not done because, like Hercules at the cross-roads, this man chooses between good and evil and is good on the basis of His choice of the good. The Son, who is obedient to the Father, could not possibly want to ask and decide what is good and evil. He could not possibly regard as the good that which He had chosen for Himself as such. No, it is as He is elected by the grace of God that the good is done. As this Elect, quite apart from any choice of His own between good and evil, He is concerned only with obedience.[20]

Again, so far as determinism is concerned, Brunner has already been quoted as saying that 'the revelation of God's will for humanity is more than this: it is a gift, and therefore a reality', and as defining Christian ethics as 'the science of human conduct as it is determined by Divine conduct'. Likewise Barth on his side had very similar things to say. Being prepared to insist, even more radically and intransigently than Brunner, that 'revelation includes the creation of the God-knowing subject',[21] he could all the more freely say of the ethical question that 'as election is ultimately the determination of man, the question arises as to the human self-determination which corresponds to this determination'.[22] He could also declare that 'what right conduct is for man is determined absolutely in the right conduct of God. It is determined in Jesus Christ'.[23]

> We cannot even incidentally make it the object of our choice. For if we do, it is no longer this good, not even if we do finally approve it. This good is chosen only in obedience, i.e., in the choice in whose making we have no choice, because we are chosen ourselves and can only make this one choice.[24]

This is by no means the whole of Barth's ethical teaching, and there is much else of great value. This *is*, however, the framework, the ground-plan, of his ethics; and although his readers can scarcely fail to be impressed by his massive attempt to be quite single-minded in his acknowledgment of divine grace, the verdict is inevitable that this is a one-sided articulation of the Christian ethic, which falls on the side of formalism, determinism, and heteronomy. It is not to be thought of course that either Barth or Brunner intended to affirm a deterministic outlook which would in its development squeeze out the concepts of responsibility and self-determination. On the contrary, these are words that they readily used; but the fact remains that, driven by the logic of Christian truth as they understood it, they rendered their use problematical and ambiguous – so problematical and ambiguous that they come to stand for something like islands lying off the land-mass which is their first and lasting thought.

Such critical comments, however, should not obscure the massive strength of the contributions made by Barth and Brunner. Perhaps the latter especially stands forth as one of the great Christian moralists who in his systematic account of the Christian ethic has gone far to grasp and exhibit the radical character of that ethic, what Professor Kraemer called its Christocentric and theocentric character, the fact, in other words, that a man cannot begin to live by it except through a radical reorientation of will whereby the man's practical outlook is centred in God rather than in himself or in humanity. There is a world of difference between this type of treatment of the Christian life and the portrayal of it as a life lived within the *theological* framework of all human existence, the kind of treatment which has flourished from the time of Schleiermacher until almost the present day. According to the latter view the Christian life, as we have argued, was a thoroughly autonomous one, albeit one which had absorbed within its ambit the teaching and *ideas* of revelation. In comparison with such a treatment Brunner's account (or, for that matter, Barth's) is both more radical and more adequate; and it is abundantly clear that for them ideas of revelation could never take the place of the reality of revelation.

If a counterpart is to be sought in the various forms which the history of the subject has produced, perhaps the nearest is to be found in those early Protestant accounts for which the words and injunctions of Scripture were taken to provide the sole and sufficient rule of conduct. At any rate they too were heteronomous; but their failure was that they did not grasp the radical and theocentric character of the Christian ethic as adequately as Barth and Brunner have done. A law may come entirely from without and may operate in complete independence of any insight the agent himself may have; but once he has accepted it as set out in a number of written prescriptions he may all too readily acquire a position of dominance in relation to it, he may very quickly come to have it 'pocketed', so that his life is marked by that self-righteousness of which unfortunately Protestant morality has not always been innocent.

Too readily the letter, the written prescriptions, though they come from without, transform themselves into a manageable code in which man himself is sovereignly at the centre. That was the ultimate defect of the scribes and the Pharisees; and the early Protestant versions of the Christian life did not sufficiently guard against the same danger. On the other hand, Brunner and Barth have much more adequately grasped and expressed the radical character of the claim which God in Christ places upon all human life. In its own way their account represents the Christian life as one which is given over in faith to the overlordship of Christ as containing within himself the whole duty of man.

*(c) Rudolf Bultmann's ethical message: the demand of love*

None the less this ethical teaching is itself one-sided in its bias towards heteronomy, and it appears as only one wing of the movement of neo-Protestantism. It is not really surprising to find, by way of reaction on the other wing of the same movement, another account of the Christian ethic, likewise seeking to grasp its radical character and marked by a negative attitude to natural morality, but substituting something like actualism for the formalism of the others, and, instead of determinism, a refreshing emphasis upon human freedom and decision. In other words, this alternative account is no less radical, but at the same time no less one-sided, in the direction of autonomy rather than heteronomy. This is the kind of account which radical Protestantism has produced on its other wing in conjunction with existentialism.

The most prominent name in this connection is doubtless that of Professor Rudolf Bultmann. Although primarily a New Testament scholar rather than a systematic theologian, he has not allowed the New Testament to remain, as it were, a closed book but has developed from it certain emphases of his own. In the issue he has diverged sharply from, and presented a vivid contrast to, the characteristic teaching on the original wing of neo-Protestantism, the more orthodox, and perhaps more biblical, thought of Karl Barth and Emil Brunner.

These peculiar emphases of Bultmann's are, chiefly, his acceptance of the modern scientific world-view (whatever that may be), his demythologizing project along with his radically anti-metaphysical temper, his historical scepticism, and his existentialism. All these combine, in a highly integrated way, to produce the distinctive theological and ethical outlook with which Bultmann's name has come to be associated. They have led him, in contrast to Barth and Brunner whose theology was essentially one of the word of God, to interpret everything theological in anthropological terms, in terms derived from an analysis of human existence, and so to bring almost every theological topic within the compass of an enlarged doctrine of man. In such an outlook ethical reality is bound to occupy an important and prominent place. The Christian faith itself is represented, not as a worldview of any kind, whether statically or dynamically conceived, but as a new *self-understanding* on the part of man, and, in turn, the Christian life is seen as a new and authentic possibility of human existence.

If this were the whole story one might well expect from Bultmann an ethic but hardly a theological ethic. There is, however, another side to his thought, in many ways nebulous but inflexible in its effect, a mere point perhaps, which as geometricians say has position but no magnitude, but none the less a limit and a quite rigid one. It is this 'side' – if the word may be used to signify only a point – which compelled one theologian to say that 'Bultmann does not carry out his demythologizing project to the bitter end',[25] and another to speak of 'the paradox in Bultmann' and to hold that he 'sets a limit to demythologizing'.[26]

What justifies such statements is the fact that Bultmann has repeatedly affirmed that both the Christian faith and the Christian life are made possible by the same act of *God* and that the name 'Jesus Christ' stands for this act. In relation to the new self-understanding which it makes possible it may be called revelation, and in respect of the new existence and life it is grace. It is further true that with reference to God Bultmann makes frequent use of such words as 'forgiveness' and 'love'. None the less, it should be noticed, Bultmann intends them in what he calls a non-objectifying sense, and he means that what is opened up before us by the reality for which such words stand, or perhaps by the words themselves,[27] must be understood exclusively in terms of *human* existence. Accordingly, unless we are to stray into the error of metaphysics, much of the traditional interpretation of these words in terms of a divine reality and of a world other than this one must be set aside as sheer mythology.

Plainly for this theological outlook there are many questions and problems. In the present context, however, it is the ethical implications that are the all-important consideration, although since this theology is virtually in its whole extent a doctrine of man these implications are by no means peripheral but lie very near the centre.

One of the defects which has already been noted in Brunner's and Barth's discussions of the Christian life was their determinism, their representation of that life as one *determined* throughout by the word and act of God. In Bultmann's thought, on the other hand, the place of determinism is taken by decision, a decision of man which is the decision of faith, a decision for God and against the world. This is a characteristically existentialist emphasis, and it is to be found throughout in Bultmann. Moreover, as one aspect of this emphasis, there is in Bultmann a clear conception of the new creation in Christ as a work of *grace*. If it is the case that Barth and even Brunner so emphasized the activity of God that there are passages in both which suggest that the Christian man is, in the most literal and absolute sense, a new creature, a new creation, Bultmann, on the other hand, takes the trouble to affirm quite emphatically that, even if Christian existence is something radically new and owes its origin and possibility wholly to God, yet there is unquestionably continuity and self-identity between man prior to faith and man under faith, between Saul and Paul. Moreover, for Bultmann, the gulf between these two diverse forms of human existence, the inauthentic and the authentic, is bridged by a human decision, the decision of faith, so that wholesale determinism here is quite unthinkable.[28] As much as Barth and Brunner, Bultmann has been unwilling to minimize the new possibilities that entered human history with Jesus Christ, but he has declined to give to this 'event' an interpretation which he considered mythological. Further, for him the characteristic expression of these new possibilities has not been that the reality of the Good is given to man in Jesus Christ and that man's life is henceforth determined by the Word of God, but that the possibility of authentic existence is opened up for man as a possibility for his decision in faith. Accordingly, as Professor Thomas C. Oden has put it in a highly sympathetic and perceptive discussion of Bultmann's ethics, the imperative and the indicative are for him 'as two sides of a coin'. 'The imperative is "hidden" within the indicative, and the indicative is "hidden" within the imperative.'[29]

Another defect to be found in Brunner's and in Barth's discussions is their formalism, their exclusive emphasis upon the form of the will, that is, upon obedience, and their strict rejection of all reasons of determination drawn from the content of that will. *On the face of it*, however, it is much more difficult to say with confidence that Bultmann for his part avoids this defect. At least there is abundant prima facie evidence on the other side. In expounding St Paul, Bultmann seems to represent faith as primarily and fundamentally obedience, a thoroughly obedient decision for God rather even than trust in God.[30] When he speaks of the decision of faith as a decision for God against the world he means that it is a decision against self-will, self-seeking and self-pleasing, and therefore essentially a decision of obedience. Christian freedom too he describes as 'freedom to obey'.[31]

On the other hand, for all that Bultmann himself has to say of obedience, its importance and centrality in his teaching is much more ambiguous than it ever was in Brunner's or in Barth's. The difficulty is that if theological thought is dominated by the category of divine determinism then the idea of obedience is quite congenial and the only problem is whether divine determinism rules out obedience because it rules out disobedience. If, on the other hand, theological thought is governed in this connection by the idea of human decision it is not immediately clear whether the question of obedience can even be raised or not. Everything depends on whether there is someone to obey, for whom to decide in obedience. It depends, in other words, on the reality of a superhuman will to which in his decision a man can render obedience.

Moreover, this question could not be more acute than it is for Bultmann. The dominant trend of his theology suggests that if a theologian allows himself to speak of the will of God that is evidence that he has been lured into the realms of mythology and metaphysics. Whenever this dominant trend in Bultmann's thought is given a free rein it inevitably carries with it the implication that over against man there is nothing, nothing but the source of an eschatological event or perhaps just that event itself, nothing that can be grasped by objectifying thought, nothing, that is, but a bare Beyond. Such a focus of faith and decision, however, seems much too meagre to attract anything that can conceivably be described as obedience. Whether we spell the word 'beyond' with a capital or not, we cannot *obey* a 'beyond'. We may be open to it and embrace it, but we cannot obey it; and the conclusion is irresistible that when Bultmann speaks of obedience he really means openness.

For Bultmann, then, the central concept in this connection is not after all obedience but openness; and by that he means openness to God, or, perhaps one should say, to the Beyond. That in itself, however, if nothing more were said, would be an entirely empty openness or merely formal receptivity; and that is certainly not what Bultmann has in mind. On the contrary, for Bultmann this openness of spirit always takes the form of a decision, the decision of faith, and that he characterizes as a decision of *love*. The decision of faith is, in terms of Bultmann's elimination of mythology and of his existentialist reinterpretation, always an openness to the demand of love in the immediate situation or encounter.

Moreover, Bultmann is most insistent that love knows of no precise definable content, no law, no pre-formulation. What love is and what it involves are only to be seen in the moment of encounter, and faith 'realizes itself', Bultmann tells us,[32] 'in knowledge of what one has to do or not to do in the specific instance'.

Accordingly no charge of formalism could ever be preferred against Bultmann as it can legitimately against Brunner. On the contrary, for the former the content of love is no merely contingent content but is of the essence of the matter. Indeed since Bultmann recognizes no general law, no norm or pre-formulation, but concentrates exclusively upon the immediate demand of the particular concrete situation, treating love as a substitute for law rather than as the fulfilment of law, he must be deemed to abstract altogether from everything that we know of right and wrong, from all our moral understanding, distorted and imperfect as doubtless it is. If this is so it means that in the end Bultmann's position does not amount to formalism at all, it amounts, at the opposite extreme, to fanaticism and sentimentalism, to moral anarchy, to an actualism or naturalism or empiricism which is quite devoid of moral significance. He ends, that is to say, not in a law without content but in life without law.

For the sake of clarity, however, it ought to be noted that Professor Oden distinguishes Bultmann's ethical account from formalism in one sense and describes it in terms of formalism in another sense. Thus Bultmann employs 'the prophetic idea of obedience' which involves the whole man, in contrast to the 'formal obedience of Pharisaic legalism' affecting only certain 'external actions'; and this emphasis of Bultmann's is in line with his contention that in the decision of faith and love a man gains for himself authentic existence, and with his distinction between a mere work on the one hand and a deed on the other or 'an act in which one's whole being participates in one's doing'.[33] This distinction between formalism and its opposite, however, relates not to the character of the act required but to the 'motive-power' from which it is done; and consequently it is logically quite distinct from the contrast between formalism and actualism in terms of which Barth and Brunner can be accused of formalism.

According to Oden, however, there is another sense in which formalism *is* a correct description of Bultmann's ethics, for '*what* the moment demands is always *that* we love our neighbor as ourselves'. 'It is in this sense that Bultmann regards the command of God as formal.'[34] This is certainly closer to the sense in which Brunner can be said to have landed in formalism; but it is exceedingly difficult to believe that the 'that' of love can be thus separated from its 'what'. When abstraction is made from the latter there is only the word 'love' left; and Bultmann's thesis would not make sense if it were not immediately added that for him the demand of love makes itself known in the moment of encounter. The thesis that what love requires in the immediate encounter of the moment is directly and unmistakably discernible may not be credible in itself; and Oden makes a sound point when he complains that 'Bultmann's ethic envisions no sense of moral ambiguity in the moment of decision' and no 'realistic understanding of the intense and endless *conflicts of values* and interests and obligations that characterize human existence'.[35] None the less, this *is* Bultmann's thesis; and without it his ethical account, with its exclusive emphasis upon a demand of love which cannot be formulated and conceptualized, would be hopelessly incomplete. Thus it seems to me more accurate to say that love is a material principle, not a formal one, but that if Bultmann's thesis of immediate discernibility is untenable his ethic of love must amount to an ethic of naturalism or actualism, an ethic of life without law.[36]

Moreover, it is worth noting, so far as the question of heteronomy and autonomy is concerned, Bultmann continues to offer a striking contrast to Brunner, and that, whereas the latter's representation of the Christian ethic is manifestly heteronomous, Bultmann's is no less clearly autonomous.

It is true that there are passages in Bultmann in which in this connection his thought becomes highly ambiguous, and that this is especially so when he emphasizes the place of obedience. For example, Bultmann can say that 'genuine freedom is not subjective arbitrariness. It is freedom in obedience. ... Freedom is obedience to a law of which the validity is recognized and accepted, which man recognizes as the law of his own being. This can only be a law which has its origin and reason in the beyond. We may call it the law of spirit or, in Christian language, the law of God.'[37] He can say too that the idea of this genuine freedom, 'constituted by law, this free obedience or obedient freedom was well known both to ancient Greek philosophy and to Christianity', whereas the product of science and technology, of the Romantic movement, above all, of 'anxiety in the face of real freedom', namely, 'the freedom of subjective arbitrariness', 'is a delusion'.[38] Into the bargain, 'it is the Word of God which calls man into genuine freedom, into free obedience, and the task of demythologizing has no other purpose but to make clear the call of the Word of God';[39] and Bultmann can even imply that this genuine freedom is 'responsible to a transcendent power'.[40]

Such passages read very strangely indeed when taken in conjunction with the contention that Bultmann's representation of the Christian ethic falls on the side of autonomy. It is odd, however, that Bultmann should place this recognition of 'obedient freedom' so firmly in the ancient world and should see in it no live option for the present day. The truth seems to be that on occasion he allows himself the luxury of a considerable sympathy with idealist thought which his thoroughgoing existentialism cannot afford – even if he makes the questionable assumption that such existentialism is the true successor of idealism in the modern world. If the late Professor R. Gregor Smith, in his book *The New Man*, was not in line with everything that Bultmann says, he was in line with what is clearly the dominant trend in Bultmann when he argued that 'the reality of the Spirit is not found elsewhere' as in 'some rule of nature, or some abstract and timeless norm', 'it is not an addition to this concatenation of events and clashing wills', that rather 'the basic Christian material permits of no flight from history, but it draws us back again and again to the singularity, the particularity, the temporality, in a word, the genuine historicity which is its dominant characteristic'.[41] Moreover he seems certainly to have been in line with the dominant trend in Bultmann's existentialist thought when he added that this outlook carries with it 'an extraordinary emphasis upon the autonomy of man'.[42]

The one case that can be argued to the effect that there is in Bultmann's ethical thought a genuine element of heteronomy must lean very heavily on the fact that for Bultmann the possibility of Christian or authentic existence is given to man by God in Christ, that is through the eschatological event which is Jesus Christ and which is repeated whenever the Gospel is preached. On the other hand, it must equally be borne in mind that for Bultmann this act of God must be understood in a completely non-objectifying manner and that therefore the eschatological event is for him without colour, character or content. According to Professor Oden, there is a radical 'distinction between Kantian and Biblical patterns of obedience';[43] and this no doubt is true. It is not, however, to be assumed[44] that on this matter Bultmann is unreservedly and unambiguously on the side of the Bible. The decisive consideration seems to be that however Bultmann envisages the possibility of authentic existence arising he does hold that a man is to love his neighbour as '*he himself would wish to be loved*'[45] just as Kant represented the moral life as one in keeping with the requirements of the agent's rational, rather than his emotional and affective nature. As Bultmann himself says, 'The little words "as yourself" in the love-commandment pre-indicate both the boundlessness *and the direction* of loving conduct'.[46]

Certainly the fact that a man knows how he would wish to be loved does not of itself impose upon him the demand that he love his neighbour in the same way. Consequently it must be supposed that somewhere in the background of Bultmann's thinking there is an element both formal and heteronomous which witnesses to the fact that he comes from the same theological stable as Barth and Brunner. None the less, because of his anti-metaphysical and existentialist standpoint, this element is doomed to remain thoroughly nebulous. It cannot enter and occupy a stable position within his ethical outlook; and the last word must therefore lie with naturalism or actualism *and* autonomy.

There is even a doubt whether this nebulous element, doomed to remain nebulous and totally incapable of development and elaboration, is really an element of heteronomy after all and not

THE GROUNDWORK OF CHRISTIAN ETHICS

one of autonomy. It apparently belongs to the ontological structure of man and can be discovered by analysis of that structure. As Oden puts it, 'Bultmann sees in the ontology of man a tension between is and ought that constitutes a preunderstanding of God's demand',[47] and man as such 'knows that his life consists in a struggle to become ... what he *ought* to be'.[48] What Bultmann needs to be able to say at this point is that man as such stands in relation to God. This, however, he cannot do because it would involve using the word 'God' in an objectifying manner, whereas for Bultmann the word is meaningless or mythological apart from an existential apprehension. Consequently the reality for which it stands, or part of it, is brought within the ontological structure of man himself.

The critical question of course is whether this autonomous representation of the Christian ethic is in the end any more defensible than the heteronomous accounts given by Barth and Brunner, whether this 'extraordinary emphasis upon the autonomy of man' is indeed authorized, as Gregor Smith alleged,[49] 'by the very fact of the Incarnation'. It is the critical question also whether in fact Reinhold Niebuhr, who morally and materially may be an even more radical thinker but who is intellectually and formally a much less radical one, is not nearer the truth when he says that 'man as a creature of both finitude and the eternal cannot escape his problem simply by disavowing the ultimate. The eternal is involved in every moral judgment.'[50]

Whatever be the answer demanded by this critical question, however, the interpretation seems sound which finds, wherever the truth may lie, a striking ethical contrast between Barth and Brunner on the one side and an existentialist such as Bultmann on the other. Indeed the contrast is not just a contrast but a dilemma, and a dilemma remarkably similar to that which Brunner professed to discover in the development of general or philosophical ethics. According to Brunner, as we have seen, that discussion is hopelessly entangled in the dilemma: Either law without content or life and content without law; but, as it now appears, it is radical Protestantism itself, in its ethical thinking, which is entrapped in this very dilemma, for Barth and Brunner supplied the formalism and Bultmann has provided the actualism.

*(d) The ethics of Dietrich Bonhoeffer: a world already redeemed*

This contrast, which is also a dilemma, is to be seen in rather a different light when Brunner's account is considered in relation, not to Bultmann's teaching, but to the more systematic treatment given by Dietrich Bonhoeffer, whose work was prematurely and tragically cut off by his death in a German prison in 1945. It is true that owing to the catastrophic circumstances of his life Bonhoeffer was never given the opportunity to complete, still less to revise, his work, and what is now available is a compilation of various papers and sections of his argument retrieved from their scattered hiding-places. None the less the last years of his life were dominated by his concern to get down in black and white his book on *Ethics*, and although incomplete and unrevised it was in design a comprehensive and systematic treatment of his theme.

Like Brunner and Barth, Bonhoeffer could speak of the will of God, but perhaps no writer on Christian ethics could really and conveniently avoid the phrase; but, as with Bultmann, Bonhoeffer's use of it is highly problematic. What is much more significant is that the really salient ethical fact for Bonhoeffer and the absolute centre of gravity for the Christian life are not simply to be found in the will of God, conceived as standing wholly outside man's life and the human world, but rather in the fact, to which Bonhoeffer returned again and again, that the world 'is always already sustained, accepted and reconciled in the reality of God'.[51] 'The will of God', he wrote,[52] 'is nothing other than the becoming real of the reality of Christ with us and in our world. The will of God, therefore, is not an idea, still demanding to become real; it is itself a reality already in the self-revelation of God in Jesus Christ.' 'Good', he said again,[53] 'is not the correspondence between a criterion which is placed at our disposal by nature or grace and whatever entity I may designate as reality. Good is reality itself, reality seen and recognized in God.' And he held,[54] 'the reality of God discloses itself only by setting me entirely in the reality of the world, and when I encounter the reality of the world it is always already sustained, accepted and reconciled in the reality of God'.

It is indeed only in God, one must add in justice to Bonhoeffer, only in the incarnation, crucifixion and resurrection of Christ, that the world is real, with its unity restored; and consequently he could say that the will of God is not 'simply identical with what is in being, which would mean that it would be fulfilled by submissive acquiescence in things as they are'.[55] The advocacy of such aquiescence would not even be nominally Christian and would provide a very crude caricature of Bonhoeffer's thought and teaching. The world for him was only a reality and was only reconciled and unified in Christ; and consequently the Christian life is essentially one of participation in, conformation to, realization of this reality. 'Christian life is the life of Christ.'[56]

The trouble is that when the crude caricature is firmly and finally rejected it is difficult to know what historical and this-worldly reality is left to take its place. If this reality is not simply 'things as they are', natural process as a whole without qualification and without discrimination, it must be, one would think, one particular strand in this process, in the series of events which is 'things as they are'. The most likely competitors for this role are such phenomena as Christianity, Christendom and the Church, but all such empirical and historical realities are as likely as is the totality of 'things as they are' to come under the judgment of God in Christ as a rock that is higher than they.[57] It is undoubtedly a merit in Bonhoeffer's thought that he treated revelation as a reality and not merely as an idea; but, even so, to substitute fact and reality for every element of oughtness is simply to eliminate the ethical.

Brunner and Bonhoeffer certainly gave accounts of the Christian ethic which are both radical and Christo- or theo-centric and which are in their different ways characteristic of radical Protestantism. None the less a quite fundamental cleavage runs between them. In general thinking about morality at large it is not uncommon to draw a line between those ethical thinkers who take as their fundamental concept the idea of rule or right, of obligation and obedience, and those who prefer to take as their fundamental concept that of end or good; and it is clear that here that old division is reappearing within the field of explicitly theological ethics. The fact that the context is theological does make a difference. For Brunner the focal ethical factor was the will of

God, the divine law for man's life, whereas for Bonhoeffer it was a reality, an end or a good already achieved, a world already reconciled and reunified in Christ. Yet the fact remains that neither succeeded in overcoming a curious one-sidedness to which philosophical ethics itself has been prone.

Alongside this divergence, however, there is another of even greater significance, so far as theology is concerned. For even when by theological ethics the moral is seen in the most intimate connection with the reality of God, a deep division has appeared between the formalism embraced by Brunner and the actualism or naturalism in which the opposing wing seems doomed to end. These are the horns of an ethical dilemma in which radical Protestantism appears to be inescapably entangled. Yet it is not unlikely that this dilemma stems from a shared assumption which, critically considered, it is virtually impossible to justify. This is the assumption on the part of both wings of the vigorous movement of modern Protestantism, rather their common attitude to natural morality, an attitude which can only be described as indiscriminately negative. For if the fact were borne in mind that human life by its very nature is moral, that human freedom is ultimately inseparable from a sense of worth or dignity, from the acknowledgment of a sovereign norm, however difficult to apprehend fully and to articulate adequately, and that from the perspective of this ultimate norm human life and history are full of unfinished tasks and unresolved predicaments, no theological ethics could ever be content to end either in formalism or in naturalism.

### (e) The negation of natural morality in modern Protestantism and the consequent dilemmas

This negative attitude may be expressed in different ways. Brunner could say that 'if I feel I *ought* to do right, it is a sign that I cannot do it. . . . The sense of "ought" shows me the Good at an infinite, impassable distance from my will.'[58] For his part Bonhoeffer preferred to say that a man 'can know God only if he knows only God. The knowledge of good and evil is therefore separation from God. Only against God can man know good and evil.'[59] Yet in relation to morality as such and not just to some moment or particular possibility in man's moral life, neither verdict is finally plausible. Both are in danger of lapsing into meaninglessness and are held in being only by the possibility of some more discriminating thought which at the same time they both express and fail to express. In itself the outright rejection of natural morality, lock, stock and barrel, is bound to issue in the dilemma, either law without content or else life without law, either formalism or naturalism. Moreover, in turn, this dilemma inevitably leads to another, to the unhappy choice between a sheerly heteronomous authority on the one side, which will arbitrarily supply the missing content, and a completely autonomous way of life on the other, without authority, norm or principle.

It is, however, necessary to recognize that both Brunner and Bonhoeffer were constrained to make room in their systems for a rough counterpart, perhaps one might even say, a rough counterfeit, of natural morality. It is noteworthy that both had a doctrine of orders, as Brunner called them, or mandates, as Bonhoeffer preferred to describe them. 'We speak of divine mandates rather than of divine orders', he wrote,[60] 'because the word mandate refers more clearly to a divinely imposed task rather than to a determination of being.' Whether they be called orders or mandates, however, they are identical with certain forms of community, certain distinguishable sets of relationships in which men stand. Thus for Brunner the orders were five in number, consisting of marriage and family, labour, government or state, culture, and the Church; while for Bonhoeffer there were four mandates, namely, labour, marriage, government, and Church, although he sometimes substituted culture for labour[61] and was plainly puzzled about the place of friendship in any such schematism.

One might well be prepared to accept one or other of these schemes as representing a rough-and-ready division of human activities and relationships inseparable from human life as we know it. God has made us in such a way that by and large all of us are involved in these various directions with other people. It is difficult to imagine human life in terms which do not include these different spheres of human interest and activity. Consequently either schematism as it stands might well be taken as a fairly reliable, but not necessarily exhaustive, analysis of the *raw material* of human life, of what Bonhoeffer called 'the determination of being', the way in which we are made, the content of life, and so of the kinds of practical and moral problems which beset the characteristic path of the human being. Even so, on this level, a good case could perhaps be made out for adding 'colour and race' as another order, for God has apparently made us of different races and colours, and it may be that the international sphere would provide still another.

In fact, however, this is not precisely and not just what is meant by the orders and mandates as they appear in Brunner's system of thought and in Bonhoeffer's. These distinguishable spheres are not understood simply as different divisions of the raw material of life, different determinations of being, different sets of moral problems. They are conceived rather as 'divinely imposed tasks', as if each sphere confronted a man, not just with an area of possible human interest and activity, but with a sphere of relationships having already its own settled rules and laws, so that if he enters this sphere in one capacity or another the behaviour expected of him is objectively determined by the objective order or mandate to which it belongs. The orders therefore do not present a moral challenge in the sense of a challenge to moral insight and creativity as well as action. Their laws are comparable to those of nature rather than of morality as something more than a matter of routine conformity. Such a representation of the case, however, in terms of orders or mandates, seems to suffer from two main weaknesses. In the first place, the enumeration of a fixed number of orders constitutes a much too inflexible approach to the delicacies and refinements of a mature moral outlook and can achieve nothing but a very rough approximation. Secondly, the assimilation of this total area to the world of nature with its objective discoverable laws and the consequent elimination of the challenge and the claim of morality misrepresent human life and human freedom by rendering its law static and dead, and by failing to reckon with human creativity. Stability is secured at the cost of life; and what is left at the end of the day is a rather doctrinaire substitute for morality, not the substance of the good life.

A somewhat similar criticism of the 'orders' has been made by Professor Gustaf Wingren when he says that, while 'a radical demand . . . follows from the Creation and bestowal of life', 'life has not been established in Creation once and for all, to be maintained and preserved subsequently under certain orders defined by God. . . . In this misinterpretation of Creation,' he maintains, 'which has generally arisen through confining God's work of Creation to a particular point in the past, there is no real understanding of God as continuing to create in the present, or of life itself as God's continuing Creation. There is rather a conception of certain static results of the work of Creation which has isolated certain abilities or qualities in human nature, or social institutions, or at times a combination of both, in some time long since past.'[62]

Perhaps, however, Brunner and Bonhoeffer themselves see something of these defects, but if they do they do not make matters any better by taking the bull by the horns or by making a virtue of necessity. At any rate there is a further important fact about the orders or mandates which suggests an even more serious criticism, for it is quite clear that they are conceived as *external* to the truly good life, the Christian life. According to Bonhoeffer, the entire area of the mandates is to be understood under two categories, that of preservation whereby a fallen world is preserved from complete disorder and chaos, and that of preparation, that is, preparation of the way for the coming of Christ. Under both categories this entire sphere belongs to what Bonhoeffer called the penultimate as distinct from the ultimate, in which alone the genuine good, the Christian life, is to be found. The Christian life is 'a justified life, a life justified by grace alone',[63] it is 'the life of Christ',[64] it belongs to the ultimate, and, although the penultimate remains, 'the ultimate entirely annuls and invalidates it'.[65]

By Brunner too the orders and their laws were apprehended under the categories of preservation and preparation; but Brunner assigned to them a third significance, a significance for faith and for the Christian life, as providing guidance.[66] It is important at this point, however, not to jump to conclusions nor to magnify this concession, for it did not take Brunner much further than Bonhoeffer and it did not qualify the negative attitude to natural morality. The reason is that, as Brunner himself made clear, this guidance does not contain any ethical sentiment but has rather 'a more technical function: that of giving the right direction'.[67]

Time and again Brunner described the orders as providing no more than a framework for the Christian life and as 'based upon a standard of law which is totally different from that which is known by faith'.[68]

Thus, in spite of apparent concessions, the attitude to natural morality remains thoroughly negative to the end. The relationship of life in the orders to the Christian life is purely external, although it is exceedingly difficult to see how this external relationship can be compatible with the fact that it is none the less a source of guidance for the Christian. Indeed, curiously enough, so far as Brunner is concerned, this puzzle is no isolated one, for in his treatment of the Church he regarded the organization of empirical churches as a substitute for the Spirit, and yet he held at the same time that these distortions of the true Church are an external means towards the growth and renewal of the latter.[69] Moreover, just as he neither raised nor answered the question: Where then is the true Church?, so he neither raised nor answered the question: What then is the Christian life? Where is it lived? Had he perhaps forgotten for the moment that it is inasmuch as we do it unto one of the least of these our brethren that we do it unto Christ?

If the foregoing analysis of Christian ethical thought in modern or radical Protestantism is correct, it is evident that of this movement there are two quite distinct wings, a right and a left, with very diverse characteristics, although both are at one in seeking to grasp the Christian ethic as indeed an ethic of revelation and reconciliation. On the one side, stemming from the work of Karl Barth, there is an interpretation of the Christian life characteristically marked by formalism, divine determinism, and sheer heteronomy, while on the other side, in reaction against these emphases and at the instigation of thinkers like Bultmann and Bonhoeffer, there has developed a view of the Christian life which reveals quite another set of characteristics. In place of the formalism of the other there is a tendency towards actualism or naturalism; in place of divine determinism there is a notable emphasis upon human decision; and finally where the other account is thoroughly heteronomous this one is no less autonomous.

Behind both views, however, there is a common rejection and

dismissal of natural morality as something of no account in the present context; and the suggestion of the argument has been that it is because of this common rejection that the subsequent articulation of the Christian ethic finds itself in the dilemma or dilemmas represented by the opposing wings of modern Protestantism, either formalism or naturalism, either divine determinism or self-creative human decision, either sheer heteronomy or else 'an extraordinary emphasis upon autonomy'.

### (f) Can the dilemmas be eliminated without the reinstatement of natural morality?

There has indeed been one further and important contribution in recent times to this discussion which merits consideration both because of its intrinsic merits and because of its relation to the present argument. It is Professor Paul Lehmann's book, *Ethics in a Christian Context*, published in 1963; and it is significant for this argument because *in certain respects* it seems to cut itself free from the dilemmas just mentioned and so to bridge the gulf between the two wings of modern Protestantism.

Reference has already been made in passing to Professor Lehmann's characterization of the ethical views of St Augustine, St Thomas Aquinas and Schleiermacher as, respectively, revisionism, synthesis and dia-parallelism; and there is no reason to quarrel with his rejection of all three as solutions to the fundamental problem of Christian ethics, what he himself calls 'the prior question'.[70] Indeed it is to his credit that he sees this problem so clearly, 'the question of the correct and fundamental starting point for Christian ethical thinking',[71] the answer to which involves an essay 'in reflective analysis, rather than in trying to prescribe how Christians ought to behave'.[72] In attempting to solve it, however, Lehmann shares what we have seen to be the presupposition of both Brunner and Bonhoeffer on different wings of radical Protestantism, that natural morality is of no significance for Christian ethics. St Augustine, St Thomas Aquinas and Schleiermacher, on the other hand, stopped short of any such total rejection, and yet in their affirmations of this natural morality they allowed themselves in their different ways to be drawn into serious error. In particular they failed effectively to represent the

Christian ethic as one both of revelation and of reconciliation; and yet modern Protestantism, which has been concerned at all costs to avoid this error, has itself become deeply involved in one dilemma after another. The critical question then for Lehmann is whether, without the reinstatement of natural morality, these dilemmas can yet be transcended.

According to Professor Lehmann, Christian ethics is to be defined as 'the disciplined reflection upon the question and its answer: What am I, as a believer in Jesus Christ and as a member of his church, to do?'[73] Further, he declares explicitly and emphatically that Christian ethics 'is oriented toward revelation and not toward morality'. It is true that in itself this might be no more than the declaration, which any adequate account of Christian ethics would have to make, that the Christian ethic *is* an ethic of reconciliation; and in fairness to its author it ought to be added that he does say that we cannot ignore 'the common moral sense of mankind, the distilled ethical wisdom of the ages'.[74] Of course we cannot, and as I have argued the Christian revelation and redemption hold us to it in fact. The trouble is that if, when it comes to the reflective discipline of Christian ethics, we assign to natural morality no positive role we seem to be doing no better than ignoring it. It is difficult to believe that 'the common moral sense of mankind' is important in practice but not in theory.

In fact the dominant trend of Professor Lehmann's discussion of this natural morality, so far as he does discuss it, is unquestionably critical. It suffers, it would seem, from one pervasive defect, that it is abstract and preceptual. Consequently it creates or at least leaves a gap, which it is entirely unable to close, between the ethical demand and the ethical act, that is to say, between the insight or (from the other side) the claim of morality, which according to Lehmann is abstract and preceptual, and the concrete act which is laid upon me as a Christian to do in this particular situation in which I find myself.[75] Lehmann refers repeatedly to this unbridgeable gap as a pervasive and fundamental defect of natural morality. He holds that for a genuinely Christian ethic 'the clarification of ethical principles and their application to concrete situations is ethically unreal because such clarification is a logical enterprise and there is no way in logic of closing the gap between the abstract and the concrete'.[76] 'Ethics', he adds, 'is a matter not of logic but of life, a certain kind of reality possessed by the concrete.'

Moreover, the philosophical ethics which interprets natural morality is treated as a rival to be expelled, and, as Brunner had done, it is treated by Lehmann as ending in a dilemma between eudaemonism and legalism. Indeed there is a sense in which there is only one possible end to the philosophical inquiry, namely, eudaemonism;[77] and in harmony with this interpretation of ethical thought it is perhaps significant that, while Friedrich Hegel, John Stuart Mill, F. H. Bradley, T. H. Green, and James Martineau are relegated to a footnote (not to mention G. E. Moore and H. A. Prichard who are passed by in silence), William James is allowed to claim a chapter to himself entitled 'The Redirection of the Search'.[78] At any rate this interpretation of the history of ethical thought does enable Lehmann to find the search culminating in an intolerable choice between ethical absolutism which has failed in sheer irrelevance and an ethical relativism which can offer no better guide than mere expediency.[79]

As for the genuinely Christian ethic it involves, as Lehmann understands it, 'the displacement of the prescriptive and absolute formulation of its claims'[80] and of 'an ethic of precept and law'.[81] This, however, is a merely negative characterization which prepares the way for a more positive account, but one which, just because it thus rejects the normative from the outset, is not a little ambiguous in its very claim to be an ethical account. For one thing, Lehmann holds that 'the starting point for Christian thinking about ethics is the fact and the nature of the Christian Church'[82] and, accordingly, that 'Christian ethics is *koinonia ethics*' so that 'it is from, and in, the *koinonia* that we get the answer to the question: What am I, as a believer in Jesus Christ and as a member of his church, to do?'[83] Once again this *might* mean no more than that the Christian ethic is an ethic of redemption, but equally it might mean, and in fact as it turns out it does mean, that the ethic of redemption is to be understood in a peculiar way.

What especially Professor Lehmann means is that the Christian ethic is not only a *koinonia* ethic but also what he calls a *contextual* ethic, one which is incomprehensible apart from the divine initiative and activity, the fact that 'what God is doing in the world is setting up and carrying out the conditions for what it takes to keep human life human'.[84] And yet, although his emphasis upon both the concreteness of the ethical situation and the divine activity, 'what God is doing', represents something like a drawing together of the two wings of radical Protestantism, even this stress upon the contextual character of the Christian ethic does not fully reveal the peculiar slant which Lehmann would give to Christian ethics. His distinctive understanding of an ethic of redemption has not yet been made plain.

There are other things, however, which Professor Lehmann is no less concerned to say and which help considerably to point out the direction of his thought. For example, he tells his readers that 'the ethical question – in the *koinonia* – is not "What *ought* I to do?" but "What *am* I to do?"'[85] Further, if the reader is at first inclined to think that this is a distinction without a difference, that 'What am I to do?' is just the same question as 'What ought I to do?' with perhaps an additional element of urgency and even desperation, he at once discovers that for the author the difference between these questions is a real one and has much to do with the fact that 'in the *koinonia* one is always fundamentally in an *indicative* rather than in an *imperative* situation'. He discovers too that this indicative is not a divine indicative but a human one, that while 'the "ought" factor cannot be ignored in ethical theory' – one would hope not – 'the primary ethical reality is the human factor, the *human* indicative, in every situation involving the interrelationships and the decisions of men'.[86] 'A contextual ethic', he is later told,[87] 'deals with behavior basically in *indicative* rather than in imperative terms.' To the question which Lehmann uses to define Christian ethics, 'What am I, as a believer in Jesus Christ and as a member of his church, to do?', we can certainly answer 'the will of God', but there is a fuller and more informative reply, 'I am to do what I am!' 'To do what I am is to act in every situation in accordance with what it has been given to me to be. Doing the will of God is doing what I am.'[88]

Professor Lehmann also – and quite rightly – speaks of the Christian's behaviour as 'expressive of confidence and hope as against anxiety and despair',[89] and he says further that 'the *ethical* factor in behavior is provided not by a rational principle but by the *sign* character of the behavior'.[90] For example, 'desegregation

is *ethical* behavior in so far as it bears the marks of God's transformation of the world in accordance with his purposes, of the
world's resistance to what God is doing, and of God's ultimate
overcoming of the world'.[91] Here the Christian knows – or should
know – what Professor Lehmann means, but the question is not
whether these things are true or not – they are true – but whether
in saying them he has uncovered the nerve of the Christian *ethic*,
so that in turn he is entitled to speak of 'the displacement of an
ethic of precept and law',[92] of the end of 'the tutelage of fear,
tabu, and law',[93] and of the substitution of an indicative for an
imperative ethic.

'Let your light so shine before men', said Jesus, 'that they may
see your good works, and glorify your Father which is in heaven.'[94]
But the situation so envisaged, indeed so created, is much too
complex to justify a simple substitution of signs for claims as the
ethical criterion. Indeed has not Professor Lehmann been guilty
of a very similar over-simplification to that of which Immanuel
Kant can be accused? For just as Kant, in concentrating upon
universalizability, allowed himself to be guided by a condition
perhaps necessary but not in itself sufficient, has not Professor
Lehmann in what he says of the sign character of Christian
behaviour directed his attention to essential overtones of Christian
action, overtones which belong to it as *Christian* action, but not
to its inner reality as Christian *ethical* action? Christian behaviour
may very well be expressive of a peculiar confidence and hope
inseparable from the act of God in Christ, but this fact scarcely
provides an adequate ethical characterization of it.

It is true that Lehmann says that 'this does not mean that there
are no ethical demands'. 'It means', he says,[95] 'that such ethical
demands as are authentic acquire meaning and authority from
specific ethical relationships, and the latter constitute the context
out of which these demands emerge and which shapes the
demands.' But it is difficult to know what precisely this can mean.
It is evident that the demand does not issue, on this interpretation
of it, from general characteristics such as honesty or loyalty or
love, which might be deemed to confer what Sir David Ross
called a prima facie obligatoriness upon certain actions possible
in the given situation, for Professor Lehmann has steadfastly set
his face against anything abstract, general and preceptual and has

already said that 'the dynamics of the divine behavior in the world exclude both an abstract and a preceptual apprehension of the will of God. There is no formal principle of Christian behavior because Christian behavior cannot be generalized.'[96]

What then can he mean when he ostensibly leaves room for 'ethical demands'? To disown the general, the abstract and the preceptual is, one would think, to acquiesce in the unpredictable, the arbitrary and the impulsive. Is that perhaps what Professor Lehmann means or at least a caricature of what he means? For he does go on to say again that the question here is not 'What ought I ...?' but 'What am I ...?' And the answer is that 'I am to do what I am!'[97]

At the most this is only verbally conclusive and there are really two difficulties in Lehmann's position at this point. The first is that if Lehmann really wishes to maintain the distinction which he makes in his opening sentence between Christian ethics and the ethics of Christians, and so to avoid some form of actualism devoid of ethical significance, his indicative must inevitably be a disguised imperative. If what God is doing to make and to keep human life human is distinguishable from what I, or any other member of the Church, am empirically moved to do then standards and norms cannot be avoided. The second difficulty arises from his attempt to concentrate always upon the concrete as distinct from, and even opposed to, the abstract, for if this attempt is rigorously maintained the alleged 'Christian' action will inescapably be unpredictable and impulsive. In the end it can only be error to set life and logic at odds, as does Lehmann; but what is true in his analysis is that the thought or rationality involved in the moral judgment – which undermines any attempt to articulate that judgment in exclusive terms of the concrete – is itself wrongly represented if it is identified with the apprehension of general principles or laws requiring only to be applied to particular cases.

Closely connected with these aspects of Lehmann's total view is his emphasis upon maturity. He has already said that Christian ethics is oriented towards revelation rather than morality; and he can go on to argue that 'what God is doing in the world to make and to keep human life human is to bring about human maturity',[98] and so to say that 'Christian ethics is primarily concerned not with the good but with the will of God; it aims at maturity, not at morality'.[99] 'Morality', he says,[100] 'is a by-product of maturity'; and he speaks of 'integrity in and through interrelatedness', holding that 'what psychology knows as the problem of integration, what sociology knows as the problem of community, Christian faith discerns and delineates as the problem of the head and the body. The resolution of the problem belongs to the possessor of the secret of maturity.'[101]

In all this, beyond any question, there is much valuable insight into the essential nature of the Christian life; but when that has been emphatically said there remains a very large doubt whether Professor Lehmann has given the correct answer to his own prior question. Is it in the least defensible to substitute maturity for morality? Would it not be closer to the Christian ethic if it were held that without morality – judged, reaffirmed and redeemed in Christ – maturity is either an empty concept or one whose content is wholly arbitrary? True it is that 'it is not man but Christ who makes ethical thinking and acting "Christian"';[102] but there remains a question whether Lehmann's account of this specifically Christian ethic represents it in the last resort as the ethic of reconciliation that it is or as an ethic of what is literally and absolutely a *new creation* and so as not an ethic at all. Lehmann speaks of 'the organic vitality of the structure of the *koinonia*' and says that '*integrity in and through interrelatedness* characterizes bodily growth toward maturity';[103] but what he says is dangerously reminiscent of another type of 'contextual' ethics, that of Leslie Stephen and Herbert Spencer, in which the indicatives of the evolutionary process took the place of what Lehmann regards as the politics of God, what God is doing to make and to keep human life human – although it is worth noting that Lehmann goes further even than Stephen and Spencer ever dared and substitutes 'I am' for 'I ought'. It is only through sin and indeed in a state of sin that 'God's will to fellowship is displaced by man's will to power' and consequently 'what was a gift has become a quest', and indeed a quest 'in which man seeks what he does not know and knows what he does not seek'.[104] Yet if the restoration of the gift in unmerited grace presents no challenge and conveys no task that, one would think, must spell the end of Christian ethics. In Christianity then ethics has been rendered redundant.

The truth is that if, while dispensing with and rejecting natural morality, Lehmann is to avoid a quite unpredictable and un-principled naturalism or actualism he requires some substitute for the guiding lights of ordinary morality, and it is extremely difficult to see where he can find it. If at this point he emphasizes the concrete and particular he is surrendering to actualism by allowing conduct to be governed by pressure of event, circum-stance or even impulse. If on the other hand he stresses what helps to make and to keep human life human or, in a single word, maturity, he has surely reintroduced the general and preceptual by the back-door, and in a form far less enlightening than the traditional ideas of general morality. And if he then insists that what is important here is the *koinonia* and what *God is doing* to make and to keep human life human, it seems to me that the mainspring of the Christian life must now be placed either in the poor, actual indicative of empirical Christianity or else in the imperative of morality rescued, reoriented and established in Christ.

### (g) The problem of the double standard

There remains still another problem for Professor Lehmann's account of the Christian ethic, and it is one that he himself recognizes. This is what he calls the problem of 'the double standard'; and of course it would be intolerable, as the present discussion has already emphasized, if on our ethical theory men were represented as subject to two supreme laws, the moral law and the law of Christ. Such a representation would undoubtedly contradict the essential nature of both as uniquely authoritative for man's life, as categorical in a way that brooks no questioning (although there may be all sorts of questions on the way to the determination of the content of their claim in any given situation), and as in the sense of 'ought' opening up a dimension of human life without which life would be less than human. The sovereignty of the moral law and the lordship of Christ taken together pose the problem of the double standard.

Professor Lehmann, however, approaches the problem from a quite different angle, for he regards natural morality as of no ultimate significance, at any rate for Christian ethics, and philoso-phical ethics as a rival enterprise doomed to failure. Philosophical ethics is thus doomed, apparently, because it cannot close the gap between the general and the particular which Lehmann takes to be 'the specifically and formatively ethical factor'.[105] This in itself is a difficult position because, as Emil Brunner wrote, 'in the last resort ... moral scepticism, like all scepticism, is a flight from one's own reality and a form of self-deception',[106] and because without some natural moral insight moral philosophy or philosophical ethics could not have got off the ground. Even so Lehmann considers that he must tackle 'the crucial difficulty of a "double standard"' – as he sees it. 'The crucial problem of Christian ethics in the context of the *koinonia*', he writes,[107] 'is how the behavior of Christians is to be related to the behavior of non-Christians. How can a *koinonia* ethic make any ethical claims upon those in society who do not acknowledge the *koinonia* as their point of departure and frankly live neither in it nor by its light? Do we have here a kind of double ethical standard: one for Christians and another for non-Christians?' Indeed in logic there seems no reason why Professor Lehmann should not have posed the question in the form: Are non-Christians amoral?

Be that as it may, in answering the question which he does pose he immediately rules out two possible solutions, both that which holds that 'non-Christians must conform in their behavior to the community of the church'[108] and that which envisages the acceptance by the *koinonia* of 'the prevailing patterns of the community at large'.[109] More significantly he rejects the solution which relies on 'middle axioms'[110] as expressing the shared moral judgments of Christian and non-Christian. In rejecting this thesis he considers the suggestion of Professor John Bennett that in the application of Christian love to contemporary American society desegregation stands out as just such a middle axiom. In more detail the argument would move from Christian love to social justice to racial justice to desegregation; but Lehmann forthrightly rejects this interpretation on the ground that it represents the transition and clarification as 'a logical enterprise and there is no way in logic of closing the gap between the abstract and the concrete. Ethics is a matter not of logic but of life, a certain kind of reality possessed by the concrete.'[111] For Lehmann's own part the problem is resolved only by a *koinonia* ethic which 'is concerned to expose and explicate the *human* reality of the concrete. A *koinonia* ethic is uniquely adequate to this concern because it describes and analyses the context within which the human reality of the concrete is being steadily shaped and exposed.'[112]

Plainly this is a quite crucial point in Lehmann's argument and its critical assessment a matter of considerable importance. At the conclusion of one major division of his discussion he allows for the possible criticism of his position that 'the mountain has labored and brought forth a mouse';[113] but whatever be said on that score it may well be alleged that on the question of the transition from the general to the particular he has made a mountain out of a molehill. His argument depends very heavily upon the insolubility of this particular problem; but, whether adequately to the Christian ethic or not, many people can and do live by general principles, recognizing the general when it occurs in particular instances.[114] Accordingly a question does arise acutely for Christian ethics regarding the status and origin of these principles, such as those which enjoin the telling of the truth, the keeping of promises, the relief of the needy, and which prohibit such things as adultery. It is not enough to say that they are produced by philosophical ethics in its attempt to 'raise a standard', for they belong in some way to the essential dignity of man and philosophical ethics could hardly begin without them but rather presupposes both them and the natural morality of which they are a part. Thus there is a real problem of the double standard.

Before pursuing this line of thought to a conclusion, however, it is necessary to take more detailed notice of Lehmann's own solution to this problem as he understands it. On the positive side this solution lays great weight upon the concept of humanity.[115] But is not this too a general principle and one by itself more deficient in specific content? 'Promote genuine humanity' seems just as general as, but less illuminating than, 'Treat humanity always as an end' or 'Love your neighbour'. Professor Lehmann would doubtless protest that this is not what he intends, since for him the indicative is ethically more fundamental than the imperative; but even so, apart from some general principles or characteristics, it is exceedingly difficult to know what he can possibly mean by 'the *human* reality of the concrete' or how to recognize what God is doing to make and to keep human life human.[116]

Apart from such difficulties, however, there remains the question of the double standard as Lehmann understands it, for if he really defines the ethical in terms of the human and the human in terms of the concrete activity of God in Christ there is a real problem as to how to conceive of co-operation between Christians and non-Christians, their living together in one society. It is not really, however, the problem of a double standard but the problem of co-operation with, of living in the same society as, those who have on this view no real standard, the amoral and the non-ethical and, strictly speaking, the non-human. And yet Lehmann can speak of 'the common ethical predicament'[117] as if this were conceivable without some measure of common moral insight; and, in the course of a highly illuminating discussion of the question 'Are you saved?', can think of believers and unbelievers 'on the level of their common involvement with the issue of the possibility and the integrity of their humanity'.[118]

The explanation appears, however, when Lehmann proceeds to a further and final instalment of his solution to what he still calls 'the crucial difficulty of a double standard between believers and unbelievers'.[119] What he says is that 'those who start with and from within the koinonia find themselves on the behavioral level, involved in situations and with people who start from outside the koinonia yet whose behavior makes the recognition inescapable that they are sheep belonging to the same fold'.[120] In support of this thesis he refers to Calvin's 'general power of the Spirit' and to Luther's 'notion of the deus absconditus', he quotes Professor Roger Mehl to the effect that 'I am genuinely authorized to consider that a new life, evidently hidden in Christ (Col. 3. 3), is in the other person as in me and that one day these lives of ours will be manifested',[121] and, most significantly, he observes that 'it makes a considerable difference whether one shifts these considerations from the first article of the creed, concerning God the Creator, to the third article of the creed, concerning the activity of the Holy Spirit'.[122]

This final comment is indeed a highly significant one, and it does make a very considerable difference if we allow ourselves to shift 'these considerations', as Lehmann is suggesting, from the sphere of creation and of man as man to the sphere of reconciliation and of redeemed and rescued man, from, to use Professor

Bultmann's words,[123] 'man prior to the revelation of faith' to 'man under faith', as if an unbelieving world were already in some sense redeemed, not in principle only but also *in practice*.

This is a highly doctrinaire thesis which it seems impossible to justify; but it is important to see that there is at this point a quite critical cross-roads for Christian ethical thought. If such thought cannot be content to hand over to the Devil the entire non-Christian world either as amoral or as exposed to the moral question to which however it has not even the glimmering of an answer – and both possibilities seem equally beyond defence – then either it must give some place to the morality of natural men or else in some way it must find already active in them Christian morality itself. And its decision at this point will have far-reaching repercussions on the interpretation of the Christian religion as a whole.

Professor Lehmann's comment seems indeed to vindicate our earlier analysis and, in particular, the contention that in the end his account represents the Christian ethic *not* as an ethic of redemption at all, but as the 'ethic' of a completely and absolutely new creation, so that the difference between creation and reconciliation, between Genesis and Gospel, is eliminated, contrary to the whole tenor of the biblical witness. The Gospel is not a gospel of creation but one of salvation; and, although it may have been an unfortunate and misleading phrase, Emil Brunner had a fundamentally important reason for speaking of the divine faithfulness as 'the historical quality of God', the resolution of a 'dialectic . . . in the knowledge of the Holiness of God', even of a 'dialectic of Holiness and Love', but in any case as 'the expression of a great and joyful amazement' which lies very near the heart of the Gospel[124] – much nearer than does a sense of awe before the inscrutability of creation.

Brunner's essential point, however, was no theological novelty. St Athanasius had grasped it when he wrote, 'It was not things non-existent that needed salvation, for which a bare creative word might have sufficed, but man – man already in existence and already in process of corruption and ruin. It was natural and right, therefore, for the Word to use a human instrument and by that means unfold Himself to all.'[125] If natural man is 'a good thing spoiled', in Christian man it is the corruptible that puts on incorruption, not the non-existent that clothes itself with existence.

To say with Lehmann that the standards of unbelievers are in a concealed and unrecognized form the very same standards as those of believers is to destroy the difference which St Athanasius so clearly acknowledged, and it is to assimilate the work of salvation to that of creation. The present point is closely connected with the broader issue of a general revelation in the creation; and, in relation to that issue, it means that those are in error who argue (as did Barth in his celebrated controversy with Brunner) that to admit general revelation is to represent man as able to make himself a first instalment towards his own salvation, and it means also that on the contrary it is those who argue thus who are guilty of representing salvation as but a second instalment of creation, and so as lacking the specific quality of saving grace and forgiveness, of *re*conciliation and *re*storation.

On the other hand, if, even in the sphere of creation and of man as man, the standards of natural morality are recognized, the problem of the double standard does indeed arise as genuinely the problem of two ultimate standards. The solution, however, is that on this view these two standards are in the last resort not two but one and have their single origin in the will and purpose of God. It is sin or the world that falsely abstracts from this one standard, the rule of God's Kingdom, and, producing the distorted sphere of natural morality, gives the appearance of duality. It is on this basis of natural morality that believer and unbeliever can contrive to make moral contact with each other and even work together, can communicate and co-operate; and it is for this reason too that at the end of the day the servants of natural morality must confess that they have been unprofitable servants and must learn to receive the Kingdom at God's hands, not only in illumination of mind but in penitence of spirit – for the ultimate good they seek is much larger and more resourceful than they have ever dreamed, is a grace and truth beyond their wildest aspirations.

*(h) The Law as the instrument of divine sovereignty*

One conclusion towards which the argument has been steadily approximating is that it is impossible to resolve the dilemmas in the current discussion of the Christian ethic unless one is prepared to affirm a doctrine of natural morality, of which the traditional doctrine of natural law was but one possible version. It is therefore of interest and importance to note at this stage that one theologian who has, from his own peculiar point of view, seen something of the substance of this thesis is the Swedish theologian, Professor Gustaf Wingren. Quite rightly he finds himself unable to follow the drift of so much contemporary Protestant theology. His complaint against it is the quite precise one that 'the dominant school of Protestant theology has reduced the Bible to the New Testament',[126] reading the Old exclusively in the light of the New, and that consequently we are 'confronted by the peculiar predominance of the second article of faith in contemporary theology and the consequent rejection of the first article'.[127] Thus, if Wingren is right, what is often claimed to be the special merit of contemporary theology, its Christocentricity, is in fact its weakness, for if for theology the Word of God begins with Christ it has no relation to, it is irrelevant to, the ongoing life of the world which none the less, Wingren insists, is the ongoing work of God's creation.

Undoubtedly there is some substance in what Wingren says. The work of God in Christ is the work of reconciliation, and the very prefix indicates that it cannot properly be interpreted exclusively in terms of itself and clearly posits a prior relationship. It points back unerringly to a situation that precedes it. Wingren is not content, however, simply to detect this influential error in the mainstream of modern Protestantism. He seeks to account for it, and his explanation is of great importance for the understanding of his own alternative position. It is due, he says, to a preoccupation with the question of knowledge. Christocentricity arises from the epistemological conviction that it is only in Christ that we know anything of God and his purposes. 'If we put knowledge into the centre and place the second article before the first, we obscure the sovereignty of God.'[128] 'We should note that it is the derivation of the content of faith from the second article that is new in modern theology. The assumption here is that knowledge is the basic question, and that the revelation in Christ provides the knowledge from which all else is to be derived. . . . It is not man's knowledge but the works of God which are central.'[132]

It is always an error when 'the acquisition of knowledge and insight is made of greater importance than the works of God';[130] and Wingren goes on to suggest that when this happened in modern theology it was a case of reacting against the liberalism of 'an earlier idealist and anthropocentric period' and landing straightway in another kind of anthropocentricity 'although in a negative way, being concerned with the lack of knowledge in man'.[131]

Yet this diagnosis is not without very serious difficulty; and if concern with the epistemological problem is a mark of anthropocentricity the word ought to be put in inverted commas, for it is an anthropocentricity which cannot be avoided except by hiding our heads in the sand. Theology is a human activity, a branch of human knowledge, whether we like it or not; and the question of its epistemological foundations is quite inescapable. In the end it is not possible to by-pass the question of knowledge; and in thinking that he can do so Wingren may be aided by the fact that he resembles Barth in one significant respect in that he seems unwilling to separate theology from exegesis of the biblical texts.[132] Thus to raise the question of natural ethics and Christian ethics is to fail 'to think of God as the One who acts in the universe'.[133] Since the one significant reality for the Bible is the Last Judgment and the separation it involves, the Bible 'has no clear answer to such anthropocentric questions as, What constitutes a departure from "the natural ethic"? and, What is characteristic of "the Christian ethic" as such?, etc. These are un-Biblical questions and do violence to the typical Biblical point of view.'[134] Likewise 'Luther had no interest in whether man has wisdom, knowledge, or insight. The whole of this problem of epistemology, which dominates theological discussion at the present time, was dealt with fairly summarily and in passing by him.'[135] Indeed such questions, he suggests for his own part,[136] are beside the theological point. But this just will not do. When Wingren criticizes the exclusive and all-sufficient Christocentricity of much modern theology he is clearly discerning something of the truth; but when he castigates its anthropocentricity in its concern with the question of knowledge he is no less clearly beating his head against the wall or perhaps like the ostrich hiding it in the sand.

Plainly this disparagement of any concern with the epistemological question as anthropocentric constitutes a very odd position; and it is bound to be a fruitful source of confusion and ambiguity as Wingren seeks to set out his own position. His main point, I have said, is sound, namely, that the Gospel of Christ posits and presupposes a situation of men before God; but how in greater detail is this situation to be described? It is in trying to discover exactly Wingren's answer to this question that one is hampered by the ambiguity which stems from his insistence that 'it is not man's knowledge but the works of God which are central'. Always the difficulty is to know whether Wingren is describing a situation of man in respect of his knowledge or claim to knowledge or a situation of man independent of knowledge altogether, something quite over his head. And it is disconcerting to be reminded that the difference is of no account.

Thus at one point he is to be found maintaining that if we follow the mainstream of present-day Protestant theology and let 'the second article alone provide us with knowledge even about the Law, order, and justice ... we are then allowing the knowledge specifically given by the second article to negate a universal *knowledge* given through Creation'.[137] Here he explicitly speaks of knowledge; but since he attaches no importance to the question of knowledge his readers do not know how much weight to give to his words. If he really meant seriously a universal *knowledge* then he might well be paving the way for a weighty doctrine of natural morality; but he would not then attach a minimal importance to the epistemological question. On the other hand, he can describe the situation in natural terms which seem to go behind and before knowledge, as if we could know something which lies entirely beyond the sphere of human knowledge. 'A relationship to God is established in the very fact of human birth.'[138] 'Our relationship to God is given in and with life itself.'[139] 'This relationship is *given* with life itself, and even when men have ceased to use the term "God" they do not cease to be related to Him, because *He is*, even though they deny Him.'[140] No doubt it is important to distinguish between what is given to men and what men make of it; but it is very doubtful if one can speak of a relationship to God which may be *entirely* over a man's head.

The question seems urgent whether in all this we are dealing with something which falls within the sphere of man's outlook upon, and response to, life or with something which may fall outside that sphere altogether.

It is beyond question that such ambiguity derives directly from Wingren's emphatic point that 'it is not man's knowledge but the works of God which are central'; but it is important to see also that this same emphatic point leads him, beyond all ambiguity, to lay the weight upon 'the Law', not as something which challenges natural man so far as he can see it and to which in his own way he makes a faltering response, something which keeps human life human and can only do so through knowledge and response, but first and last as an instrument in the hands of God, whether men hear or whether they forbear. Thus under the logic imposed by his strangely negative attitude to the epistemological question, Wingren enunciates, not a doctrine of natural morality at all, but a doctrine of the two uses of the Law, the first use which places disobedient man in bondage so that in the end he must die, and exercises compulsion upon him so that life, the gift of God, does not vanish from the earth, and the second use which brings to bear upon him accusation and the sense of guilt. These are 'the works of God', and fundamentally the Law is 'a restraint and tribulation exercised by God in the world'.[141] 'In His continuing Creation God uses men, and their opposition and unwillingness do not prevent Him from using them.'[142]

In itself this position of Wingren's is not without difficulty. It implies, not that the doctrine of sin presupposes some doctrine of the Law, but that the doctrine of the Law presupposes sin, and consequently it virtually proclaims that it is incomplete – unless the gap is filled by something more ultimate than the Law itself, perhaps by what Wingren calls 'the unrecognised demand',[143] a 'demand in Creation for faith and love'.[144] Further, although it is true that seeing faith and love impressively as different sides of the same thing, Wingren can the more readily enunciate a doctrine of 'the total depravity of the whole human race',[145] such a doctrine in the end is no more credible in one context than another. It is difficult too to reconcile it with the concession that natural men are free to criticize and reform the divinely instituted earthly government because it is ruthless and tyrannical,[146] and with the

THE ETHICS OF NEO-PROTESTANTISM

apparent recognition that not all men all the time are the totally
unwilling instruments whereby the first works of the Law are
accomplished. It may well be that, as one traces the thread of
Professor Wingren's thought, the ultimate and inflexible factor
which makes coherent sense of these various tenets is a belief in
two essentially different human natures, the 'old corrupted nature'
and the 'new nature';[147] but that belief hardly makes the whole
position more tenable, demanding as it does demythologizing at
the hands of Bultmann and his thesis that there is continuity and
self-identity between Saul and Paul.

Whatever difficulties there may be in Professor Wingren's discussion in respect of coherence or of credibility, however, the
main comment for the purposes of the present argument must
refer to his refusal to deal with the question of knowledge and in
particular to consider a doctrine of natural morality. This refusal
is the more unfortunate because in various judgments on modern
theology Wingren seems to point logically in the direction of just
such a doctrine, as when he says that 'Protestant ethics has either
shown a relative indifference to existing social structures, or has
accepted them too uncritically',[148] or again that 'it is a fact that . . .
the universal Law creates a problem for any theological ethic that
seeks a specifically Christian ethos'.[149] It is such a doctrine of
natural morality that his criticism of exclusive and all-sufficient
Christocentricity in modern theology seems to demand, a doctrine
of general revelation and a theological account of natural morality;
but to insist that what is important is not the question of knowledge but the works of God is almost to substitute politics as
more ultimate than ethics. It may have been 'the central point in
Luther's doctrine of the "earthly government" – not that men
have any knowledge of God and His law apart from the revelation
in Christ, but that in dealing with the world, God uses human
beings in order to give good gifts to men or chastise them with
His wrath';[150] but this means that Luther's contribution to Christian ethics was a limited one. Moreover, to treat a concern for the
epistemological question as a resurgence of anthropocentricity is
really to bring the theological debate to an abrupt end, by setting
up another theological science in mid-air alongside that already
set up by Barth, with no possibility of communication between
them. No doubt Professor Wingren's fear is that to speak of

*natural* morality is to deny the continuing activity of God the Creator; but if a distinction is allowed – and it seems to be demanded – between a reality and what man makes of it in his grasp of it, which may very well be a sinful grasp, this fear may turn out to be unfounded.

## (i) A theological digression: nature and grace

It has been one of the main theses of the present argument that Christian ethics is not just related to dogmatics but is a part of dogmatics. If that is so it is only by a somewhat arbitrary fiat that dogmatic topics can be completely excluded from an essay on Christian ethics; and in fact the discussion, in its critical conversation with other forms of Christian ethical theory within the movement of modern Protestantism, has reached a point at which for the sake of clarity it is desirable to make an excursion into dogmatics beyond the confines of Christian ethics. For behind some of the most intractable of the obscurities and difficulties in Christian ethics may well lie ambiguities and uncritical assumptions elsewhere in dogmatics, and especially, at the present time, in dogmatic anthropology. This is so because in the vigorous development of contemporary Protestant theology the doctrine of God and Christology have overshadowed the doctrine of man, and by and large the latter has not been construed in the dynamic terms now characteristic of the former.

Thus, for example, Emil Brunner, in his articulation of the doctrine of God, justifiably complained that the traditional treatment of the attribute of omnipotence, which he regarded as symptomatic of the traditional treatment of the entire doctrine of God, had represented it as a quite abstract ability to do everything instead of an active power over the creation.[151] It has not, however, been sufficiently realized that the traditional treatment of man as a sinner has been content to represent him in terms of an almost equally abstract inability to do anything. Professor Lehmann holds that this is the point of the doctrine of total depravity and that Christian ethical thought, which is not content to be marked by 'crypto-Romanism', should not be squeamish about this doctrine;[152] but the possibility remains that those who defend the doctrine share uncritically with medieval theology a much too static conception of human nature, and that therefore in the very act of expressing an important evangelical insight they distort and misrepresent it. Certainly the heated controversy at one time between Barth and Brunner as to whether sin had or had not (respectively) destroyed the form as well as the content of the *imago dei* may well seem to have been conducted at several removes from the reality of actual man and so to have been largely academic and abstract.[153]

The truth is that theology has been much too prone to think of the world of men in terms of *human nature* as if the latter were something like an inert mass from which each man on arrival drew his ration. This mass might be polluted or not; and the evangelical teaching has been that it was. Its substance had been altered. Its appropriate properties had been lost and eliminated, in part or in whole. The *imago dei*, some said, had been destroyed, in content alone according to Brunner or in form as well as content according to Barth. This whole way of thinking, however, is much too static and abstract. Sin is not inert. Sin is not a death but a form and direction of life. Sin is active and affirmative. Sin is rebellion. Sin is not just destruction but itself a destroyer. Sin may use the armoury of its Opponent against himself. Sin can twist the argument and give its own slant to the reasoning. Sin can actively kill its Enemy, and it can build a tower and create a world against him. Professor Lehmann may frequently describe God's activity as doing what it takes to make and to keep human life human, but it remains a fact that only human beings could possibly sin.

Consequently it seems clear that the Christian doctrine of man requires dynamic terms for its proper articulation, more dynamic than those traditionally used such as that of a corrupted or totally depraved human nature; but this does not mean that the evangelical view must simply give way to the customary philosophical view of man as essentially a rational being. On this latter view man's rational endowment seems to be the distinctive thing, and there is a tendency to regard his status as a moral being as simply a function of his rationality, and perhaps even his religious potentiality as a further development of reason and morality. This, however, is not the Christian view and certainly not the view of evangelical Christianity which, as it seems to me, begins decisively at the other end. 'Man's chief end is to glorify God and enjoy him for ever.' What distinguishes man amongst all God's creatures is not simply his rationality as such, not even his morality, but a certain dimension of that morality, that man is made for fellowship and communion with God.

This dimension is certainly inconceivable by Christian faith without the horizontal or social dimension of morality which reveals itself in our duties towards our fellows. Jesus said, 'Inasmuch as ye have done it unto one of the least of these my brethren, ye have done it unto me.'[154] On the other hand, this horizontal dimension of morality *is* conceivable without the vertical; and it is strictly upon the latter that the doctrine of the *imago dei* seems to fasten. Similarly, morality, both in its vertical and in its horizontal dimensions, is inconceivable apart from rationality; but on the other side rationality *is* conceivable without morality. The doctrine of the *imago dei* does not mean that man is rational and that that entails morality and fitness for the divine fellowship. It is rather an attempt to explicate the fact that man is essentially made for this fellowship and that this carries with it both morality and rationality.

In all this the doctrine of the *imago dei* does not err; but there is a further point of equal, if not greater, importance. It is that the doctrine of the *imago dei* makes use of a metaphor which may well lead the theologian astray by tempting him to unreal rigidities and inflexibilities in his thought, to static conceptions where only dynamic conceptions answer to the realities of the situation, and to unreal problems comparable to those which attended the articulation of the divine omnipotence as an abstract and static ability to do everything. In particular, in spite of the metaphor of the image of God in man, it is a mistake to think of man's capacity for fellowship with God as something which can be expressed exclusively in terms of the concept of humanity or of human nature. It is a mistake to think of it as anything like a self-sufficient and self-contained endowment. Doubtless there is endowment involved, for otherwise sin and disobedience would not be possible; but, however the metaphor may drag our minds in other directions, it is clearly not a self-contained and self-sufficient endowment. How could it possibly be? How can man by himself have fellowship with God? There can be no fellowship with God except God himself should will it and seek to establish it. Consequently, man's capacity for fellowship with God, what the doctrine of the *imago dei* is trying to convey, is certainly not a self-contained and self-sufficient endowment falling entirely within human nature. It is rather an endowment which carries with it the possibility of morality and rationality, but an endowment always *within the sphere of a divine activity of calling and invitation, of revelation and self-disclosure.* It is in other words an endowment *within a relationship* to God established by God in grace from his side.

It is evident that one consequence of this account of the doctrine of the *imago dei* is that it complicates the relationship of nature and grace, for there is a clear sense in which there is no nature devoid of grace and yet no less there is point in the distinction and even the contrast between nature and grace.

From the standpoint of a moral philosopher Professor W. G. Maclagan has discussed this distinction with reference to modern radical Protestantism in the book from which I have already quoted, *The Theological Frontier of Ethics.* He holds that in modern Protestantism there is 'a crucial ambiguity about the expression "natural man", to which the use of the term "matter" by Aristotle and in Aristotelian scholasticism, in the doctrine of "matter" and "form", affords a parallel.'[155] The point is that in the metaphysical sense in which Aristotle spoke of form and matter the latter is necessarily the correlate of the former, distinguishable but not separable from it, whereas in a common-sense usage the word 'matter' is often applied to material things which in the more refined metaphysical sense are comprised, not of matter only, but of matter and form.

Similarly, according to Professor Maclagan, the word 'nature' may be used by theologians as the necessary correlate of grace and in that case it would make sense to say that apart from grace there is no good in man. The word might, however, be used also in an ordinary sense of actual men apart from Christ, and in this case, if Professor Maclagan is right, it would be quite false to say that without grace there is no good in man. To think otherwise, he says,[156] 'would be to affirm of the whole antithesis of "nature" and "grace" consistently employed in one sense something that can only reasonably be maintained with reference to the whole antithesis when consistently employed in the other sense'.

As it seems to me, however, the situation is even more complex than Professor Maclagan has allowed, for, in the interests of clarity, a distinction must be made between the grace which is *constitutive* of nature and the grace which is *redemptive* of the human world, that is to say, the saving grace of our Lord Jesus Christ.[157] Moreover, this distinction must be made even if in the last resort it must also be said that the latter grace is the former coming to grips with a world gone wrong. Thus it is the grace that is constitutive of human nature which ensures that man the sinner, natural man, remains a moral being. Of this grace it can be said that there is no good amongst men apart from grace; but then likewise there is no evil in a moral sense apart from this grace, and it does not prevent men from turning human life and history into a thoroughly man-centred (though not necessarily self-centred) enterprise. This indeed is the inner spiritual reality of 'the world' theologically conceived; and it seems to me that the reality of human sin can be more adequately and more dynamically described in terms of 'the world' than with reference to a totally depraved but entirely abstract human nature. The human world – this is the thesis – would not be human did it not stand by grace in the presence of God its Creator; but it would not be 'the world' did not man in his pride contradict his real situation and pose as sovereign of *his* moral universe. 'My river is mine own, and I have made it for myself.'[158]

On the other hand, it is by the saving grace of God in Christ that Christians live. 'For me to live', said St Paul, 'is Christ.' And it is presumably this grace which, in a part of his argument where we maintained he mistakenly assimilated redemption to creation, Professor Lehmann alleges to be operative in the lives of unbelievers, making co-operation between believers and unbelievers a possibility. 'The difference between believers and unbelievers,' he had already written,[159] 'both of whom are involved in the new humanity, is . . . the difference between being in a situation which is hidden and being in one which is open . . . and it is this new humanity which gives a new and different actuality to *the humanity and behavior of every man*.' It is perhaps unfortunate that Professor Lehmann does not appear to have asked whether the hiddenness of the unbeliever's situation had anything to do with human pride and sin, for then he might have questioned whether after all unbelievers could be said to be involved in the new humanity.[160]

Indeed, unless a clear distinction is drawn between constitutive and redemptive grace, theology is in danger of talking nonsense in one or other of two different directions. On the one hand, it may leave the student with the impression that Professor Lehmann sometimes gives, that all men are really Christians, or, in the opposite direction, it may suggest that non-Christians are not men, a thesis which seems to be required by Professor Paul Ramsey's discussion of the *imago dei* in his *Basic Christian Ethics*. In that discussion Professor Ramsey quite rightly distinguishes two possible views of the *imago*, on the one side, 'the definition of the image of God as some capacity native to man or some part of the substantial form of his nature',[161] and, on the other, the 'relational'[162] view according to which 'the image of God is rather to be understood as a relationship *within which* man sometimes stands, whenever like a mirror he obediently reflects God's will in his life and actions'.[163] Accordingly, we are told, 'man is a theological animal to the root of his essential being'; but if it is really intended that the image thus understood as a relationship to God appears only *sometimes* in the lives of those we are accustomed to call men – and Ramsey does say explicitly that it 'may be entirely lost'[164] – it seems to imply that after all non-Christians, and even Christians in their disobedient moments, are not really men. As if God's work of creation could really be undone by man's sin! As if man could really escape from the hollow of God's hands!

Whether or not, however, a firm distinction is drawn between what I have called constitutive grace and redemptive grace, the recognition of the former is important for the contemporary understanding of the doctrine of the *imago dei*, that is, as affirming an endowment within a divine activity of calling and invitation. Moreover, as I have already hinted, it is this interpretation of the doctrine which enables theology to see beyond the dilemma between autonomy and heteronomy in which the contemporary Protestant debate seems to terminate. Christian ethical thought of the type favoured by Karl Barth and Emil Brunner comes down, we have seen, on the side of sheer heteronomy, while, in reaction against the one-sidedness of this view, an ethical account such as Dietrich Bonhoeffer's or Rudolf Bultmann's lays 'an extraordinary emphasis upon autonomy',[165] one might say, an excessive emphasis upon autonomy. At an earlier point I suggested that Professor Lehmann's contribution to the subject was of great importance because *in certain respects* it seemed to bridge the gulf between these two wings of modern Protestantism; and yet in the end I cannot believe that it does so by integrating the insights of both into a single system but rather by alternating, up to a point, between them. So far as Professor Lehmann assimilates redemption to creation he is perhaps veering towards the heteronomous side of modern Protestantism; but in the last resort by stressing that 'I am to do what I am' and by finding this new humanity operative even in unbelievers he seems to come down on the side of complete autonomy.

Yet on this matter the truth lies exclusively with neither side. The concept of autonomy, and even talk of man's maturity and of his coming of age, enshrine an important insight; but even so man remains a creature and a moral being,[166] whom, in a paraphrase of certain words of the Psalmist, God has beset behind and before and laid his hand upon him. If the complete truth about man were that he is a rational being, then doubtless autonomy alone would contain the truth; but man is, rather, a free, rational being standing ever in the presence of his Creator and consequently autonomy by itself is only part of the truth and when affirmed as the whole is error. The law of man's being is not his own but God's, and as law and task is yet a gift of grace *constitutive of man's very nature*, so that, as St Augustine saw, God has indeed made him for himself alone and his heart is restless till it rests in God.

But, it must be said, this is not the gift of the Gospel which is, when seen from within the original gift or rather from within *what man has made of it*, the quite unimagined and unimaginable restoration of man by the act and intervention of God and the creation of a kingdom of love within a self-willed world of man's devising. As a result human life and history are neither a drift nor a rat race, neither a slippery ascent nor a headlong downfall. Rather they have a creative centre in Christ and the promise of its consummation. And yet this consummation is the promised fruit of a divine *restoration* and the fulfilment of the potentiality of the original nature. 'I will restore to you the years that the locust hath eaten ... and ... I will pour out my spirit upon all flesh; and your sons and your daughters shall prophesy, your old men shall dream dreams, your young men shall see visions ... And it shall come to pass, that whosoever shall call on the name of the Lord shall be delivered.'[167]

Accordingly the idea of autonomy is right, but it is the autonomy of the *creature*, a secondary and derivative autonomy which combines the valid elements of both sheer heteronomy and pure autonomy, it is the autonomy of one whose nature it is to stand by grace in the presence of God his Creator.

*Chapter 9*

# THE CHRISTIAN WAY IN THE
# CONTEMPORARY SCENE

*(a) The sphere of the Christian ethic is human life, that is,
historical existence in the world*

The task of Christian ethics is never finally accomplished. Each generation has to work at the problem as best it can; but it is important to see that there are two quite different reasons why this should be so.

The first arises from the change of outlook which has taken place in the nineteenth and twentieth centuries, and it consists in the realization that divine revelation is not composed of divinely guaranteed truths and edicts but is to be found in 'the mighty acts of God' and supremely in the life, death and resurrection of Jesus Christ. What revelation achieves therefore is not in the first instance a new intellectual situation but a new situation in life out of which theology and Christian ethics take their rise. There are therefore no final answers, no final theology and no final Christian ethics. William Temple hit the nail on the head when he wrote, 'There is no such thing as revealed truth. There are truths of revelation, that is to say, propositions which express the results of correct thinking concerning revelation; but they are not themselves directly revealed.'[1] And what he said had implications for Christian ethics as well as for theology.

The second reason why the task of Christian ethics is never accomplished is peculiarly relevant to the second half of the twentieth century. It is that, since Christian ethics as a form of ethics has to do with life and the problems of living, it must be as keenly alive as possible, if it is to be marked by ethical reality, to the contemporary situation. It is this fact that leads one writer to argue that 'the action of God occurs through what theologians have sometimes called "historical events" but what might be better termed "social change". This means that the church must respond constantly to social change, but this is just the trouble. . . .

We are all trying to live in an age of accelerating change with a static theology.'[2] 'It has been said', he continues, 'that history "is merely past politics," and there is real truth in the claim. This means, however, that politics is also present history, so our task is that of developing a theology of politics, and in particular a theology of revolutionary social change.'

The point is an important one, for Christian ethics at the present time can have ethical reality only if it is sensitive both to the rapidity of social change and to the increasing interdependence of different peoples, the fact that what happens in one part of the world has almost immediate repercussions in many other parts. Thus the modern consciousness frequently considers it more relevant to protest on behalf of the starving children of Biafra or the suffering people of Vietnam than to perform the task which their 'station and its duties' might seem most directly to impose. Accordingly, to have ethical reality, Christian ethics at the present time must be able to comprehend the ethics of protest as well as the ethics of revolutionary social change.

On the other hand, it is salutary and sound to remind ourselves that, while history has its novelties and is sometimes marked by changes both rapid and radical, it has no complete breaks. If there is continuity between Saul and Paul, as Bultmann has taken the trouble to affirm, there is certainly continuity between man in the thirties of the twentieth century and man in the seventies; and if there is at the present time 'a generation gap' that phenomenon is to be understood, not in terms of a new creation or a new species, but as a moral failure in mutual understanding due to the increasing pace of social change. If, however, there are no complete breaks in human history Christian ethics in its own interest, in the interest of truth, cannot afford to fall out of dialogue and communication with its own past, nor can it afford to pay merely lip-service to such dialogue by allowing itself to hear only from the past a feeble and confused echo of its own contemporary voice.

This is the justification of the foregoing analysis and argument; and if that argument and analysis are to be trusted the discussion of the Christian ethic has reached something of a climax in modern radical Protestantism, but a climax deeply involved in the dilemma which presents an exclusive choice between formalism and naturalism. This is so, it has been maintained, because neither side to the

225

debate has grasped the distinctive character of the moral which ties together the human realms of nature[3] and of grace and to which the very title of Christian *ethics* bears eloquent, though frequently unheeded, witness. None the less it is this discussion, we think, which makes the nearest approach by theological thought to the reality of the Christian life.

Accordingly, the next task which presents itself is that of re-stating the radical account of the Christian ethic – and any account of that ethic which reckons seriously with its character as an ethic of revelation and reconciliation is bound to be radical – in the light of the critical analysis of such thinkers as Barth, Brunner and Bultmann, Bonhoeffer and Lehmann, in an attempt to correct their defects and to escape from the uneasy dialectic between law without content and life and content without law. Moreover the fundamental correction in this context may be viewed from one or other of two sides.

From one point of view it consists of the refusal to relegate ordinary human life and its moral laws to some secondary, static and, in the end, irrelevant sphere to be described in Bonhoeffer's word as the penultimate. The correction seen in this light has itself several elements.

Of these perhaps the first is the recognition of the scheme of orders or mandates as no more than a rough and ready division of the raw material of human life, of the determination of being, of the kinds of moral problem with which men have to deal in the course of ordinary life. Such a recognition explicitly falls short of any claim that the scheme of orders is exhaustive, for there may well be other distinguishable spheres. Equally it falls short of any claim that the different spheres are rigidly separate, as if each order were completely self-contained and had its own peculiar set of rules and regulations. No doubt in any society there is, in each of these departments of life, a system of customs or rules, written or unwritten, which is peculiar to that depart-ment and which can therefore be described as, in a sense, tech-nical.[4] Yet beneath these and pervading them all there is the morality of the society in question, and the departmental, tech-nical systems of custom and rule are the expression, in diverse directions, of the moral insight and moral code of this society, of its way of life. About this morality and moral code there is in any society a unity, an *esprit de corps*, which overflows the provisions it creates in any one department and which holds these departments together as departments within the same society.

If this is so, however, it means that the second corrective element has already come into view, for then the argument has eliminated, not only the self-contained character of the orders or spheres of life and action, but also the static and dead quality with which Brunner seemed to endow them, their assimilation to dead natural law which is just there and does not begin to summon us to life, the sheer and mere objectivity of it all, as if a system of law could be final and leave no room whatever for the creativity of the human spirit, and as if at the same time it could be finally irrelevant to the larger promise and destiny of man's life, the ultimate. This static and dead quality is eliminated in the very act of recognizing a perhaps elusive, but no less pervasive, moral quality and significance, an element of oughtness, of claim upon us, perhaps even of destiny pressing in upon us, to live this way rather than that way and to organize our relationships one to another on this basis rather than on that.

Parenthetically, it ought perhaps to be said at this point that to a large extent the doctrinaire and unrealistic character of much systematic Christian ethical teaching stems from the traditional theological preoccupation with human nature. If Christian ethical thought is dominated by this abstract concept it may very well in its approach to the dynamic reality of human life and human history propound a doctrine of more or less static and stable mandates or orders; and this is really a Protestant version of the doctrine of natural law. There are of course differences, and important ones, between the two doctrines; but what they have in common is perhaps even more significant, namely, their reliance, in seeking a clear view and a defensible interpretation, upon anything as fixed, final and unchanging as natural law and the orders or mandates. The theory of natural law is, as we have seen, but one ethical account of moral reality, and in rejecting it it would be foolish indeed to reject also that of which it is an account; while on the other hand that reality, with all its imperious authority, so that certain possibilities of human existence are humanly, morally, quite intolerable, does not fit readily into a schematism of mandates. Certainly, whatever the ultimate explanation, there is behind both the schematism of orders and the theory of natural law a failure to appreciate the moving scene of human life and history.

Already, however, a further corrective element has been foreshadowed in what has just been said, for if morality is taken seriously in its character as the moral it cannot be relegated to any secondary sphere of the penultimate, and it cannot possibly be set in a merely external relationship to the Christian life. Natural morality is a highly complex phenomenon which expresses itself in different moral codes in different societies, and each of these expresses itself in turn in practical systems of custom and rule in the various orders and departments of human interest and activity. Some of its provisions, considered in isolation, may seem trivial in the extreme; and yet the answer to the moral question has, by the nature of the case, a unique but characteristic authority,[5] and behind all the detailed provisions of any moral code there is, providing its moral quality, a claim which in the last resort is final and unquestionable. That is to say, it is final and unquestionable in the sense that while it may legitimately be questioned whether this claim is adequately expressed in the particular provisions of a given code the claim itself cannot be questioned except in the way of denial and defiance. Accordingly, it is inconceivable that there should be two self-contained systems of morality, two ultimate yet separate claims of morality. On the contrary, the claim of morality is by the nature of the case single and self-consistent. And it is this natural morality, judged, reoriented and transformed, brought under the forgiving and reconciling lordship of Christ, which constitutes the Christian life.

From a different perspective this same central correction involves the strenuous affirmation that, just as the moral cannot properly be relegated to some secondary, penultimate and even irrelevant sphere, so, from the other end, the Christian life itself, the subject-matter of Christian ethics, cannot be placed in some elusive 'beyond', pitched, as it were, in a theological no-man's-land between heaven and earth, or withdrawn into a kind of monastic retreat separated off from the ongoing life of the world. Christian ethics, just as much as philosophical ethics, is concerned with a life lived under terrestrial conditions. Its subject-matter is not the life of heaven; and it was on a dusty earthly road that the good Samaritan found himself confronted by his neighbour and commended by Christ. To *this extent*, at any rate, the contemporary existentialist protest is justified, with its emphasis upon the concrete historical encounter of the moment.

To say this is not indeed to go very far in agreement with existentialists, for their characteristic affirmations are much more radical and the present point is, in comparison, a relatively elementary one. Yet even this elementary point can in the course of systematic thinking be obscured by a variety of unexamined presuppositions. For example, if in its theoretical examination the Christian life is placed within an ecclesiastical and institutional context, the effect can be well-nigh indistinguishable from the outright denial of this somewhat obvious point, as if life in the organized Church were not life on earth or life in the world, as if clerics and monks did not bring the world with them into the Church and make of the Church but a department of the world's life distinguishable only in respect of that which cannot be organized or controlled by man – just as the Pilgrim Fathers were to carry the world with them across the Atlantic and, so far from achieving an escape from history, were rather writing a further chapter in its tale.

Again if the systematic treatment of the Christian life is governed by an attempt to be loyal at all costs to the biblical witness and the biblical situation then even the impact of various strands of Scriptural teaching itself may be blunted by the overruling concept or impression of the Christian life as that of a separated sect and minority group. Thus the passing political conditions of the first centuries B.C. and A.D. may be allowed illegitimately to provide a permanent intellectual context for the subject-matter of Christian ethics. Moreover, this may happen, not only in spite of certain definite strands of biblical teaching which underline the religious man's involvement in the life of the world,[6] but also in spite of the fact that the 'separated sect' did not itself regard its separation as unambiguous and unproblematic, and not only embraced a mission to the outside world but sought an interpretation of its continuing life, as when St Paul declared that 'the powers that be are ordained of God'.[7]

These, however, are only minor ways in which the Church's

involvement in the ongoing life of the world may be obscured; and even if they are designed to achieve or maintain the purity of the Christian ethic, they do not really lift the Christian out of the historical stream, although they run the risk, for this Christian and for that, of arbitrarily halting the process of history at one point or another and accordingly of achieving an effect which is essentially anachronistic. Consequently, it is legitimate to suppose that the explicit theological affirmation of a sphere beyond the penultimate in Protestant ethical thought has a more profound source than such incidental features of the Church's life and thought.

## (b) The mythological 'beyond' in Protestant ethical thought

In thoroughgoing Protestant thought, then, there is presumably an operative factor other than, and more important than, the rather casual influences so far mentioned. This factor, defined simply in terms of its logical function or negatively by way of contrast to that with which moralists deal, is the concept of a sphere beyond, and more ultimate than, that within which there fall the precepts of morality and the so-called orders or mandates. It is more difficult to define this factor positively because it appears to enter theological thought by way of assumption rather than as the result of reflection and analysis. Nevertheless two things may fairly be said. Behind this assumption is an awareness, correct in itself, that what God was doing in Christ was not simply making a smooth extension of, or addition to, man's natural life as the culminating thought of the Middle Ages seemed to suggest in its characteristic synthesis. He was not simply adding revealed truth to the accepted truths of natural theology, nor divine law to natural law, nor theological virtues to the natural ones. Rather he was dealing with a situation that had gone wrong, he was *re*conciling the world to himself, bringing it back to its original and proper relationship to himself; and its lost condition was most readily understood in terms of a fallen *human nature*.

Consequently, in the second place, the assumption itself seems to include the concept of a life which is rightly understood as hid with Christ in God but which is curiously represented as in some way apart from, and beyond, human life as occurring in history.

It seems at the same time to be the concept of an existence which is in some way more real and more ultimate than existence in the world. One is almost tempted to think of it as a life or existence which is out of the body; but then inevitably the question would arise whose life or existence this is. In any case, whether it is truth or fiction, it is hardly the subject of Christian ethics which is concerned with the life of the Christian in history and the world.

This operative factor can also be described as faith; and accordingly one writer, Canon Lindsay Dewar, is to be found, in criticism of Brunner, alleging that for the latter 'faith is all that is required for the living of the Christian life, faith that works by love'.[8] What Canon Dewar finds objectionable in Brunner's position is its antinomianism, although it may be doubted whether the charge can really be made out against that position in all its many-sided complexity. What is more objectionable, however, and more clearly objectionable, is that Brunner tends to treat faith as if it were a substance or an organism, an *alter ego*, something that can fill and occupy a sphere. It is indeed truly remarkable that thinkers, who would avoid such crude misconceptions most strenuously in the context of sacramental theology, are none the less driven to posit something like them when dealing with Christian ethics. Yet that this is so in Brunner's case, for example, may be made plain by an analysis of what he said.

'The meaning of the whole doctrine of justification by faith', wrote Brunner,[9] '– indeed, the meaning of the whole message of the Bible – is this: that it is not man's efforts by way of the Law – and the human way is always the way of the Law – but that God by the way of grace gives the true relation to God and therefore the true existence.' 'This', he added, 'is the great inversion of existence. Previously, life, even at its best, is always a life directed *towards* God; now, henceforth life is lived *from* God as its centre.'

In such a passage Brunner did two distinguishable things, and clarity of thought on these matters demands that they be clearly distinguished. On the one side, he quite rightly assigned absolute centrality to the truth for which the doctrine of justification by faith stands, and acknowledged that the Christian life as a redeemed life has its origin in the reconciling action of God. On the other hand, he articulated this genuine insight in terms of a 'new possibility of life', 'the true existence' and, one might well add, a changed heart, a redeemed nature, a new creature. It is possible of course to pay scant attention to the precise terms of this articulation, and to refrain from inquiring too closely into their exact meaning. So long as one follows this course one sees nothing in the articulation save that of which it is an articulation, namely, the acknowledgement that the Christian life, whatever else it is, is a life reconciled by God to himself. When, however, attention is directed to the precise terms of the articulation and their exact meaning, difficulties abound and the threat of meaninglessness becomes acute. It is as if it were being maintained that the moral agent is lifted out of his own historical context and placed in another context, historical or otherwise. It is this kind of persistent implication which provokes an existentialist protest and invites the quite salutary reminder of Bultmann that there is continuity between man prior to faith and man under faith, between Saul and Paul, an elementary reminder that should really go without saying.

As it happens, Brunner was not entirely unaware of the force of this kind of criticism, for he did raise the question quite explicitly and quite urgently: 'does this Christian person, who owes no one anything save love, and who still owes this love, really *exist*? Or is this itself an ideal?' 'If it were simply an ideal,' he answered,[10] 'all that I have written would be sheer nonsense. For an ideal implies law, and a life controlled by ideals means a life of ethical effort, not one of spiritual power. When we talk of the New Birth and of Conversion we must speak of something real – or all our speech is vain. So we may answer the question by saying: "yes, this free Christian person does exist wherever faith exists".' 'Wherever faith exists', he said; and that clause is of quite vital importance. 'Faith exists only in the actuality of decision, thus as something which must be continually wrestled for and won out of unbelief. This faith only exists alongside of unbelief: "Lord, I believe! help Thou mine unbelief!" . . . For faith, in faith, the law has been abrogated; for man, however, "round whose neck there still hangs the old Adam", there exists at the same time the *demand* of God.' 'Hence faith is obedience, just as obedience is only genuine when it is faith.'[11] 'This does not mean that there are two kinds of Gospel. But these two points of view are like sentries who are commanded to stand and keep watch – at two opposite points – over the one sanctuary. God *demands* the obedience of faith. God *gives* the earnest determination to do something. Faith does not consist simply in passive acceptance; it always means, at the same time, an act of "pulling oneself together", just as believing confidence is only genuine when it is accompanied by the horror of the possibility of being lost. . . . The Epistle to the Romans interpreted by Matthew, and Matthew understood in the light of the Epistle to the Romans: this would provide the basis for an evangelical ethic.'

Few passages could be more important for the unravelling of the various elements in Brunner's thought and for catching a glimpse of the very core of his position – especially his declaration that, while for faith the law is abrogated, for man it remains. In other words, what Brunner was saying is that whereas for faith there is no law, for man the sinner the law is still there; and this contention is most illuminating, for it discloses the rationale of the Christian life as he understood it and it offers a thesis which, kept clearly in view, can be seen to exercise its influence in a variety of directions.

Thus for one thing it is possible to see here the ultimate source of Brunner's formalism, his insistence that there is no determination by content but only by the form of obedience to God. But for sin, there would be no law whatsoever; and consequently the whole drive and force of law is to bring men into alignment with God – not with goodness or honesty or justice or love, but with God. In a sense, the ultimate and all-comprehensive demand of law has nothing to do with its detailed contents, but is first and last a demand that sin be overcome, that faith should triumph, that law itself should come to an end. Law is essentially suicidal for at its very core it aims at its own destruction. In a sense, there is only one edict of the law, namely, that we believe in God, that we have faith.

At the same time, another underlying characteristic of Brunner's ethical thought momentarily appears on the surface, and this might be called a high-minded but pervasive eudaemonism and, linked with it, an incipient and pragmatic other-worldliness. It is a curious fact that, on the one side, not distinguishing carefully between anthropocentricity and egocentricity, Brunner could accuse natural morality and ethics of the latter defect, and could hold, not very convincingly, that 'even where the *summum bonum* is regarded as Divine favour and Divine life, and even where duty is regarded as the Divine command, it is man's *self-interest* which moves his will',[12] and that 'even in his service to others the legalistic man remains shut up within himself . . . even where he is dealing with others, in the last resort, he is only dealing with himself'.[13] It is an even more curious fact, on the other side, that in his own exposition of the Christian ethic he should come very close to laying himself open to precisely the same charge. None the less, that he should do so can be understood, for if the demand of the Gospel is conceived in entirely formal terms as a demand that I should have faith it is difficult to avoid the implication that the overruling consideration here is *my* salvation. Brunner even held that 'believing confidence is only genuine when it is accompanied by the horror of the possibility of being lost';[14] and although some such language is an inalienable part of the Christian gospel it seems clear that something of that gospel has been lost if in the last resort this horror is a purely natural, and not a moral, phenomenon.

Indeed a further characteristic of Brunner's ethical thinking is underlined at this point, for it seems a fair charge against him that, in spite of an extensive and often illuminating treatment of the subject, he had not really grasped the unique character of the moral, the normative, that reality which constitutes a law for man in his freedom and sets the sphere of the distinctively human apart from, even if linked with, the natural. On the contrary, so far from appreciating and expressing the unique character of the moral, Brunner's ethical thought was pervaded by the naturalistic fallacy, the error of deriving 'ought' from 'is', the moral from the natural, the mistake of subordinating the former to the latter instead of affirming its supremacy as the true supernatural.[15]

This characteristic of Brunner's ethical thought is apparent in his treatment of the various orders, as when he attempted to derive the ideal of marriage as a lifelong relationship between one man and one woman from the bare natural facts that every child is the offspring of one man and one woman and that two people in love resent the intrusion of a third party.[16] Perhaps, however, the instance *par excellence* of the naturalistic fallacy in Brunner is to be found, not in what he regarded as the penultimate, but in the ultimate itself where he did not just derive the moral from the natural but allowed the latter to swallow it up and actually substituted the natural, even if it was the supernatural naturally conceived, for the normative. But for sin, Brunner would have represented the Christian ethic in exclusively descriptive terms. The Good is that which God does. 'Christian ethics is the science of human conduct as it is determined by Divine conduct.' Ultimately, even if it be ideally, law and morality are non-existent. The imperative is lost in the divine indicative and it is only because of sin that 'the indicative of the Divine promise becomes the imperative of the Divine demand'.[17]

Thus the sense of ought is deemed to be a by-product of sin, and accordingly Brunner could hold that 'the sense of "ought" shows me the Good at an infinite, impassable distance from my will. Willing obedience is never the fruit of a sense of "ought" but only of love. This is the paradox: that the sense of "ought", through which alone I learn at all what freedom is in this sense of "ought", unveils to me my formal freedom – announces to me that I am in bondage to sin.' 'If I feel I *ought* to do right, it is a sign that I cannot do it. If I could really do it, *there would be no question of "ought" about it at all*.'[18] The ethical rigorism of such passages, which confuses a psychological 'ought' with the logical one, is highly questionable, even if Brunner learned it from Kant; but his amoralism, his elimination of the genuinely moral, is even more significant and is as important an element in his total position as is his formalism on the one side and his incipient and pragmatic other-worldliness and eudaemonism on the other. Indeed all three cling together as indispensable parts of Brunner's thesis that while for faith there is no law, for man the sinner the law remains.

The main purpose of this analysis, however, has been to disclose what Brunner really meant by the ultimate; and it seems clear that he posited, whether wittingly or not, what I have called a sphere, a life, an existence, a nature, a heart, which is on every side and in the most absolute sense the gift of God. Even for the Christian, however, there is alongside this gift another reality, an *alter ego*, the sinful ingrown self; and between these two there is, one can only suspect, an unremitting warfare. Yet, if this is a fair assessment, it means that in the immediate background, behind Brunner's explicit treatment of the Christian life, there lurks a highly mythological statement of the case, and that it is exceedingly difficult, rather that it is impossible to see what Brunner's treatment would mean if for a moment it were deprived of the substance of this hidden support. The background of ideas is entirely indispensable; but at the same time it is highly, and, for a systematic treatment of the Christian life, intolerably mythological. The reader would not have to agree with the main behaviouristic thesis of Professor Gilbert Ryle's *The Concept of Mind*, in fact he could retain the most substantial reservations about the adequacy of that thesis, and yet he might find incredible the presupposition of Brunner's discussion that there are, not just one 'ghost in the machine', but two – and a ghostly warfare between them.

The truth seems to be that, while radical Protestantism has done well to think of God always in dynamic rather than in static terms, it has conspicuously failed to realize a like achievement in its thought about man. Too often the concept of an abstract and hypostatized human nature is indispensable to its thought, whereas it seems clear beyond all peradventure that there is no such thing as human nature except as a generalization about the ways in which actual men and women behave. The reality here is not in the generalization but in the individual men and women, in their day-to-day lives and historical existence, and in the world which has made them and they have made. Accordingly, if theological thought is to be sound and realistic, it must be translatable into terms of the reality and not just into terms of some abstract generalization about the reality; and so long as this translation is quite impossible it is inevitable that within radical Protestantism itself there should be the kind of protest that existentialism has made.

*(c) The existentialist protest and its mythological historical moment*

The misfortune is that in an excess of zeal existentialism tends to fly to an opposite extreme and, instead of correcting a misrepresentation, to deny that which is misrepresented. Thus, in a context which demands a more adequate account of a divinely reconciled life, it begins to lay what has been called an extraordinary emphasis upon the autonomy of man,[19] which for Brunner, not altogether without reason, is the devil itself – at any rate with sufficient reason to ensure that in due course the protest will give rise to a protest against the protest.

The crucial problem at this point is to determine what would constitute a more adequate account of the Christian ethic and the Christian life; and the first approximation to a solution lies in the realization that a more adequate account would be both more ethical and more dynamic than that which Brunner has provided. Consequently it would neither relegate the moral to the penultimate nor deal with the ultimate in mythological terms. It is because this would be an approximation to a solution that the existentialist protest carries so much weight, for it provides, so far as man is concerned, a more dynamic treatment and one which has grasped something of the unique character of the moral. Accordingly it places the life of the Christian quite firmly in an historical context, in its place in the continuing movement of human history. Thus Professor Bultmann lays all the emphasis upon the concrete historical encounter of man with man. Yet this existentialist emphasis and apprehension is a one-sided one which, as we have seen, so emphasizes autonomy that it cannot comprehend the heteronomy of genuine morality. Into the bargain, by virtue of its anti-metaphysical temper and its radical distrust of any form of supernaturalism it is at a disadvantage in trying to understand without unnecessary ambiguity anything which owes its origin to the reconciling activity of God.

Certainly the existentialists are right to emphasize the decision of faith and to emphasize it as a decision of love. It is because they do so that their teaching is both more dynamic and more ethical than that which comes from the other wing of radical Protestantism. Even so three points must always be made.

In the first place, love is not totally independent of law or whatever reality it is that man apprehends and expresses as the moral law. On the contrary, the demand of love can be apprehended, articulated and met only in terms of the diverse insights of the ordinary moral consciousness; and apart from these the moral agent is at the mercy of mere sentimentality and sheer fanaticism. Thus it is not only interesting but significant to note that at precisely this point Dr J. A. T. Robinson, in his controversial book

*Honest to God*, begins to waver in his allegiance to existentialism. To begin with he quotes with approval Professor Joseph Fletcher's defence of what Pope Pius XII had condemned as 'situational' ethics, not in the sense in which we have already used this word to indicate a pioneering and *ad hoc* ethical inquiry, but in the sense of a fully blown and deliberate interpretation of the Christian ethic independently of moral principles. Then, however, Dr Robinson maintains that 'such an ethic cannot but rely, in deep humility, upon guiding rules, upon the cumulative experience of one's own and other people's obedience. It is this bank of experience', he adds, 'which gives us our working rules of "right" and "wrong", and without them we could not but flounder.'[20] It is true that he leaves the impression that these are but an *external* pointer, since they are understood 'without respect of persons' whereas love '*does* respect persons'; but since love too can be without fear or favour it is clear that the equivocal phrase 'respect of persons' cannot make the separation it is here designed to make. What is even more important is that if experience is not moral from the beginning no mere accumulation of it will ever produce a guide to morals. Laws may be inhuman but love may equally be blind; and Christian love is intrinsically the fulfilment and completion of law or whatever moral insights law seeks to embody.

In the second place, faith is not a spontaneous, self-sufficient decision which a man makes quite out of the blue, but it is on every side a response to divine revelation, and in particular, to the fact that God was in Christ reconciling the world to himself. Once again, however, the existentialists are abundantly right in holding that faith is expressed in terms of a social and historical context, and that apart from such expression it is empty and meaningless, and in fact not faith at all. Faith is certainly faith in God as other than man and other than any element of this world's life, and any articulation of faith, any system of religious thought, which minimizes this truth is so far misleading; but faith in God is the faith *of* men, even if it owes its possibility to divine grace, it is faith in him who is worshipped and served on earth and in history, and any representation of the matter which obscures that fact is to that extent a misrepresentation. None the less, this faith *of* men is still faith *in* God.

It is true that Bultmann, whatever some of his followers believe

– for in them there has been a tendency to deny this kerygmatic side to Bultmann's own thought – has himself strenuously insisted that the new authentic existence in love becomes a possibility for man only through an act of God, indeed by *the* act of God, the eschatological event, which is Jesus Christ, which is repeated whenever the Gospel is preached, and which is essentially a demand for decision. At the same time, however, he has been no less emphatic that this act of God must always be affirmed in a completely non-objectifying way, and that on no account must it be given any kind of metaphysical magnitude as would be the case in the development of what is sometimes called a world-view. So far as world-views go modern man is committed to what Bultmann calls the modern or scientific world-view.

Yet if Bultmann is taken seriously in this insistence, as he certainly means to be, the act of God becomes a sheer point or a sheer event, lacking all colour, character and content. It becomes in other words a sheer irrelevance; and it is not therefore surprising that some of those who are concerned to develop Bultmann's thought, such as Professor Fritz Buri, are prepared to dispense with it altogether. What is important to notice, however, is that even in Bultmann, if the act of God is affirmed in a completely non-objectifying way, there can be no rational connection between it and what it is alleged to make possible in human existence, a decision of love in the concrete encounter of the moment. It is only by drawing illegitimately and inconsistently upon the more traditional understanding of Christianity that we can continue to say that we love him *because he first loved us*. If Bultmann's position is consistently maintained there can be no rational connection (only a blind causative one) between the sheer act of God and the demand and decision of love. Accordingly, the kerygmatic side of Bultmann's thought, upon which he paradoxically insists, does not in the least infringe the autonomous character of the Christian life as he understands it.

In the third place, plainly, all this means that the particular moment of history, the concrete encounter with a neighbour, is by the existentialist so packed with meaning that it becomes transformed into a mythico-mystical reality. In it, if anywhere, is to be found the entire meaning of Christian faith in God as Creator of the universe and as the reconciler of human life to his divine purpose of the Kingdom of God. Into it too, by itself in splendid isolation, is compressed the whole demand and decision of love, the fulfilment of human destiny. Clearly, in this concentration upon historical existence, attention is restricted to a discrete moment of history, and this discrete moment of history is not allowed to point beyond itself, *either* on its own level to the continuum of history past and gone, and within that to the fate of the moral in man's experience, *or* beyond itself to a transcendental sphere whence history may derive its meaning, its purpose and its goal. This, however, is to pack the historical moment to bursting-point and to give it a mythico-mystical quality as unacceptable as the mythology in which the other wing of radical Protestantism is unwittingly involved.

### (d) Secularization and situationalism

If it is true that the *locus* of the Christian life and so of the Christian ethic is neither a mythological 'beyond' nor a mythological moment of history, those moralists seem to be on the right lines who emphasize instead the life of the world and even the politics of God. It was, as we have seen, a main concern of Dietrich Bonhoeffer in his *Ethics* to speak of a world 'already sustained, accepted, and reconciled in the reality of God';[21] and there is no doubt that, although in his distinction between the ultimate and the penultimate and in his doctrine of the mandates he made contact with the other wing of modern Protestantism, for him the centre of gravity fell here. Consequently, although he was a critic of the kind of Christian existentialism favoured by Bultmann,[22] his own ethical position, like Bultmann's, falls on the side of naturalism or actualism as opposed to formalism.

This characteristic emphasis of Bonhoeffer's is to be found also in what he had to say about religionless Christianity and about living in the world before God '*etsi deus non daretur*';[23] and it is to be seen also in the fact that, unlike Bultmann who turned his back upon it,[24] Bonhoeffer was ready to embrace the technological age into which man was entering. It is present too in the theme of 'Christian worldliness' to which he devoted considerable attention.

It is true, as Professor John D. Godsey has reminded us, that this worldliness 'of which he speaks is *not* the world's understanding of worldliness, not the "shallow this-worldliness of the enlightened, of the busy, the comfortable, or the lascivious" . . . , but a worldliness deriving from the knowledge of Christ, a knowledge in which death and resurrection is ever present'.[25] The trouble is that what distinguishes one kind of this-worldliness from another must itself be a this-worldly reality, and it is exceedingly difficult to see where it is to be found. Is it a present reality or an historical memory and example? For Bonhoeffer, according to Professor Godsey, 'the *resurrection* and *ascension* mean that "Jesus Christ has overcome sin and death and that he is the living Lord to whom all power is given in heaven and on earth", and that his Lordship "sets creation free for the fulfillment of the law which is its own, that is to say, the law which is inherent in it by virtue of its having its origin, its goal and its essence in Jesus Christ" . . .'[26] Even so, however, the difficulty remains unabated, and indeed it remains in aggravated form when it is further declared, in Bonhoeffer's own words, that 'now that it has come of age, the world is more godless, and perhaps it is for that very reason nearer to God than ever before'.[27] We are to take with full seriousness the fact, Professor Godsey expounds Bonhoeffer as holding, 'that the whole reality of the world is already drawn into Christ and bound together in him, and that the movement of history consists in the world's being accepted and becoming accepted by God in Christ . . .'[28] The problem posed by all this could scarcely be more acute. Is Christian living simply a matter of swimming with the tide? And are there no cross-currents and no contrary winds?

It is one of history's tragedies that Dietrich Bonhoeffer was denied the opportunity to develop his thought and answer himself some of the questions which his writings pose. There is no doubt, however, that, whether systematized and integrated or not, his ideas have had an extensive influence, and others have tackled the problems that he bequeathed. Professor Lehmann, as we have seen, deals with the subject on the same profound level, emphasizing what God is doing to make and to keep human life human; but, if our analysis of his argument is sound, he too ends in actualism or naturalism. Nor indeed may we expect any other outcome, unless, by a somewhat tenuous thread and with, we may suspect, a loss in profundity, the logical successor to Bonhoeffer is to be found either in secularization or in situationalism, working respectively with a present reality and an historical memory.[29]

Perhaps the clearest and most persuasive presentation of the former thesis is to be found in Professor Harvey Cox's book *The Secular City*; and there is no doubt that it contains a valuable account of life in the contemporary scene and an illuminating diagnosis of such particular moral problems as those of sex and work. What is important, however, in the present context is the framework within which these discussions fall, the general thesis that the process of social change has thrown up three distinctive eras, those of the tribe, the town, and what Harvey Cox calls the technopolis. This last which has appeared in our time is marked by urbanization and secularization and constitutes the secular city. This city has both shape and style, that is to say, it carries with it a social system and a culture, the former marked by anonymity and mobility, and the latter by pragmatism and profanity.

As a diagnosis of the contemporary condition of man all this is of great interest; but, it should be noticed, Cox's thesis is that in this diagnosis he has uncovered the basic thrust to be found in the process of social change, and that this thrust, so far from being resented by the Church or by the Christian believer, should be welcomed as a movement which has its roots in the Bible. Indeed it is Christianity, along with technology, which has produced this development in the process of social change; and the secular city is an image which, not only helps us to develop a *theology* of social change and revolution, but even enables us to understand the concept of the Kingdom of God. 'Our struggle for the shaping of the secular city represents the way we respond faithfully to this reality in our own times.'[30] What it stands for in our secular age, marked as it is by 'the liberation of man from religious and metaphysical tutelage',[31] is described as 'maturation and responsibility'[32] or again as 'maturity and interdependence'.[33] 'The grammar of the Gospel is not a categorical imperative; it first of all points to what *is* occurring, only secondarily does it call for a consequent change in attitude and action. The Kingdom of God is at hand; therefore repent. The syntax of the secular city is identical. Through its irrepressible emergence it establishes a new situation which renders former ways of thinking and doing wholly obsolete.'[34]

The biblical sources which authenticate this process Cox describes more specifically as 'the disenchantment of nature', enshrined in the story of the creation, 'the desacralization of politics', taught by the narrative of the exodus, and 'the deconsecration of values', inherent in the record of the Sinai covenant. As a result of this threefold liberation man is in a position to take control of his own destiny, to create his own values, and to apply to his specific problems the skills and techniques developed by his technology. 'The Bible does not deny the reality of the gods and their values; it merely relativizes them. It accepts them as human projections, as "the work of man's hand", and in this sense is very close to the modern social sciences. It was because they believed in Yahweh that, for the Jews, all human values and their representations were relativized.'[35]

In this way man is prepared for life in the secular city, with its anonymity and mobility, pragmatism and profanity. In the secular city, for example, many of modern man's personal contacts must be merely functional; and 'urban man has a wider variety of "contacts" than his rural counterpart; he can choose only a limited number for friends'.[36] Further, modern man 'will be more open to change, movement, newness. There is no reason why Christians should deplore the accelerating mobility of the modern metropolis.'[37] Moreover, life in the secular city is marked by pragmatism – 'the world is viewed not as a unified metaphysical system but as a series of problems and projects'[38] – and by profanity – 'profane man is simply this-worldly'.[39] These are elements in the outlook of contemporary man in the secular city; and not only is this outlook authenticated by the Bible, but the Church, even if it has rarely recognized it, has the task of promoting it, of acting as a cultural exorcist. 'Jesus calls men to adulthood, a condition in which they are freed from their bondages to the infantile images of the species and of the self. Exorcism is that process by which the stubborn deposits of town and tribal pasts are scraped from the social consciousness of man and he is freed to face his world matter-of-factly.'[40]

Enough has perhaps been said to indicate the tenor of Cox's principal thesis; and what is most basically puzzling about it is that this is essentially a *sociological* thesis, perhaps highly speculative and perhaps also extremely simplified, but essentially a *sociological* thesis, and yet one for which the author deems it relevant and necessary to secure a *theological* sanction, grounding and authentication. It is not just that this enterprise involves the crossing of barriers between different disciplines. That in itself would be a small thing and perhaps even a merit. The real problem lies in the particular connection that is forged. For, on the one hand, the theological grounding is far from convincing and requires a large measure of special pleading. To mention only one point, although a central one, it is difficult to see how the deconsecration of values can be held to arise out of the Sinai covenant or, for that matter, any other part of the biblical witness. The argument is that the prohibition of idols prevents the treatment of values as absolute, although the prohibition of killing, adultery and theft is on the face of it every bit as categorical as the prohibition of idols.

This does not mean that we may not recognize idolatry where the children of Israel would never have recognized it. We may, for example, quite legitimately regard as idolatrous the treatment of one's own interpretation of the moral law as inflexible and absolute, but hardly the view that, whether we have adequately grasped them or not, there are objective values, not just 'human projections'. In fact Cox himself admits that 'it is in the realm of values and ethics that the nurture of secularization becomes most ambiguous and problematical'.[41] Yet not only does his thesis lead him to ride roughshod over the biblical revelation and theologies that are based upon it, it also tempts him to spurn 'academically trained people who specialize in the humanities', who, he says, occupy 'a perceptual context where what they say can be safely ignored'.[42]

On the other hand, the design of giving to the sociological thesis a theological grounding is no less puzzling when considered from the other end. After all, the sociological thesis in question is that man has taken control of his own destiny, creates his own values and tackles with his technological skills his own problems, he is 'master of his fate . . . captain of his soul'; and to attempt to give to that thesis a theological grounding and authentication is simply to contradict it. If man really has come of age in this absolute sense he does not need, he ought to reject any suggested theological sanction for his new stature. Such a man, one would think, might well speak, as did Auguste Comte, of the regency of God during the long minority of humanity; but one would not expect him to seek, as if through some lingering inferiority complex, a theological grounding for his new-found freedom.

As it happens, Cox himself is not unaware of the problem and the possibility that 'all we have said about secularization as the work of God for man is nonsense and the whole thesis of this book is erroneous';[43] and in facing up to this prospect he explicitly relates his discussion to the thought of Bonhoeffer. None the less he believes that the difficulty can be overcome. 'All words,' he says,[44] 'including the word *God,* emerge from a particular socio-cultural setting. No language was ever handed down from heaven.' In keeping with this fundamental principle he goes on to maintain that 'in secular society politics does what metaphysics once did' and that 'the mode of theology which must replace metaphysical theology is the *political* mode'.[45] Indeed it is not theology alone that is affected. In the secular age politics 'brings unity and meaning to human life and thought' and instead of being 'unified ... in metaphysical systems' truth 'is functionally unified by bringing disparate specialties to bear on concrete political perplexities'.[46] But so far as *theological* meaning is concerned Cox suggests that perhaps in the secular city 'like his relationship to his work partner, man's relationship to God derives from the work they do together',[47] and that for the rest we must believe that 'a new name will come when God is ready. A new way of conceptualizing the Other will emerge in the tension between the history which has gone before us and the events which lie ahead.'[48]

This way of escape from the danger of talking nonsense is not, to say the least, without its difficulties. For one thing, it is not easy to take seriously that God is to be thought of mainly as man's partner, as a member of the team assembled for the solution of a specific problem; and it is tempting to ask which particular technical skills are to be deemed divine. Nor is it easy to believe that truth has really been significantly unified when 'disparate specialties' are pragmatically brought together to deal with concrete problems.

The decisive consideration, however, is that this representation of the situation is a curious inversion of what the development of the traditional understanding of Christianity seems to us to suggest and that on examination this inversion proves not to be viable. It has already been hinted that the truth about man is that essentially, by his nature or constitution, he stands inescapably in the presence of God his Creator, that is, in relationship to God, and that it is this that binds him to his fellows. What Cox is holding on the contrary is that the basic thing about man is the relationship in which he stands to his fellows, and that the meanings of the words he uses, that even the meaning of the word 'God', is a function of this relationship and of the ways in which it changes. That this is an inversion of the traditional understanding is not fatal to it; but what is fatal is that when critically investigated it shows itself an impossible position. If it were true, if the meaning of words were indeed a function of our social relationships, changing as they change, it would be impossible to speak significantly of social change itself, and yet this is the very thing that Harvey Cox succeeds in doing.

It is true that human beings do not occupy a supra-historical perspective, that their views and beliefs are coloured by the place they hold in the stream of history; but this does not mean, this simply cannot mean that man creates his own values (still less that this is the secret meaning of the Bible) nor that truth is a function of man's historical and social location. Change is an important factor in man's attempt to understand himself, but the thesis that it constitutes the whole truth is indistinguishable from nonsense. Perhaps, for all his contempt for those academically trained in the humanities, Harvey Cox should have paid more attention to Heraclitus.[49]

Our basic problem at this stage of the discussion, it will be remembered, is to discover whether, on the assumption of Bonhoeffer's thesis of a world already redeemed, it is possible to find some reality which would help to distinguish, as Bonhoeffer himself deemed essential, between Christian worldliness and non-Christian worldliness and so to avoid naturalism or actualism. Such a reality, I said, was by no means easy to find, whether conceived as a present reality or as an historical memory and example; and the investigation of the theme of secularization has confirmed this suspicion so far as the former possibility is concerned. The secular city is a legitimate, if radical, development of Bonhoeffer's thought, and there was in the articulation of that thought no built-in corrective which would have rendered this development illegitimate.

As for the historical memory and example it is necessary now to turn attention to situationalism. Some notice of this outlook has already been taken when reference was made to Dr J. A. T. Robinson's book *Honest to God*; but a more extensive treatment of the position has been provided by Professor Joseph Fletcher in his volume *Situation Ethics*. Once again the thread connecting with Bonhoeffer's thought is a tenuous one, and once again, there is, we may well suspect, some loss in the level of profundity; and yet if Professor Fletcher can make out his case he can perhaps rescue Bonhoeffer by supplying the missing criterion which distinguishes Christian worldliness from non-Christian worldliness. Certainly his aim is to bring ethics to 'the growing edge of the human enterprise',[50] and his approach is marked by an unashamed pragmatism. 'We have seen the light', he says,[51] 'when we recognize that abstract and conceptual morality is a mare's nest. Bonhoeffer was correct in his distaste for metaphysics, as Kierkegaard was in his hatred of systems.' 'What is precisely and exactly and starkly unique about the Christian ethic is *Christ*. It is a Christological ethic, not simply a theological ethic. When Bonhoeffer speaks of how Christ "takes form" among us here and now, this is his rather mystical but nonmetaphysical way of saying that every ethical imperative is contextual or situational, not propositional – but it is Christ who takes form with us when we conform to his commandment.'[52] And this commandment is to act in love as the contemporary situation demands.

So far there are certainly points of contact with the thought of Bonhoeffer and with his theme of Christian worldliness, although there may be no firm perception of a world already redeemed. The further development of Fletcher's ethical thought, however – of his ethical *method*, for he does not profess an ethical *system*[53] – is marked by three salient and defining features. The first of these is situationalism itself as offering a middle way between legalism and antinomianism. That is to say, situationalism neither holds to a variety of fixed and binding moral principles or laws, nor does it disown all principles and rely instead upon some kind of inspiration. 'The situationist', says Fletcher,[54] 'enters into every decision-making situation fully armed with the ethical maxims of his community and its heritage, and he treats them with respect as illuminators of his problems. Just the same he is prepared in any situation to compromise them or set them aside *in the situation* if love seems better served by doing so.' And more than once he refers to Bonhoeffer's participation in the plot to take Hitler's life.

The second salient feature is relativism. 'In our attempt to be situational,' he says,[55] 'to be contemporary in our understanding of conscience, we can pin another label on our method. It is relativistic.' Yet not completely so. 'There must be an absolute or norm of some kind if there is to be any true relativity.'[56] 'Only love is a constant; everything else is a variable.'[57] Love 'is not a virtue at all; it is the one and only *regulative principle* of Christian ethics.'[58] 'There is only one thing that is always good and right, intrinsically good regardless of the context, and that one thing is love';[59] and apart from that 'there *are* no "values" at all; there are only things (material and nonmaterial) which *happen* to be valued by persons'.[60] 'Only love is objectively valid, only love is universal.'[61]

The third defining feature of Fletcher's ethical theory is his utilitarianism. 'As the love ethic searches seriously for a social policy it must form a coalition with utilitarianism. It takes over from Bentham and Mill the strategic principle of "the greatest good of the greatest number" . . . replacing their pleasure principle with *agape*.'[62] Fletcher even holds that in this coalition 'the hedonistic calculus becomes the agapeic calculus, the greatest amount of neighbor welfare for the largest number of neighbors possible';[63] and in his later book, *Moral Responsibility*, he maintains that 'justice is love balancing interests and claims, calculating . . .'[64] and suggests that 'every time we think "love" we should *say* "justice".'[65]

In its pragmatism and situationalism, in its relativism and in its utilitarianism this view of Christian ethics is thoroughly contemporary; and, although it seems to lack any clear affirmation that this world is already a redeemed world, it can perhaps in its worldliness claim to be something of a legitimate successor to Bonhoeffer, while in its occasionalism or situationalism it matches Harvey Cox's emphasis upon specific problems as they crop up.

The crucial question, however, is one concerning its adequacy, and on this score a negative verdict must be entered.

In its situationalism it may indeed contain or disguise a legitimate protest against the concept of moral *law*. We have already suggested that, while this may be a fairly natural and obvious metaphor, it fails to comprehend the creativity of genuine morality. It is, however, one thing to make such a protest and quite another to treat the protest as if it were a distinctive type of Christian ethics.

In its relativism, on the other hand, it seems to lose touch with morality. It is important to grasp this point as clearly as possible even if the alternative to relativism must certainly avoid the idolatry which Harvey Cox condemns and the legalism which Professor Fletcher abhors, and is therefore by no means easy to articulate. None the less, if every good but love is relative, how can one possibly love one's neighbour? Is loving one's neighbour a matter of doing good to him? But if so, which good, good as relative to the neighbour or good as relative to me the agent? If a comprehensive relativism which permits love as the only absolute is taken seriously – and this is what Fletcher seriously means – it confronts the moral agent with an unanswerable question, and in the absence of an answer it throws the gates open wide to caprice and impulse, to sentimentalism and fanaticism, to naturalism and actualism of one kind or another. Love may bring food to the starving neighbour but not to the glutton who has already more than enough, although food may be the very thing that both most desire. Love needs to know how persons *ought* to be treated, as Dr J. A. T. Robinson in spite of himself was compelled to admit. Even Professor Fletcher, in distinguishing his situationalism from antinomianism, allows himself to be 'fully armed with the ethical maxims of his community and its heritage, and he treats them with respect as illuminators of his problems'; but if love is really the only absolute and if all other goods are completely relative to the person for whom they are goods, these maxims look extraordinarily like rabbits pulled out of the conjurer's hat.[66]

Clarity of thought requires more attention to the well-known distinction between deontological and teleological ethics than Fletcher is prepared to give when he says that 'one's "duty" is to seek the goal of the most love possible in every situation, and

(1)

(2)

one's "goal" is to *obey* the command to do just that!'[67] Love, no doubt, is the Christian's universal duty; but such a single universal duty requires the recognition of more specific requirements, and these in turn the recognition of specific goods. Fletcher poses a curious question regarding the relationship between the law and the commandment of love: 'Is the Summary to be taken as a compendium or as a distillation?'[68] He himself clearly favours the latter; but the truth is that it is neither, it is the fulfilment which is at the same time the redemption of the law. Love may define the extent (not one mile but two, not seven times but seventy times seven) and the range (the neighbour who may be a stranger or even an enemy) of the Christian's duty, but *by itself* it does not give the direction.

Fletcher's utilitarianism also presents considerable difficulty. It is well known that John Stuart Mill's hedonistic calculus was a source of weakness rather than strength for his brand of utilitarianism. How could pleasure be calculated on the basis of the diverse criteria which Mill was constrained to recognize? But equally, or indeed more so, how can one possibly seek 'the goal of the most love'? How can love be measured? In any case love is transitive, its very nature is not to be self-contained and something that can be measured, it is concern for the other and in its concern for the other it cannot be, it *refuses* to be measured – it may have to measure what it dispenses and conveys but not itself.

In a more recent book, *Christian Freedom in a Permissive Society*, Dr J. A. T. Robinson has continued the theme of situationalism, insisting that 'in Christian ethics the only pure statement is the command to love: every other injunction depends on it and is an explication or application of it'.[69] This does not mean that he is prepared to abandon moral codes and social orders. On the contrary he emphasizes the need for these,[70] and holds that 'the deeper one's concern for persons, the more effectively one wants to see love buttressed by law';[71] but he seems to think of these codes and social orders as the very variable expression of love and so as thoroughly relativistic. Accordingly he argues that 'the raw material of an ethic is provided by the ethos of a society or a century or a group',[72] and he regards this as a 'relativistic factor'.[73]

Indeed his own *radical* position has on his own confession much in common with that of the *revolutionary* who seeks to destroy the social structure in contrast to the *reformer* who is content to modify it here and there. For the revolutionary 'absolutes are out. Ethical relativism is the order of the day',[74] and he has taken his stand, 'quite correctly, against any subordination of the concrete individual personal relationship to some alien universal norm'.[75] In all this the radical can join with one 'decisive exception'. For him too there is 'nothing prescribed – *except love*, in the New Testament sense of intense personal care and concern. And this is the decisive exception.'[76] Moreover this love, this 'utter openness to persons in all their depth and uniqueness',[77] is the 'root' of the social structure and the moral order.

All this means that on Robinson's view love by itself provides 'direction' for the moral life. 'Love alone can afford to be utterly open to the situation, or rather to the person in the situation, uniquely and for his own sake, yet without losing its direction.'[78] This indeed is 'the profoundly constant element in the distinctively Christian response in every age or clime. For it produces in Christians, however different or diversely placed, a direction, a cast, a style of life, which is recognizably and gloriously the same.'[79] On the other hand, '*what* precisely they must do to embody this claim will differ with every century, group and individual'.[80] No doubt, Robinson admits, many Christians will find disturbing this ready acknowledgment of variability and indeed extensive relativism, an acknowledgment of all-comprehensive relativism apart from the single demand of love; but if they are disturbed they should examine for themselves the moral teaching of Jesus. There they will find that the various principles which constitute their own moral code and which they regard as constant have no place in that teaching. 'The moral teaching of Jesus . . . says nothing whatever, for instance, about how a man is to pursue what after all occupies most of our waking hours . . . namely, our everyday work, or how one is to be a good citizen and a positive and useful member of society.'[81]

The crucially critical question for this so-called radical combination of the absolute of love with an otherwise all-pervasive relativism is whether it is ethically viable; and one aspect of that question concerns the truth of the contention that love by itself gives direction. This is a matter on which, as we have already seen,[82] quite opposite positions have been held; and it is perhaps unfortunate that, on this particular aspect of the general question, Dr Robinson himself seems to offer a seriously variable opinion. On the one hand, he says that without guiding rules we are bound to flounder; and yet again and again he insists that love is the one and only absolute demand and that 'persons matter more, imponderably more, than any principles'.[83] Nor is the situation made any clearer by his contention that unlike love the guiding rules are without respect of persons, for the lack of respect for persons in the one case is not, as Robinson seems to assume, the opposite of respect for persons in the other. On the contrary, it is the equivalent of 'without fear or favour' or 'without respect for mere position' which is not necessarily inconsistent with, which may very well be a part of, respect for personality as such.[84]

The reason for this ambiguity in Robinson's discussion is, however, more important than the ambiguity itself, and it is that in truth love does require the law which it fulfils, the sense of social justice and human dignity which the law enshrines and which unwittingly Robinson packs into his concept of 'persons in all their depth and uniqueness'. Love does not destroy the law, it fulfils it; but – and this is the grain of truth in situationalism – in fulfilling the law love does destroy its form as *law* and makes it a creative and liberating force in human affairs. It is only thus that love has the 'direction' which Robinson sees to be necessary, and it is only thus that sense can be made of what he has to say in defence of the inductive approach to moral problems[85] consistently with his own realization that 'no "is" can of itself supply an "ought".'[86] Moreover, when he claims support for his view in the moral teaching of Jesus and especially in the fact that it does not tell us how to spend our working lives, he is surely abstracting quite indefensibly the explicit teaching from what is implicit and presupposed, the whole moral world to which it was addressed.

There is further in Robinson's ethical outlook an inherent atomism, a concentration upon the particular situation and the particular relationship which we have already found in some degree in the thought of Professor Paul Ramsey and which is no more defensible when it comes from Dr Robinson's pen. Indeed within this atomism there is also a concentration upon the sexual relationship which is calculated to raise many a storm in Anglican tea-cups.[87] Because of this concentration, and even more because of the underlying atomism, there is in Dr Robinson's ethical teaching no sense of an ethic supplemented by a doctrine of history, no apparent concern for the fate of the moral in history at large which is characteristic of the Old Testament prophets at their best. Consequently there is likewise no sense of the enormity of the Christian demand to love one's enemies. Loving one's paramour is one thing and loving one's persecutor quite another; and I would have thought that the 'direction', the 'cast', the 'style of life which is recognizably and gloriously the same', is normally more evident in the latter connection than in the former. Thus Professor Gustaf Wingren refers to the goodness of God becoming flesh in Christ and speaking 'in the commandment of love of one's enemies and prayer for one's persecutors'.[88]

Once again, moreover, this ethical aberration, if such it is, in Dr Robinson's thought has its root in his handling of the moral impact and significance of Jesus Christ and in a further abstraction which vitiates his treatment of this subject. For not only does he abstract the moral teaching of Jesus from the moral world to which it is given and which therefore it posits, but he also abstracts that teaching from the career of which it was an element. Although he quotes often with approval from Professor Paul Ramsey's *Basic Christian Ethics* I cannot find that he has given the weight that Ramsey gave to the fact that God was in Christ reconciling the world to himself, as the source and sanction of the Christian ethic of unlimited and unrequited love, of an ethic of love in a world gone radically wrong.

Perhaps, however, the final comment on these various contributions to Christian ethical thought should be the perceptive judgment of James M. Gustafson that 'the umbrella named "contextualism" has become so large that it now covers persons whose views are as significantly different from each other as they are different from some of the defenders of "principles".'[89] This is perfectly true; and to find the way forward it is necessary to reckon with the dialectic of the Christian ethical discussion as a whole and to come to terms with the diverse dilemmas already diagnosed.

Before attempting to do so, however, it may be well to glance at another contribution to the debate which combines situationalism with secularization and yet owes something to the existentialism of Rudolf Bultmann. That these different movements can be brought together in this way is certainly an impressive indication of a contemporary mood, but that in itself of course is no guarantee of truth. The contribution I have in mind is contained in R. Gregor Smith's book *The New Man*[90] which carries the subtitle 'Christianity and Man's Coming of Age'. Here Gregor Smith maintained that the new view of man lays 'an extraordinary emphasis on the autonomy of man'[91] and this is authenticated by 'the very fact of the Incarnation'.[92] On this view, he said,[93] 'history had fully taken over; nature was but the raw material, metaphysics and a possibly more real world only a misleading dream. Man had come of age'; and Christianity is no longer to be seen as a religion 'which imposed standards and norms upon society' but 'to be in the very substance of society'.[94]

At this point the critical reader may realize that the problem of distinguishing between Christian worldliness and non-Christian worldliness is still acute. He may well wonder whether the meaning of the Incarnation is that God became man or that man became God, and what difference remains between the Gospel of the Incarnation and Auguste Comte's thesis concerning 'the regency of God during the long minority of Humanity'.[95] Gregor Smith held, however, that in society Christianity is not only 'a positive hopeful element' but also 'a critical dissolvent element';[96] and 'in the historical situation of man', he said,[97] '. . . it is necessary to recognize that freedom and obedience both have their place'. Obedience to what? one may very well ask; and on the present terms it cannot very well be to any supra-historical reality. There are apparently no limits within the human spirit to the possibilities which it may unfold, but there must be 'strict obedience to the facts out of which these possibilities flow', namely, 'the given objects, the things and people' – 'man is made by his free acceptance, in unlimited openness, of what comes to him out of the surrounding darkness'. 'It is the otherness of the other' which 'is the basic manifestation of transcendence in human life'.[98]

Clearly, on this view, obedience really means openness, and it is complete openness that is the essential mark of genuine maturity. It may well be doubted, however, whether, without the insights of the ordinary moral consciousness, openness any more than love can function in human life as the key to maturity. By itself it seems to herald the reign of unrestrained and unrestricted naturalism; and although conscience can be misused by man, hedging him in instead of leading him out and on, and although it may be overlaid in a thousand ways, it is the one thing that can give directional content to the demand for openness or love and that can act as a barrier between the stream of history and the processes of nature.

### (e) The moral character of historical existence

It appears then that the truth lies somewhere between the characteristic forms of radical Protestantism and the existentialist and secularist reactions to them. So far as Christian ethics is concerned this truth is safeguarded by the recognition of the Christian life as essentially the life of faith, as a life, that is to say, given over in faith to the overlordship of Christ as containing within himself the whole duty of man and as fulfilling, while transforming, the moral aspirations and convictions of natural man. Such an account seeks to grasp and describe, not the varied and detailed content of the Christian life, but its abiding and definitive reality.

The truth it expresses can be distorted in one or other of two opposite directions, for faith may be represented either as an existence or a life other than, and unrelated to, the various possibilities of human historical existence, or else, contrariwise, it may be set forth as something wholly explicable in human and historical terms. Accordingly, to the dilemmas already recognized in which modern Protestantism is deeply involved – those between formalism and naturalism, between a system of divine determinism and one that gives a central place to human decision, and between a heteronomous account and an autonomous one – there must be added the dilemma between a representation of the Christian ethic which finds the heart of the matter in a mythological warfare beyond history and one which is severely this-worldly and concentrates either upon the concrete, immediate, wholly particular encounter of the present historical situation or else upon the immanent movements and claims of history itself.

What then are the implications of this long analysis for the correct account of the Christian ethic? The analysis has revealed that on one wing of radical Protestantism there is ultimately affirmed what when it is made explicit can only be regarded as a mythological warfare, not between two cities as St Augustine held, but almost between two souls or substances, two lives, existences, hearts or natures, one of faith which is the gift of God and one of unbelief which is the result of sin. The sphere of this warfare is regarded as the ultimate, a mythological 'beyond', whereas the everyday decisions and choices which make up the tale of each man's life and the narrative of history are relegated to a sphere called the penultimate. As against any such view it can hardly be too strongly affirmed that the spiritual warfare is waged, not in any mythological 'beyond', but in the sphere of historical existence, in and through those very choices and decisions which, we have said, make up the tale of each man's life and the narrative of human history. 'Work out your own salvation with fear and trembling. For it is God, which worketh in you both to will and to do of his good pleasure.'[99]

Consequently, the existentialists and the secularists are right so far when they concentrate upon historical existence; but the discussion has also demonstrated that history by itself, whether as a concentrated moment of encounter or as a broad movement of social change, is not enough. History is not just a discrete moment of encounter but a developing and ever-changing continuum of personal relationships, which owes much of its character at any one time to the human choices and decisions which have gone before. Christian and non-Christian alike find themselves part and parcel of this moving reality, their existence is historical existence, and it is in and through the everyday choices and decisions involved in this existence that the Christian must work out his own salvation. There is no other sphere in which he may do so. Although, however, the word 'historical' may not immediately and directly say so, and although it may certainly be used in a reductionist sense, it becomes clear on reflection that historical existence *is* moral existence, and that, we have seen, introduces a supra-historical reality. The attempts to treat history as moral and yet as self-contained inevitably break down.[100] Culloden Moor is doubtless an historical battleground and so has historical existence in some sense, but only derivatively through the part it has played in human affairs; and these affairs have in

THE CHRISTIAN WAY IN THE CONTEMPORARY SCENE

turn an indefeasible moral quality in the absence of which they would not be human at all but would lapse into the natural, perhaps as an extension of natural evolution.

Even Professor Bultmann has paid eloquent testimony to the moral reality of man in words that are not easy to fit into an existentialist context. 'Genuine freedom', he once wrote,[101]

is not subjective arbitrariness. It is freedom in obedience. . . . Freedom is obedience to a law of which the validity is recognized and accepted, which man recognizes as the law of his own being. This can only be a law which has its origin and reason in the beyond. We may call it the law of spirit or, in Christian language, the law of God. This idea of freedom, constituted by law, this free obedience or obedient freedom was well known both to ancient Greek philosophy and to Christianity.

It is indeed true that Bultmann adds that in

modern times, however, this conception vanished and was replaced by the illusory idea of freedom as subjective arbitrariness which does not acknowledge a norm, a law from beyond. There ensues a relativism which does not acknowledge absolute ethical demands and absolute truths. The end of this development is nihilism.[102]

But how could it possibly *vanish*, so that if, as Bultmann elsewhere maintains, there is continuity between Saul and Paul there is none between medieval man and modern man or between eighteenth-century and twentieth-century man? Has man changed in his essential nature? Is modern man really to that extent a new creature, a new species? Or was the idea of freedom constituted by law never more than an idea of man's own in his efforts at self-understanding, never more than a theory which in the end did not work out? And was therefore the law of that freedom not really from beyond but only from within?

Neither alternative is readily compatible with the earlier part of this passage in Bultmann; but if one overlooks this fact for the moment – in the long run of course it cannot possibly be over-looked – one must suppose that it is the latter alternative which governs Bultmann's thought at this point. If so, one can further detect some common ground between Bultmann and Professor

Lehmann when the latter, having dealt with 'The Search for the Good' with special reference to Immanuel Kant, goes on to speak of 'The Redirection of the Search' with special reference to William James, and then of 'The Powers of Man' with special reference, first, to Professor Paul Weiss and, then, to Dr Erich Fromm, holding finally that 'depth-psychological humanism is significant not only as another attempt to get beyond ethical relativism. It is also the most important alternative to Christian ethics confronting our contemporaries.'[103]

Does, however, this development in man's *thought* about himself – this is a quite crucial question – justify or even begin to justify Bultmann or Lehmann in treating the 'idea of freedom, constituted by law' as if it had altogether *vanished*? It may play no part, or hardly any, in the *theories* by which man systematically *thinks* about himself; but this is *not* the decisive question. The decisive question is concerned with man who is thought about and who, for all the theories, continues to go about his daily business. The decisive factor is not the theories presently current but actual man about whom they are theories, without whom indeed the theories would be set free on a sea of relativism, they would be exercises in the free play of speculative imagination. The decisive question is whether actual man has no sense of 'freedom constituted by law', no sense of 'ought' whatsoever.

Both Bultmann and Lehmann avoid this question, and get over this gap in their analysis, by using the phrase 'ethical relativism'; but this is simply to beg the question. A great deal of relativism there may be in the modern period, in contemporary society accepted standards of conduct may be challenged and very radically challenged indeed; but this is on a social scale what often happens in the growing life of the individual moral agent, the one thing it does not mean is that basically modern man has ceased to be a moral being. He may not be very sure where he is going nor by what road he ought to travel; but at the very least he is aware and often profoundly aware of some of the pitfalls he ought to avoid, as the passage already quoted from Professor Paul Weiss makes clear. If modern man had really ceased to be a moral agent with no sense of 'ought' whatsoever, without even a vague concept of human dignity and social justice, there would certainly not be any significant continuity between his life and that of his predecessors. Something like a complete break would have to be recognized; but then human society would have disappeared in any familiar sense of the phrase, and neither 'depth-psychological humanism' nor Christian ethics could then get off the ground. If the sense of 'ought', the moral dimension, is lost to man who is thought about, man who thinks about him cannot pretend to conjure it up like a rabbit out of a hat.

In discussing critically the whole enterprise of moral theology Professor Lehmann holds that it 'rightly sees that the crux of the problem of freedom and obedience is the conscience',[104] and he also acutely maintains that it 'assumes *de facto* that the moral counselor is in a *different* situation from that of the man under instruction and guidance' whereas 'the truth of the matter . . . is that the counselor and the counselee are in the *same* ethical situation'.[105] What I am suggesting is that Professor Lehmann himself and those who think with him within radical Protestantism may be guilty of something like the same error in a more subtle form, driving a wedge between man who is thought about and man who thinks about him.

Doubtless it is arguable that man has so advanced in knowledge that he has become a new creature; but is man who has landed on the moon *fundamentally* different from man who can but gaze at it across some earth-bound sea? More plausibly it is perhaps arguable that man has so advanced in knowledge *of himself* that he has become a new creature; but can the depth-psychologists – or the depth-theologians – carry the ordinary man with them? Can they help him over the gulf which on this view separates the modern world from what has gone before? Or must we all become depth-psychologists in order to remain human – or rather to become human in the new sense of the word? Against the background of such thinking what I have said regarding the *ordinary* moral consciousness may be understood as a plea for the common man; but if so it is not a sentimental plea but a logical one. Thoroughgoing relativism is a position impossible to defend. Thoroughgoing ethical relativism would be unable to distinguish the ethical from the non-ethical. As it is it is a confession of failure rather than a logically possible theory.

It is man as man who drives himself as the one who thinks about himself to transcend the limitations of ethical relativism and so to correct his *self-understanding* in the light of his own *reality*. It stands to reason, however, that unless man as man is irrevocably a moral being this search of man the thinker is nothing but a wild-goose chase. No doubt man needs a compass; but that is a metaphor and the plain fact is that unless he had one he could not possibly find one nor could he recognize it if he did. Certainly, a self-contained compass which operated quite independently of the direction of the pole would hardly meet the case. Kant thought that man was essentially a rational being and that it was therefore appropriate to regard his morality as a function of his *rationality*; while depth-psychologists and depth-theologians may plumb the depths of man's being in search of some factor which will perform the same function. Whatever the fashionable appeal of such endeavours there seems to be a fallacy attached to the very project, precisely the naturalistic fallacy of deriving the moral from the non-moral.

The truth seems to be that, however deep we go and however far back, we cannot get behind or below man as man confronting an objective claim upon his freedom as part of his very being. For the Christian theist this means that by his very nature man stands essentially in the presence of God his Creator, so that his life is haunted, however dimly he may apprehend it, by the claim of human dignity and social justice.

If this is so believers and unbelievers do indeed share historical existence, and that means that they have in common many moral insights, many moral doubts, perplexities and ambiguities, and underlying them all an indefeasible and irreducible sense of 'ought', some sense of human dignity and of the true humanity of man. To say this is to enunciate what seems a quite incontrovertible doctrine of natural morality, that there is such a thing; but it is not to set forth a theory of natural law or indeed any other systematic presentation or interpretation of this natural morality. Morality is not a dead, static, unchanging thing, as the theory of natural law tends to represent it; and at the root of the present-day criticism or suspicion of objective norms and ethical absolutism there may very well lie a confusion between the traditional representation of a reality and the reality itself.

The moral outlooks of different ages and of different societies in the same age may vary quite widely from each other, and while it may be easy to underestimate the degree of moral unanimity that obtains amongst different peoples and times, it is no less easy to exaggerate it. To understand the moral outlook of any given society one would have to live in it and acquire at first hand some acquaintance with its customs, conventions, institutions, legislative code, and the personal standard of behaviour of its members; and, in addition, one would have to try to grasp the *esprit de corps* which animates and unifies these various factors as facets of a single, more or less integrated, moral outlook. The theory of natural law mistakenly fails to acknowledge this *esprit de corps* and falsely assumes that the diversity of moral custom and prescription, to be seen as one passes from one society to another, rests upon a common denominator of universal moral insight. In other words, it associates, rightly enough, morality with *humanity*; but it tends to think in terms of an abstract human nature, not in terms of human beings caught up in a process of social change. Thus it fails to see that this quite necessary association between morality and humanity is in and through an ever-changing pattern and plurality of social groupings with no finality and no permanence.

None the less, behind all the diversity, unless I am mistaken, there is, there must be an objective and original claim which imposes upon man the sense of 'ought' and so some sense of human dignity and social justice. This claim is not itself, however, an explicit system of specific moral laws. Such a system arises at a logically subsequent stage as, in his creative response to this original claim, man seeks to articulate a moral code by which to live. And no such system or code is morally inviolable or incorrigible. All are coloured by the particular historical conditions which gave them birth.

The Christian's historical existence, then, is within one social grouping rather than another. He is a member of such and such a family, he speaks such and such a language, he stands in such and such a particular strand of history, and he is moving towards such and such a national destiny. In a word, he belongs to an historical and quite temporary grouping; and from that he derives the stuff of his daily life and the subject of his everyday choices and decisions. He shares in some measure the moral outlook of this society, which may colour his moral judgment even on issues and at points at which explicitly he disowns it; and it is in and through his handling of the raw material of life, with which it confronts him, that he must work out his salvation.

If he reflects on this situation he may well be tempted, on the natural level, to ethical relativism; but as he reflects on it he himself sets a limit to any such temptation and to any such tendency, for he finds himself entering with sympathy and understanding into the moral outlook of some other society, past or present, at one point or another. He is forced indeed to recognize a moving line of moral agreement and alignment running through the various societies of humankind. No matter how divergent they may be these societies do not utterly fall out of the possibility of mutual moral communication; and this is highly significant, even when points of concurrence are of a negative character, underlining what is morally intolerable rather than outlining what is morally desirable.

Indeed it may be that moral agreement is more readily available on what is wrong than on what is right; and it is to be noted that, like the Ten Commandments, the statement of moral unanimity already quoted from Professor Paul Weiss, is predominantly negative.

Wanton murder, injustice, betrayal are absolutely wrong, all of us believe. The wrongness, all of us hold, does not depend on how we happen to judge such acts; it is not jeopardized by changes in customs or morality, by shifts in goals or in the nature of our chosen ultimate ends. These acts are essentially wrong, intrinsically wrong; they and wrongness together make an irreducible ethical fact which it would be folly to deny.[106]

Likewise who would dare to deny that the fear of life on the face of a child is morally intolerable? Indeed it may even be the case that there is a predominantly, not exclusively, negative slant to man's natural morality, and that this is a symptom of his lost condition, so that more readily he can recognize wrong turnings than find his way forward, as if it were a relic, the broken fragment, of a wholeness he once had – or for which in his very heart he was made.

Be these things as they may, however, even a predominantly

negative morality stands as a barrier against ethical relativism, and against what Brunner calls 'moral scepticism', and against what Bultmann calls 'nihilism'.

There is a further fact about social groupings which ought to be recognized, for it would be a mistake to regard them as self-contained and as static. They are certainly not self-contained for, as I have already mentioned, there is the possibility of mutual moral communiction, and, more than that, there are even moving areas of common moral conviction and of co-operative action. Besides a French or a German outlook there is also a Western European outlook, and an incipient human outlook. Harvey Cox is right when he says that 'contemporary man has become the cosmopolitan'.[107] Moreover, each social grouping is anything but static; and that is why the word 'grouping' seems more accurate in the present context than the word 'group'. In some ways it is a rather gross oversimplification to speak of a social grouping as having a moral outlook, for, wherever one draws the line of moral conviction in such a society (and even this will vary from time to time), there are many who fall below it and stand condemned by it, while there are always some who condemn it and would seek to reform it in one respect or another. Yet operative in any society there is some vague but complex idea of social justice and of human dignity, which gains for itself some degree of stability by being embodied in social structures and institutions, which can venture out beyond the confines of its own society, and which can make contact with similar ideas in other societies and can even, by a process of cross-fertilization, help to yield other such ideas over a wider field of social relationships.

The moral life is certainly not a matter of applying a number of fixed immutable principles to a succession of practical and particular situations. It is much more a matter of following, amid all the confusions, complexities and compromises of life in society, a gleam of light which may yet shine differently in different situations and may often be so obscured that the suspicion is born that it has no more substance than the traveller's mirage in what is really a desert. None the less, without it life in society, human life, would cease altogether to be specifically human, it would become a completely natural phenomenon like a rat race – although of course normally to describe it thus is already to deny that it is so, it is to deny that it can be understood in purely natural terms.

Indeed what makes the situation difficult to conceptualize in any adequate fashion is the fact that history is a moving stream and that our problems are the problems of today in which yesterday lives on and in which the future towards which it is moving is already in part anticipated. Perhaps, however, we can say that our moral rules are the solutions to yesterday's moral problems and provide the springboard for the creative response to those of today. The genuinely moral solution to a moral problem cannot be routine and mechanical; it must be creative, even if it echoes those that have been offered a thousand times in the past. This means that there are no final moral principles requiring only to be applied to successive moral problems as they occur; but of course if we were not moral beings already, that is to say, apart from our ordinary moral consciousness we should not even recognize these moral problems as moral at all. There is thus communication with the past out of which we have come in the recognition of any problem as moral. Moreover, the moral principles we have gathered are articulations, so far as they go, of the sense of human dignity and social justice; and so the fact that most of us most of the time can most effectively follow the gleam by having relatively fixed but not inflexible rules and principles does not alter the fundamental nature of our historical situation.

*(f) Christian ethics and the problem of the double standard*

Christian and non-Christian alike, then, find themselves involved in historical existence, in the life of a social grouping such as we have been trying to describe in its inner reality. They are not only involved in it, this is their life. For the Christian it is in and through the choices and decisions which there confront him – not in some mythological 'beyond' or no-man's-land – that he must work out his own salvation. The Christian can no more abstract from this context than can the non-Christian. To do so would be to empty his life of all content. He may indeed make a distinctive, a unique, and on occasion by the grace of God, what might be called a redemptive, contribution to it; but what he cannot do is to abstract from it. And no more, one would think, should Christian ethics.

Charity begins at home, and so should Christian ethics, but of course the slogan means something here very different from its usual meaning. It means that charity, that is, our charity, begins in history and not in heaven; and so should Christian ethics. It means something much nearer to the biblical estimate of Jesus than some theologies contrive to reach, 'A bruised reed shall he not break, and smoking flax shall he not quench';[108] and it is in line with Christ's own declaration, 'Except your righteousness shall exceed the righteousness of the scribes and Pharisees, ye shall in no case enter into the kingdom of heaven'[109] – not 'shall be entirely separate from and quite unconnected with', not 'shall occupy an entirely different world from', but 'shall *exceed* the righteousness of the scribes and Pharisees'.

Certainly, such a text taken in isolation cannot claim to have grasped the Gospel either in its entirety or in its essence. That is more nearly achieved by St John's declaration: 'God so loved the world, that he gave his only begotten Son.'[110] The world, however, which is thus posited as the object of God's love is the world of men, and it is the object of God's love, not because of its morality, perhaps in spite of its morality, but certainly with its morality. Without that morality a quite different and far less comprehensible situation would in 'grace' (if 'grace' would then be the correct word) be put before us. Likewise, in the opposite direction, it is inconceivable that it should be a matter of complete indifference to Christian faith when an unbelieving society uses its resources of time, wealth and human effort, to bring relief to the needy and the suffering, whether within its own bounds or beyond. It is much more than a directionless movement, a mere manœuvre, within a total depravity of human nature.

The truth is that, just as the universe is a sacramental universe wherein the non-human natural sphere provides the means whereby person communicates with person so that it is not possible to abstract from this natural sphere without emptying human life of all its content, so the human world which is the object of God's love is essentially a moral world, historical existence is moral existence, so that to abstract from this and to ignore it is to lose the human world altogether – and it is to compel Christian ethics to deal either with a mythological 'beyond' or with a no less mythological moment of encounter. On the other hand, it is precisely because Christian ethics may not abstract from this historical and moral world in which man lives, it is precisely because Christian ethics must start here, that *at its very foundation* it confronts the problem of the double standard; and it is one of the great merits of Professor Lehmann's discussion that he explicitly acknowledges this aspect of the subject.

It is true that, as it seems to me, it is only by a violent and highly arbitrary device, with potentially far-reaching repercussions, that he resolves the problem, finding the Christian ethical factor operative in unbelievers.[111] Some other solution than this must be found; but equally it must be a solution, not an evasion nor a denial of the problem as in so much contemporary Protestant thought. Christian ethics must begin with Christian man where it finds him, in the world, and with his historical, human, moral existence; and it must squarely confront the problem of the double standard, which is a problem because by the nature of the case the claim of morality cannot be other than single and self-consistent. Confronting this problem Christian ethics is bound to have the curious character which I have already noted at an earlier point in the argument, namely, that it enters upon a ground already occupied.[112] That is why Professor Lehmann is perfectly right when he says that 'the decisive issue affecting the validity of an evangelical or Protestant ethic in distinction, on the one hand, from moral philosophy and, on the other, from moral theology is this: *Which account of the conscience is correct?*'[113]

That, however, is also why we cannot in the end accept either Brunner's conception of Christian ethics as the science of human conduct as determined by divine conduct, or Lehmann's own definition of it as 'reflection upon the question, and its answer: What am I, as a believer in Jesus Christ and as a member of his church, to do?'[114] In different ways they both deny the *ethical* reality of the Christian life. Instead, we must think of Christian ethics as the systematic account of human conduct as given over in faith to the overlordship of Christ as containing within himself the whole duty of man.

Christian ethics, then, begins with the Christian in the world, and that means with the Christian as a moral being in a particular form of human society. Christian ethics accordingly enters upon a ground already occupied by general ethics; but that does not at all imply that Christian ethics can ever be content only to echo what it finds there in possession of the field. None the less, it is in and through the choices and decisions of his social setting, and nowhere else, that the Christian must work out his own salvation.

Moreover the Christian is not in any position of privilege so far as the *technical* aspects of these choices and decisions are concerned. It may or may not be true to say that for humanity at large the centuries have brought a considerable increase of moral wisdom; but there is no doubt that there has been a very large technical progress over the years, and that in relation to it the Christian is in precisely the same position as the non-Christian. Whether it be methods of birth-control that are in question or ways of applying economic sanctions, there is no specifically Christian view so far as technical efficiency is concerned. On the contrary, Christians may differ amongst themselves on such matters as readily as non-Christians, and indeed they may do so without clearly realizing that the difference between them is not one of Christian ethical judgment but of the technical assessment of a given situation.

On the other hand, the means of achieving a certain goal is not exclusively a technical matter but may well be itself the subject of moral considerations and moral judgments, as when hitherto the Roman Catholic Church has exempted from condemnation one particular method of birth-control, apart altogether from questions of technical efficiency, on the ground that it retains in the sexual act a certain objective orientation towards the procreation of children.[115]

What is even less often realized, and is indeed much more difficult to recognize, is that, as Christians live and work in the same social setting, with the same moral problems, as non-Christians, Christians may differ amongst themselves on *moral* issues just as readily as may non-Christians. Moral issues are by no means always clear-cut, presenting a simple choice between black and white; and it is not to be expected that all Christians will deal with those issues in exactly the same way. The day is gone when men could think that they had in their hands an infallible yardstick or route-map which had dropped miraculously down from heaven. There are no infallible, divinely revealed, not-to-be-questioned, solutions to our moral problems. Consequently, the Christian who imperiously urges upon his fellow-believers allegiance, in the name of Christian faith, to the same political party, is suffering from an excess of zeal and a lack of judgment. In any society there are operative moral standards which permit of differences of moral judgment, at one point or another in relation to one complex situation after another; and these sincere and conscientious divergences are clearly to be found amongst Christians as well as non-Christians. Consequently, in many respects Christians *do* echo the moral judgments of the society to which they belong, and their choices and decisions are, from the standpoint of an external observer, frequently indistinguishable from those of non-Christians. As Professor Lehmann has noted, 'Christian ethical analysis shows a slowly and steadily emerging awareness of the difficulty of marking precisely what the distinction between Christian and non-Christian behavior is'.[116]

The explanation is, however, that the non-Christian is still a man, a moral being, not that, somehow or other, he is a secret Christian.

## (g) The Christian transformation of historical existence

Christian ethics in its search for clarity requires what is conspicuously lacking from some recent contributions to it, namely, as clear a conception as possible of the nature of man. It has already been suggested in this essay that essentially, by nature, man stands in the presence of, or in relation to, God his Creator, so that for him there is no nature without grace. It is because this is so that what has just been said about the morality shared by Christian and non-Christian cannot be the whole truth. Certainly, autonomy is part of the truth; and because it is so the reconciling act of God reaffirms this common morality. Because, however, autonomy is not the whole truth, that reconciling act, in reaffirming this morality, corrects, restores and fulfils it, giving it its true centre in God.

Because the true autonomy of man is the responsive autonomy of the creature, because in other words the truth contains both autonomy and heteronomy, this truth has unavoidably two sides. On the one hand, as we have already said more than once, it is in and through everyday choices and decisions, sometimes coincident so far as can be seen with those of non-Christians, in situations common to both, that the Christian for his part must work out his own salvation. On the other hand, as it stands this statement is seriously elliptical. It is in and through these choices and decisions, we ought to say, that the Christian must work out his own salvation in fear and trembling, for it is God who is working in him both to will and to do of his good pleasure.

Here is the fundamentally distinctive quality of the Christian ethic, that it is God who works in the Christian both to will and to do of his good pleasure; and this is likewise the source of the characteristic statements of the various accounts of the Christian ethic already brought under review. It is the source, for example, of Brunner's contention that the good is what God does. It is the source, perhaps somewhat less directly, of Bultmann's thesis that what is demanded of the Christian is a decision of faith and love in the concrete encounter of the moment, made possible, it should be remembered, by an act of God. It is the source too of Lehmann's emphasis upon what God is doing to make and to keep human life human, and also of his belief that the Christian ethic is an indicative, not an imperative, ethic. Yet, if the analysis of this essay is sound, all of these distort the point in the act of making it; and the question remains how the point is to be made without distortion. Brunner, as we have argued, places the ultimate warfare, which is between faith as a gift of God and unbelief, in a mythological sphere, and withdraws the everyday choices and decisions of men into a penultimate sphere where 'technical' considerations seem to be uppermost. Bultmann appears to treat the moral habits and standards of a society as an external framework within which there occurs the real thing, the concrete encounter of the moment, requiring a decision of love which is independent of all standards and admits of no preformulation. And Lehmann seems in the end to deny any, even relative independence to the standards of society, but finds in them a concealed or hidden work of God whereby human life is made and kept human.

In contrast to these articulations of the Christian ethic, however, we have been maintaining that it is in and through the moral choices and decisions of daily life that the Christian must work out his own salvation, and nowhere else. It is therefore a mistake either to withdraw these choices and decisions into some penultimate and perhaps 'technical' sphere or to treat them as no more than an external framework for the decision of love. On the other hand, it is no less a mistake, while insisting that it is after all in and through the moral choices and decisions of daily life that the Christian must work out his own salvation, to minimize the difference between belief and unbelief, so that the latter is no more than a matter of ignorance[117] and other consequential defects such as a lack of 'confidence and hope'. It is true, as we have argued, that the moral standards of natural morality have their ultimate origin in God and nowhere else; but this does not justify us in saying that in the unbeliever too it is God who is working both to will and to do of his good pleasure. We may say rather that, although he does not know it, the unbeliever may be doing God's work so far as he is able. We must, however, say further that by sin and unbelief, not only is man ignorant of the origin of his moral standards, but the standards themselves have been centred in man and so distorted and fragmented, though not destroyed. This is indeed what is meant by the world; and the seemingly unqualified emphasis by Bonhoeffer as well as by Lehmann that this is a redeemed world can be, because of its lack of precise qualification and discrimination, seriously misleading.

More fully, then, we must say that it is in and through the moral choices and decisions of everyday life, in a social setting which is part and parcel of an alienated world (not in the sense of being totally depraved but in the sense of being thoroughly *man*-centred, for in traditional terminology natural man is a sinner but still a man), that the Christian must work out his own salvation in the knowledge that in some sense it is God who is working in him. Accordingly, he may not abstract from, nor contract out of, these choices and decisions. To do so would be to empty his life of all content and perhaps to fill it with a pseudo-content, what I think R. Gregor Smith may have had in mind when he spoke of 'a false and separated Thou'.[118] Often his choices and decisions will be externally indistinguishable from those of unbelievers. Yet, whether on this occasion or that there is any visible difference or not, the choices and decisions will be different with a difference which makes all the difference in the world. They will be imbued by the faith that it is God who is working in him, and not just God in heaven, if I may so speak, but God who was in Christ reconciling the world to himself.

To put the same point in another way, the Christian not only acts as one whose life has been set in a particular social and historical setting, but also, *in and through that very action*, he acts as one who has been called to a place in the body of Christ, in his Church, in the fellowship of his Spirit. Professor Lehmann is so far right, then, when he defines Christian ethics as 'the reflection upon the question, and its answer: What am I, as a believer in Jesus Christ and *as a member of his church*, to do?'[119] He is right too when he says that 'Christian ethics is *koinonia* ethics',[120] and he is right again when he declares that 'the *koinonia* of which Jesus Christ (Messiah) is meanwhile the head is faithful to its foundation and to its ethical resources when it celebrates in the world over which he rules as Lord, in recollection and in hope, his sovereign presence and power in the midst of the people'.[121]

Christian behaviour, consequently, 'celebrates' in the world – not elsewhere, but in the daily choices and decisions of the world – Christ's 'sovereign presence and power'; and, owing to the complexity of the practical situation, Christian behaviour may be otherwise indistinguishable from non-Christian behaviour. On the other hand, its character as celebration, what Lehmann elsewhere [122] calls its 'sign character', is not merely a matter of knowledge and its consequences; and in thinking that it is Lehmann distorts the truths he has grasped. It is true that Christian behaviour is 'expressive of confidence and hope', but the distinctively Christian quality of behaviour is not confined to such characteristics. On the other hand, as *koinonia* behaviour its secret is not to be found either in obedience to the teaching of the visible Church, whether identical with that of Scripture or not, or in following the moving stream of empirical Christianity (or, for that matter, of a world redeemed).

It is true, as Lehmann says,[123] that 'the complexity of the actual human situation, with which a *koinonia* ethic tries seriously to deal, is always compounded of an intricate network of circumstances and human interrelationships bracketed by the dynamic of God's political activity on the one hand and God's forgiveness on the other.' If, however, the contribution of faith to action is exclusively one of knowledge and so of confidence and hope, why should Lehmann speak of God's *forgiveness*? Of compassion, yes perhaps, but surely not forgiveness – unless the contribution of faith to action is decisively more extensive than Lehmann has apparently represented it to be.

What more then is involved? What must be said is that the Christian's existence is genuinely historical existence like any other, but that he acts historically between the times, between the time of God's reconciling act in the fullness of time and the time of God's fulfilment of time itself and history. If our argument is sound even natural morality is in the last resort inexplicable apart from a superhuman *purpose* in men's affairs; but for the Christian that mysterious purpose has become both a no less mysterious *presence* and a no less mysterious *promise*.

The moral standards of society and the world are not left inviolate by the action of God in Christ. On the contrary, they undergo a two-sided transformation, wherein also their fragmentary character is overcome and healed; and these two sides consist in this, that Christ *fulfils* the law, fulfils and completes natural morality and the standards by which (watered down as they are) human society contrives to remain human in divorce from God, and that in fulfilling the law Christ *centres* it once again in its source and origin in God the Creator. Thus it becomes the bond of fellowship once more, not just between a man and his neighbour, but between both of them and God, whose resources and purpose transcend all things human and historical, who created all things to his own glory, who in Christ has already given the world 'the dream come true', and whose dynamic purpose is that neither they without us nor we without them should be made perfect but that all should abide in him. There are then three respects in which the contribution of Christian faith to moral action cannot be confined to knowledge, confidence and hope, and in which consequently it overflows the description of Christian behaviour in terms of its 'sign character' or as an indicative ethic.

## (h) Love, the Summum Bonum, and Gloria Dei

In the first place, it must be said that the Christian ethic is an ethic of love and that love is not content simply to reaffirm the law, even with confidence and hope; love fulfils the law and completes it. It restores the law in concentrated strength and purity. John Stuart Mill was of the opinion that his utilitarian ethic, which was concerned with the greatest happiness of the greatest number and for which each was to count as one and none as more than one, had caught the very spirit of the Golden Rule and was in effect a systematic re-articulation of the Christian ethic; but hardly anything could have been further from the truth. Christian love knows no limit and is prepared to go not one mile but two. To love one's neighbour as if he were oneself, to put oneself unreservedly in his place, is certainly not to treat him as one of many, one but not more than one. To love one's neighbour in this way is to treat him not as if he were one but as if he were I.

This is part of the truth which Professor Bultmann has grasped in his insistence upon the demand and decision of love in the concrete encounter of the moment, and even in his contention that this love knows of no preformulation. In so far as preformulations would be the same thing, or serve the same purpose, as predetermined limits Bultmann is clearly right. None the less, preformulation *is* required in the shape of conscience in order that love may have some moral content or direction,[124] and not just an arbitrary one like the contents of sentimentalism and fanaticism, in other words, that love may genuinely do good to the uttermost.

When the rich young ruler was commanded to sell all that he had and give to the poor there was no suggestion of an equal distribution amongst the greatest possible number. Professor Bultmann is much nearer to the Christian ethic when he emphasizes the limitless going out of love in the concrete encounter of the moment. Even so, however, it is important to remember, such love is the fulfilment of morality, of alms-giving, for example, and of altruism in relation to specific needs. Moreover, it might conceivably take the form of an equal distribution amongst a given number in a restricted social situation (rather than concrete encounter) impinging upon the agent. What love will do may be unpredictable, and there is about it an irreducible element of divine vocation and divine givenness; and yet none the less it operates always through a good, rather, a redeemed, conscience.

Further, whatever we may learn from the contemporary concentration upon the concrete encounter of a man with his neighbour, upon what Dr J. A. T. Robinson has called 'utter openness to persons in all their depth and uniqueness', this concentration can be seriously misleading. As we have just seen, openness by itself is not enough, not even when it is given the name of love, for if love is not understood as the fulfilment of the law it is without direction. In other words, the openness to persons must already be moral. More than that, however, it must be noticed that the whole Christian ethic cannot be poured into such concrete encounters without remainder. The moral commitment and outlook of the Christian man overflows any succession of concrete encounters, embraces the ongoing life of the world in its entirety, and cannot avoid difficult questions of social policy simply by enclosing itself within some concrete encounter with a particular neighbour.

For example, provided the technical and medical considerations are favourable, the contraceptive pill must be seen as a godsend if it frees a fully personal relationship between husband and wife from the dilemma of frustration or fear; but the question cannot be ignored whether the contraceptive pill should be made available to unmarried and promiscuous women in order to avert the tragedy of unwanted and illegitimate children. The question is an exceedingly difficult one; but perhaps in an age of maturity and non-paternalism and in a pluralistic society there is in the end no escape from the conclusion that in the name of social justice no one has the right to withhold it. But who will say that Christian love can make this decision and *rest content*? Who will deny that 'the acknowledgment of somebody as a person . . . can achieve justice without creating a relationship'?[125] The decision may be morally inevitable, but for Christian love it is tragically incomplete and must end with the confession: 'We are unprofitable servants: we have done that which was our duty to do'[126] – a confession before God revealed in Christ who spoke the parables of the lost sheep and the lost coin.

In more general terms, when Martin Buber distinguished the two primary words which man speaks, 'I-Thou' and 'I-It', he made a point of great ethical significance which has been taken up by those who concentrate upon moments of encounter with a neighbour. It is that in dealing with a person we ought to deal with the whole person in all his 'depth and uniqueness', in the full substance of his personality, and not just with an abstraction, with an image[127] whether projected by the person himself, defined by some general moral principle, or manufactured by our own desire.

Martin Buber, however, was misleading, so far as ethics is concerned when he classified 'I-He' and 'I-She' along with 'I-It', for if love is the fulfilment of the law every 'He' and every 'She' is a potential 'Thou'; and love *is* the fulfilment of the law *both* when it is able to go a second mile with a particular neighbour *and* when it sees only the bankruptcy of law without love and yet dares to hope and believe – in God who has provided some better thing than that we without them should be made perfect.

Moreover, while it is true, as Professor Fletcher and others have pointed out, that in concrete encounters love may require the abrogation of some moral maxim, such as that which requires truth-telling, it is also true that frequently in such situations there is moral regret and even on occasion a sense of guilt that circumstances should require this abrogation. Clearly, atomism and situationalism cannot assimilate this fact but can only seek to explain it away; but the truth seems to be that the Christian ethic cannot be packed into isolated concrete situations without remainder and that love is ever the fulfilment of the law. Persons morally deserve the truth, the whole truth and nothing but the truth.

*A slogan!*

Curiously enough, there is a further respect in which the concentration on concrete encounters is misleading and ultimately breaks down, for, although Bultmann's distinction between a *work* involving only a part of the self and a *deed* involving the whole self is ethically significant, it is difficult to believe that this distinction justifies the exclusive attention to particular moments of encounter. The whole self is not engaged except in relation to the whole moral universe of which it is a part; and thus to 'see whole' is an indispensable aspect of 'being whole'. Accordingly, the action which is, in Bultmann's terms, deed and not just work, is not simply action in relation, exclusively, to a thoroughly concrete and particular situation, but action between the times, between Incarnation and Consummation;[128] and this action is an action of love as the fulfilment of the whole law.

I suggested, however, that another respect in which natural morality is not left inviolate by the Christian ethic is that in the latter the fragmentation of the former is overcome and healed. On the natural level morality and the *summum bonum* disintegrate into an aggregate of duties and another aggregate of virtues. These all have their imperative character. Promises ought to be kept. Honesty and uprightness commend themselves to the natural conscience. Our moral codes are, so far as they go, creative articulations of the human spirit in response to the ineluctable dimension of the moral. Yet so long as duties and virtues remain in their multiplicity the Good has still escaped from the grasp of men. This remains true even if this multiplicity can be reduced to the twin demands and principles of social justice and human dignity; and yet on the face of it this fragmentation is not overcome by the decision and response of love in the concrete encounters of historical existence.

To this problem the answer, so far as there is one, seems to come in two stages. For one thing, the Christian ethic, as we have already argued, does not belong to an isolated, insulated, and discrete encounter, but operates through the daily decisions and choices of human existence in a particular social setting, over the whole range of its common life. These in their complexity offer a varying resistance to the spirit of Christian love, of outgoing and limitless love. Most of the time, perhaps, the Christian cannot break through the practices of the world in their entrenched and loveless legalism. Even when they are modified by that spirit and a new social setting arises, it in turn offers resistance in other forms and, as one of the central tenets of Professor Reinhold Niebuhr's ethical teaching affirms, comes under the judgment of God.

Certainly, the Christian may not be a defender of the *status quo* come what may; the Christian life is not exclusively one of law and order. Rather the Christian must be alive and alert to the in-breaking of God's Kingdom at this point or that, the advent of the personal realm in the fullness of its substance, and his ethic consequently must have room for an ethic of social change and even of revolution. It is here that the so-called middle axioms have their place. On the other hand, the Christian knows that if the Kingdom breaks in at this point and at that, it does not *come* at this point and that, by social change and revolution; and the new social structure will in turn come under judgment, at best as a system of law and order without love, but doubtless also as one marked by man's inhumanity to man, what Niebuhr calls 'the tribal limits of his sense of obligation to other men'.[129] The

Christian must seek to discern 'the politics of God' but he can never shut out the politics of man – a truth of which the relief of suffering at the end of the Biafran war provides a graphic illustration. The Christian's action therefore in response to the discerned in-breaking of God's Kingdom is incomplete without the prayer, 'Thy Kingdom come'.

This in itself does not take us very far and may seem even to move further away from any possible solution of the fragmentariness of natural morality; but the other correction is this, that, just as the concrete situation is misconceived when it is shut off from the 'intricate network of circumstance and human interrelationships' of the social setting, so the love which meets the demand of the situation is misconstrued if it is thought of as an individual response. On the contrary, it is *in a way* the response of God – of God who for us men and for our salvation became man and uses men in the work of his Kingdom. More strictly, of course, it is the response of X but of X as a member of Christ's Church. It is the love of God's Kingdom which is God's gift and God's promise, and, between the two and under them both, each man's salvation and his task, a salvation to be worked out in the life of the world. Thus, because its source and centre is in God, even in the most concrete and particular of all situations, it is ultimately a love which embraces every child whom God has made. In *this* kingdom social justice and human dignity are altogether one under the sovereign grace of God. It is as if by action the Christian extended every situation both backwards and forwards, backwards to the time of God's reconciling act in Jesus Christ in the fullness of time, and forwards to God's fulfilment of all time and history.

A further aspect of this point is that Christian ethics cannot properly accept as the last moral word either the opportunism of Professor Fletcher's utilitarian situationalism or the atomism both of Bultmann's existentialism (an atomism of situations or encounters) and Harvey Cox's secularization (an atomism of problems). Yet the Christian alternative to these is not easy to state. Harvey Cox is quite right when he says that 'contemporary man has become the cosmopolitan'; and certainly modern man, far more than his predecessors, is acutely aware of the diversification and dispersion of humanity. On the other hand, although there is realism in Harvey Cox's plea for 'a viable theology of anonymity' and in what he says about 'those public relationships . . . which we do not allow to develop into private ones' ('These contacts can be decidedly human,' he says,[130] 'even though they remain somewhat distant'), yet this cannot be a final attitude for the Christian ethic. We may choose our friends but not our neighbours (in the sense of the parable); and human choice is not the final factor. In the Christian ethic there must be some echo of the prophetic vision,

> I will say to the north, Give up; and to the south, Keep not back: bring my sons from far, and my daughters from the ends of the earth; even every one that is called by my name: for I have created him for my glory, I have formed him; yea, I have made him.[131]

These considerations lead to the third respect in which moral standards are not left inviolate but are redeemed by the Christian revelation, for in Christ these standards are not only integrated and fulfilled but are also centred in their true source in God and so established 'come wind or weather'.

Once again, however, the logical point, unlike a mathematical one, has several sides. It means for one thing that the *summum bonum* is a divinely purposed and established *fellowship*. Ultimately and in origin the moral order is personal. It is not just an impersonal realm or reality to which it is the distinctive merit of persons to give peculiar attention. It does not *become* personal through the obedience of such persons. *Ab initio* it is itself personal; and only in such an order could love ever be the fulfilment of the law. Here is the truth contained in the suggestion sometimes made in modern Protestantism that the divine fatherhood is the prototype, not the projection, of human fatherhood. Here too, as it seems to me, the merely humanitarian account of Jesus Christ, 'the man for others', at most the discoverer, the propounder, and the observer of the commandment to love, borders on ethical absurdity. How can law disclose itself as love while clinging to the abstract and impersonal form of law? Rather as a New Testament writer saw, 'herein is love, not that we loved God, but that he loved us . . .'[132] The moral order is personal through and through, and, whether we know it or not, the moral life is something of a partnership. In the last resort it is not a case of *Athanasius contra mundum*, nor can it properly be said, as Bertrand Russell did say, that 'blind to good and evil, reckless of destruction, omnipotent matter rolls on its relentless way; for Man . . . it remains only to cherish, ere yet the blow falls, the lofty thoughts that ennoble his little day.'[133] This does not mean that there is any easy answer to 'the slings and arrows of outrageous fortune' or to the question of Jeremiah the prophet, 'Wherefore doth the way of the wicked prosper? wherefore are all they happy that deal very treacherously?'[134] Our task has not been to justify the ways of God to man but to analyse our human situation. What we can say is that for the Christian such questions as that of Jeremiah arise within the fellowship in the form of a prayer, already an expression of fellowship.

Nor is the sense of 'ought' abrogated by this fellowship as some exponents of Protestant ethics have been concerned to maintain. If it were really abrogated then ethics, Christian and non-Christian, would be abolished. The sense of 'ought', however, like the content of natural morality, is rather renewed and transformed. It becomes what Karl Barth called a 'permission';[135] it takes on the character of privilege and grace. It points to a calling, a vocation; and it makes explicit the true nature of man as man, that he is made in the image of God his Creator, not in the sense of a self-contained and self-sufficient endowment, but in the sense of an endowment within the divine activity of grace, the divine activity of self-disclosure and invitation.

Again, when morality is set free from its source and origin in God and cast as bread upon the waters of history, it is at the mercy of man's will, which has no resource beyond indignation when the standards and authority of morality are set at nought. Man's inhumanity to man cannot be purged by man. 'Who can forgive sins but God only?'[136] On the natural level morality must either remain detached, in abstraction from the ambiguities and complexities of actual historical existence, oblivious to its own fate at the hands of men, or else it can only condemn the breach of its own requirements. To forgive is to condone. Even if forgiveness were prescribed by our moral standards, how could we deal with unforgiveness except by condemning and resisting it? And I suspect that when we obscure this situation it is because unwittingly we have contracted out of a moral concern as long and broad as history itself. It is by no means difficult to pay lip-service

THE GROUNDWORK OF CHRISTIAN ETHICS

to the ethic of love without recognizing that this is an ethic which is not content simply to deny its own denial and reject its own rejection.

There is an interesting passage in John Calvin's *Institutes* in which he says,

> Assuredly there is but one way in which to achieve what is not merely difficult but *utterly against human nature*: to love those who hate us, to repay their evil deeds with benefits, to return blessings for reproaches. It is that we remember not to consider men's evil intention but to look upon the image of God in them, which cancels and effaces their transgressions, and with its beauty and dignity allures us to love and embrace them.[137]

'What is not merely difficult but utterly against human nature', wrote Calvin; and the point is a sound one, except that when it is made in this psychological form it suggests a corrupt and even a totally depraved human nature which, if it were a fact, would not be human. The truth here is not a psychological one but a logical one, a truth concerning, not the motives, but the moral reasoning of natural man. By the nature of the case natural morality has no resource with which to deal with the defiance of itself save that of condemnation. It can do no other than support and uphold those who do good, and oppose, defeat and even destroy the evildoer.

This, however, is not the way of the Christian ethic which is essentially an ethic of love, but not of love only, rather and quite specifically of love towards our enemies and towards men who do evil, transgressors and malefactors. It may well be that many Christians are prone to treat the peculiarly Christian character of the Christian ethic of love as a matter of course, as something that can go without saying; but in fact this ethic does not make moral sense except on the foundation of Jesus Christ, as the way of his Kingdom. 'Herein is love, not that we loved God, but that he loved us, and sent his Son to be the propitiation for our sins.'[138] And 'God commendeth his love toward us, in that, while we were yet sinners, Christ died for us.'[139] Much has been said by contemporary moralists to the effect that moral words are 'commending' words; but the present point is that the Christian ethic of unlimited and unrestricted love, of love towards those opposed to love, can be commended only by action and that the sovereign action of God himself.

In his particular historical social setting Jesus contrived to make evident this inversion of moral reasoning when he both summoned men to himself and sent them forth to all and sundry without condition and without moral bar. 'Come unto me . . .' 'Go ye therefore, and teach all nations . . .' 'Ye have the poor always with you; but me ye have not always.' 'Inasmuch as ye have done it unto one of the least of these my brethren, ye have done it unto me.'[140] If there is one single incident in his career which illustrates the point it is that 'before the feast of the passover, when Jesus knew that his hour was come', he washed his disciples' feet and said to them, 'If I then, your Lord and Master, have washed your feet; ye also ought to wash one another's feet.'[141] This incident, however, is by no means an isolated one, it is rather a parable which underlines the whole tenor of his career, the fact that he was 'obedient unto death', that he gave himself to the uttermost, even to the point of death, and that on the Cross his prayer was, 'Father, forgive them; for they know not what they do.'[142] Within the Christian faith it is thus that the ethic of love is commended to us.[143]

Thus, quite correctly, Calvin entitled the section of his argument from which I have already quoted: 'Love of neighbour is not dependent upon manner of men but looks to God.' It is because of the theological context of the Christian's action, the context of God's work of reconciliation, that Calvin could say, 'Whatever man you meet who needs your aid, you have no reason to refuse to help him', even if he be a 'stranger' or 'contemptible and worthless' or has no special claim upon you or even 'has deserved something far different'. On no other ground could the Christian ethic be justified. Moreover, it is because of the same theological context that, when the Christian finds his endeavour frustrated and obstructed by the complexities of the historical situation and by the resistance of the world, he is bound, in solidarity with that world, to confess his own unworthiness, and so to acknowledge what Professor Reinhold Niebuhr has called 'the relevance of an impossible ethical ideal'[144] – impossible, that is to say, to men, but in Christ God's gift and God's promise.

Yet we have not completely grasped this aspect of our subject, and we are bound to misrepresent it, if we think of the theological context, God's action in Christ, as providing a reason in the argument which is fundamentally *our* argument, as functioning only as a premiss in the argument. It is not only a premiss but a presence – *the* presence and so the conclusion as well and the ultimate demand itself. The Christian life, the moral life reconciled, is the life of God's Kingdom which is not our kingdom, even if we were made for it. In learning to love our enemy we learn to love God, and we do all things *to his glory*. If the Christian's action did not thus point backwards and forwards but also upwards to God it would fail to make sense.

From this perspective we can understand what Emil Brunner had in mind when he said that the Christian life is lived, not towards God, but from him. He meant, for example, that the Christian is not in the position of the natural man, either blind to his solitude and isolation and vulnerability or desperately anxious in his effort to hold human society, or some particular social relationship, together. Rather the Christian lives and acts by, and in, God's gift and God's promise – that is his strength. From the present perspective, however, it must also be said that the Christian life is lived *to* God's glory which is infinitely greater than the Christian's obedience here and there – that is the Christian's wisdom and insight. God is in heaven and the Christian is on earth, seeking to give what he has received, so that here in history amongst the affairs of men God's Kingdom may come.

'Wherefore', says the Epistle to the Philippians, '. . . work out your own salvation with fear and trembling. For it is God which worketh in you both to will and to do of his good pleasure.'

# THE ETHICAL THOUGHT OF
# PAUL TILLICH

One of the most interesting and valuable discussions in modern times of morality in general and of Christian ethics in particular is that of Paul Tillich; but, largely because it is part and parcel of his total theology and peculiar philosophy of religion, it is apt to receive much less attention than it deserves, and certainly it has not featured prominently in these pages.

Tillich's distinctive approach reveals itself when, having rejected the project of a Christian philosophy as an enterprise with predetermined results and therefore dishonest, he similarly disowns the idea of theological ethics as 'consciously prejudiced ethics'[1] and as therefore unworthy of a serious thinker. In its place he puts what he calls theonomous ethics, and, in contrast both to the 'autonomy of practical reason' and to 'the heteronomy of revelatory divine commandments',[2] 'actual theonomy is autonomous ethics under the Spiritual Presence'.[3] What Tillich seems to mean, however, by an autonomous ethics is a somewhat trivial point that ethics is an independent discipline free from 'external ecclesiastical or political authority';[4] and he appears to assume that any discipline independent in that sense must be one in which the operative reason is not only independent but quite sovereign. In other words, he does not envisage a science of ethics in which, without any interference with its intrinsic rational responsibility, reason recognizes the moral situation or, for that matter, the religious situation as one in which man *as such* is a being under authority – something very different from the fact that here and there men in fact find themselves contingently under some visible authority, ecclesiastical or political. Perhaps it was his reaction from the latter situation in pre-war Germany which blinded him to the former situation. At any rate he did not seem to envisage ethical science as an independent science in the sense just described, but thought of it as essentially moral philosophy wherein a quite sovereign reason began by laying an ontological foundation for morality in an independently articulated philosophy of being. Such a discipline was free to use – or not to use – intellectual and other elements drawn from one concrete religious tradition or another, such as the Christological dogma, as symbolizing its own interpretation of reality.[5]

If this assessment is valid, and the analysis upon which it rests, it means that a quite outstanding importance attaches to a passage in Tillich in which he rejects the whole idea of *levels* of reality,[6] for this rejection carries with it the affirmation of the absolute sovereignty of reason in the sense already indicated. It is significant too that, as Tillich sees it, what he calls 'the Protestant and the democratic principles' negate, not just certain forms in which the recognition of different levels of reality might express itself, but the very idea and metaphor of any such levels. It is no less significant that for his own part he prefers the metaphor of dimension to that of level, and that he understands the former in such a way that for him 'the replacement of the metaphor "level" by the metaphor "dimension" represents an encounter with reality in which the *unity* of life is seen above its conflicts'.[7] Such an affirmation almost predetermines the results, in general but not of course in detail, of the philosophic quest it announces, although no charge that it 'would inevitably betray the honesty of search'[8] would be in order. Yet the general type of philosophy of being to which the argument will lead has already been implicitly laid down; and while, for example, the notion that the universe is sacramental in character, so that nature can provide the medium whereby spirit communicates with spirit, seems to require the recognition of different levels of reality, it should be no surprise that Tillich who denies such levels emphasizes rather the experience of ecstasy.

None the less, even if such presuppositions ensure that morality will be seen through a glass darkly, it remains an impressive fact that Tillich does see at least the outline of morality and does grasp something of its reality. Thus, as a first approximation, he does see that the truth about morality must lie somewhere between the errors of relativism and what he calls graceless moralism. He knows perfectly well that 'since the eighteenth century, at least in Europe' the word 'moral' 'has carried the implication of "moralism" in the sense of graceless legalistic ethics';[9] but the truth of human life, he contends, can rest with neither 'graceless moralism' nor 'normless relativism'.[10]

This means that for Tillich there is an objective and absolute moral standard; but, as a further point, it does not mean that there is an objective set or system of moral laws, known to man, which man has the unchanging duty to observe and apply. That there is such a system has been a very common assumption in the past, but it fails to take account of two facts both of which Tillich appears to recognize. One is that man's apprehension of the moral standard is not infallible and is, in particular, frequently conditioned by his social setting; while the other is that the genuine response to the moral demand is much more creative than would be the mechanical application of universal rules to particular situations. Thus Tillich sets aside the traditional conception of natural law on the ground that its contents are 'historically conditioned'[11] and, more broadly, he holds that 'there are no principles which could be applied mechanically and which would guarantee that justice is done. Nevertheless,' he adds immediately,[12] 'there are principles of justice expressing the form of being in its universal and unchanging character'; and he suggests that 'creative justice is the form of reuniting love'.[13]

In *Morality and Beyond* Tillich has a chapter entitled 'Ethics in a Changing World', reprinted from his earlier book *The Protestant Era,* in which he says significantly that 'there must be something immovable in the ethical principle, the criterion and standard of all ethical change. There must be a power of change within the ethical principle itself. And both must be united.'[14] The solution to this dilemma he finds in love or *agape.* 'Love, *agape,*' he says,[15] 'offers a principle of ethics that maintains an eternal, unchangeable element, but makes its realization dependent on continuous acts of a creative intuition.' 'Love alone', he holds,[16] 'can transform itself according to the concrete demands of every individual and social situation without losing its eternity and dignity and unconditional validity.'

It is, I suppose, inevitable that because of such statements Tillich should sometimes be hailed as a situationalist; but so to regard him would simply introduce endless confusion into the subject. Accordingly, as a further point concerning his ethics, it should be unambiguously noted that for Tillich justice and love are inseparable and that both together are inseparably connected with the nature of being. Hence for Tillich there is no place for lawless or unprincipled love and no place for ethical relativism. 'Justice', he says quite clearly and firmly,[17] 'is immanent in love. A love of any type, and love as a whole if it does not include justice, is chaotic self-surrender, destroying him who loves as well as him who accepts such love.' Justice, he insists, 'is the form in which and through which love performs its work. Justice in its ultimate meaning is creative justice, and creative justice is the form of reuniting love.'[18] Moreover, it is precisely this characterization of love as reuniting which unveils the ontological status of love beyond every realm of relativity. 'Being precedes value,' he says,[19] 'but value fulfills being'; and 'love in all its qualities drives toward reunion'.[20] 'Life is being in actuality and love is the moving power of life.' 'Love is the drive towards the unity of the separated', but it would be quite 'wrong to give to separation the same ontological ultimacy as to reunion. For separation presupposes an original unity' and 'unity embraces itself and separation, just as being comprises itself and non-being'.[21]

In these statements there is to be discerned quite clearly the ontological grounding which Tillich provides for morality, and it is a grounding determined by an ecstatic vision of the unity of being reminiscent of the ecstatic vision of Plotinus for whom separateness was the ultimate evil as was manifoldness for Origen or transience for Plato.

It is plainly impossible to combine this account of morality with ethical relativism; and indeed there is a grandeur about the former conception of the moral life to which the latter could never lay claim. As Tillich himself put it, 'the religious source of the moral demands is love under the domination of its *agape* quality, in unity with the imperative of justice to acknowledge every being with personal potential as a person, being guided by the divine-human wisdom embodied in the moral laws of the past, listening to the concrete situation, and acting courageously on the basis of these principles'.[22] However much some thoroughgoing relativists may covet the support of Tillich they cannot possibly make room in their own systems for what Tillich genuinely and consistently regarded as 'the divine-human wisdom embodied in the moral laws of the past'.

As still another point, however, it has to be said that if Tillich's account stands decisively aside from ethical relativism, in the end it also stands apart from the kind of view towards which the argument of these pages seems irresistibly to have moved. There are several stages in which this point requires to be made; and in the first of these the preliminary query arises whether the ontological grounding which Tillich carves out for morality really serves the purpose he requires of it. The difficulty is to know whether, if the unity of being is posed as ultimate, separateness can possibly appear upon the scene, nor is this difficulty really diminished when it is fully recognized that Tillich takes a dynamic, not a static view of being and also emphasizes the place of non-being as well as the *power* of being. 'The power of a being is the greater the more non-being is taken into its self-affirmation. The power of being is not dead identity but the dynamic process in which it separates itself from itself and returns to itself. The more conquered separation there is the more power there is. The process in which the separated is reunited is love.'[23] Behind such statements there may lie an ecstatic vision of reality but the statement is not in itself logically compelling and seems to demand more than 'intelligent recognition'[24] if it is to supersede alternative accounts which may be more congenial to Christianity.

The same difficulty reappears at the other end of the process of reunion, for a community of love stops short of absolute unity; and it is exceedingly difficult to believe that, given his presuppositions, Tillich is really entitled to say that 'it is the superiority of the person-to-person relationship that it preserves the separation of the self-centred self, and nevertheless actualizes their reunion in love'.[25] If, on Tillich's philosophy of being, separation does not have the same ontological ultimacy as reunion, as it clearly does not, this cannot possibly be the last word, or else it is a most ambiguous one – as is his reference to God 'with whom I have a person-to-person encounter'.[26]

Indeed, in so far as Tillich professes to occupy the ground of Christianity, it is necessary to press home the criticism at this stage, for if in his thought there is a suggestion that from ultimate unity separateness derives with logical inevitability – 'unity is not identity. An element of separation is presupposed when we speak of unity'[27] – it very much looks as if, whereas for Barth sin was an ontological impossibility, for Tillich estrangement is an ontological necessity!

The second stage of this critical assessment involves the recognition of a prominent element of rigorism in Tillich's ethical thought. He holds that there are 'two different meanings of law, law as structure and law as the demand to actualize this structure';[28] and he insists that in the latter sense it is itself 'an expression of man's estrangement from his true nature'.[29] For Tillich the command and the struggle to obey are inextricably linked together;[30] and indeed, whereas in Kant a rigorist conception of the moral law was combined with the belief that practical reason, recognizing the law, had within itself the motive-power to obey it, in Tillich the opposite conclusion is drawn, that 'the law makes for the increase of estrangements'.[31]

On the face of it, so far as specifically Christian ethics is concerned, this contrast suggests that Tillich is much nearer the truth than Kant, and there is a sense in which that is undoubtedly the case. This does not mean, however, that Tillich is right for it may well be that both he and Kant are wrong in their rigorism. The crucial question in this connection is: Is the moral law in some way a function of man's disobedience or estrangement? Is therefore Emil Brunner right when he says, 'If I feel I *ought* to do right, it is a sign that I cannot do it. If I could really do it, there would be no question of "ought" about it at all'?[32] Is there really for the saint no question of 'ought', no question of a moral command or law, no question of being a man under authority? It seems to me that, while both Brunner and Tillich are right, against Kant, to emphasize grace, they are both wrong to interpret grace with the help of a rigorism which they share with Kant, which indeed exceeds the rigorism of Kant – for in his concept of holiness Kant did transcend his own rigorism.

Within Christian ethics, in contrast to general ethics, it is important in this context to emphasize grace; but the evaluation of Tillich's thought at this point depends on how grace is to be understood, as something which eliminates the 'ought' or as something which does not, as something which posits the Christian as quite literally – but quite incredibly – a new creature in the most absolute sense or as something which creates a new context and a new relationship of life.

There are certainly passages in which Tillich comes close to recognizing the point I am here making. Thus he speaks of what is morally motivating as 'the driving or attracting power of that which is the goal of the moral command – the good';[33] but clearly from the ethical standpoint it matters much whether this power is conceived as driving or as attracting, and whether the attraction is naturally or morally construed.

Since this power is for Tillich the power of being there can be little doubt how in his mind the ambiguity must be resolved; and it is clear that his rigorism is but one side of a coin of which naturalism and the working of what he calls the Spiritual Presence is the other. 'Every organism, natural as well as social, is a power of being and a bearer of an intrinsic claim for justice because it is based on some form of reuniting love.'[34] This power of being is love, and 'love, through compulsory power, must destroy what is against love. But love cannot destroy him who acts against love. Even when destroying his work it does not destroy him. It tries to save and fulfil him by destroying in him what is against love.'[35] The power of being, which is thus conceived as life and love, is, however, construed in the last resort impersonally. Love does not act as something 'added to an otherwise finished process'. Rather, 'life has love in itself as one of its constitutive elements', and 'love reunites that which is self-centred and individual'.[36] No wonder Tillich can lay down as the basic formula of love something which, so far from commanding instant assent, requires his whole philosophy of being for the articulation of its very meaning, namely, 'Being taking Non-Being into itself'.[37] No wonder when he speaks specifically of the religious man he says that 'the Spirit takes the personal centre into the universal centre, the transcendent unity which makes faith and love possible' and which 'is the unity of the divine life'.[38] 'The Spirit', he says,[39] 'elevates the person into the transcendent unity of the divine life and in so doing it reunites the estranged existence of the person with his essence.'

Thus rigorism, a new naturalism, and something like possession by the divine Spirit all hang together within the texture of Tillich's thought. 'Grace is, so to speak,' he says explicitly,[40] 'the "possession from above", overcoming the possession from

below.' Together these characteristics of Tillich's thought render
ambiguous and problematical his references to person-to-person
encounters, whether between humans or between man and God.
They do so because unmistakably they point towards an ultimate
pantheistic monism and mysticism in which is fulfilled 'the drive
toward reunion with essential being in everything ... with
things and persons in their essential goodness and with the good
itself',[41] and for which inevitably 'the moral stage is a station on
the way'.[42] The centrality of the concept of love in Tillich's
thought should not be allowed to deceive us. It was an important
idea too of Benedict Spinoza.

# AGAPE, EROS AND NOMOS

One of the most important books on Christianity published in the present century is *Agape and Eros* by the Swedish bishop and theologian, Anders Nygren; and no student of Christian ethics can rest content until he has taken account of Nygren's argument and related his own thinking to it. This is especially so since Nygren is refreshingly clear and unambiguous in maintaining that 'Christianity knows nothing either of a non-ethical fellowship with God or of non-religious ethics. The Christian Religion is a thoroughly ethical religion and its ethic is a thoroughly religious ethic.'[1] Yet, impressive as Nygren's argument undoubtedly is and instructive in the light which it throws upon the development of Christian ideas in the ancient and medieval periods as well as in the work of Martin Luther, it presents considerable difficulties to the Christian moralist in his attempt to come to terms with it. It may very well be that the very conception of the book, even its title, involves a subtle twist or bias or even oversimplification given to its material in the very act of grasping it; and in the end, so far as Christian ethics is concerned, it represents the production within Lutheran theology of a position bearing certain striking resemblances to that of Karl Barth within the tradition of Reformed theology.

The book is designed as a piece of what Nygren calls motif-research, which is related to but distinguishable from historical-genetic research, and which is, like the latter, a thoroughly empirical investigation[2] and properly prior to and independent of any commitment and decision on the part of the scientific investigator.[3] Motif-research is concerned with the content and manifestation characteristic of fundamental motifs, and fundamental motifs are answers to ultimate questions such as the ethical question about the good or the religious question about the eternal. Moreover, according to Nygren, in the field of ethics and religion there are two such fundamental motifs, precisely Agape and Eros, and the history of Christian ideas is very largely the story of their interplay. It is true that from time to time a third fundamental motif is brought into the picture, namely, Nomos, the Law; but the title of Nygren's book is not misleading if it suggests that any role assigned to this is bound to be a subordinate one; and it is interesting to note that on this score Nygren has been the target of criticism by other Scandinavian theologians such as Gustaf Wingren. Indeed, according to the latter, this aspect of Nygren's thought not only misrepresents Christianity but renders impossible its task of making contact with whatever idealism there is in the contemporary world, since, as Wingren puts it, 'when the Law disappears as an independent factor alongside the Gospel, and when the problem is reduced to one of "*eros* and *agape*," this means that we are regarding idealism exclusively as being at variance with the Gospel'.[4]

Be that as it may however – and the point is a strong one – Nygren undoubtedly treats Agape and Eros as the two motifs, far beyond anything else, with which he has to reckon in the field of ethics and religion; and further, not only does he concentrate almost exclusive attention upon them, but all along the line he regards them as mutually opposed. To this point he returns again and again and holds explicitly that in origin and properly speaking, that is, save by confusion, they have nothing to do with each other, they are thoroughly alien to each other. Eros is 'the born rival of the idea of Agape'.[5] So emphatic is Nygren on this inherent opposition that the purported scientific detachment of his empirical standpoint seems hardly credible. Not that his real standpoint is thereby discredited. It is only that from the outside a mixture of Agape and Eros is as much a reality as either by itself, and it is really from the perspective of an evangelical faith that Nygren can be so sure of the essential divergence of his two fundamental motifs.

If his real standpoint has thus been accurately diagnosed it is possible to understand how Nygren can represent Eros and Agape as standing for two entirely different, 'two diametrically opposed types of religion: the *demonstrational* and the *revelational*'.[6] It is possible to understand too how he can see the history of Christianity in the ancient and medieval periods as the interplay and the varying synthesis, in more or less stable forms in spite of their inherent opposition, of these two ideas, the result of which was always 'a self-contradictory compromise'.[7] It is likewise possible to understand how he can find in Marcion and Irenaeus, and in their limited recovery of Agape in its pristine purity, not synthesis, but something of reformation, and how above all he can find in Luther a 'criticism of the Catholic idea of love' which is not only 'radical' but 'irrefutable'.[8]

From the particular standpoint of Christian ethics, however, the matter of main concern must be the contrast between Eros and Agape as Nygren understands it; and fortunately Nygren presents the contrast quite firmly in the clearest possible form, even in the shape of a table of specific points of divergence.[9] There is apparently nothing in common between the two ideas and the principal conflicting features are that whereas 'Eros is acquisitive desire and longing', 'Agape is sacrificial giving', that whereas 'Eros is an upward movement', 'man's way to God', 'Agape comes down' and 'is God's way to man', and that whereas 'Eros *recognizes value* in its object – and loves it', 'Agape loves – and *creates value* in its object'. If all this can be accepted it is easy to see how Nygren can hold that in ascending order of importance Eros must place neighbourly love, love for God and self-love, while Agape must place love for God, neighbourly love and God's love, and that whereas Eros has really no room for God's love Agape has no room for self-love.[10]

At first sight indeed it may not be altogether clear why certain items should occupy the place they do in this scheme, why, for example, under Agape love for God should find a lower place than neighbourly love, but there is a firm unequivocal answer to all such questions. Since Agape *creates* values there is something odd and inappropriate about the thought of love for God and one should speak rather of faith, of being possessed by God's love.[11] Further, under Agape love of others comes only second to God's love and is indeed, almost literally, an extension of the latter so that it is not too much to say that 'it is Christ who is the real subject of the Christian life',[12] nor to speak of 'the new, Spirit-given Agape-life, of which the subject is no longer the man himself, but God, Christ, God's Agape, God's Spirit'.[13] On the other hand, under Eros which *recognizes* values and is by no means confined to sensual love, the higher must take precedence over the lower, so that even the love of neighbour is ultimately seen as a stepping-stone to God conceived as man's highest good – and consequently even man's love of God is but a form of self-love. On the one hand, accordingly, man seeks to have and to possess, and his ultimate end is to possess the highest. On the other hand, love is essentially a giving which has its origin in God and Christ – 'Agape is Christianity's own original basic conception'[14] – and its motto is to be found in the words of Jesus, 'Freely ye have received, freely give',[15] which is supremely seen in the love of enemies.[16] So different is Agape from Eros that Luther can say that 'such love is not a natural art, nor grown in our garden',[17] and Nygren can say logically – but not perhaps credibly – that 'the Christian is not an independent centre of power alongside of God' but that 'Christian love is through and through a Divine work'.[18]

Thus the scene is set and the argument proceeds to portray the interplay of Nygren's two fundamental ideas in considerable historical detail, first in a preliminary way in post-apostolic times, and then definitively in St Augustine with his conception of Caritas, and so subsequently through the Middle Ages right up to the Reformation and the work of Martin Luther. Many Protestant historians of dogmatic theology find an unbroken succession in Paul, Augustine and Luther; but whatever truth there is in this interpretation it represents for Nygren a serious oversimplification. As he sees it, it was not Augustine's teaching on sin and grace, it was not even his conception of the Church, which prevailed in the medieval Church. It was 'at another point that was really more central for him' that 'his view has set its seal on the Catholic type of piety',[19] and this was his synthetic conception of love as Caritas under which he thought it right to bring the whole reality of Christianity. In his doctrine of Caritas Augustine contrived a synthesis of Agape and Eros, 'trying to unite things which by their nature cannot be united';[20] but this means that it is no straight line of continuous development or straightforward succession which leads from Augustine to Luther. Rather, 'what the former builds up, the latter tears down, and erects on the vacant ground an edifice of a totally different structure.'[21]

The main points of resemblance between this characteristic

teaching of Nygren and that of Karl Barth are, so far as Christian ethics is concerned, in the first instance two in number. For one thing, for both theologians the Christian way, when it comes upon the scene, finds a ground that is already occupied,[22] and its proper reaction is represented by both as one of wholesale annexation and annihilation. Accordingly, Barth has no solution to the problem how man can be said to be exposed to the ethical question from the outset without any inkling of the reality which poses the question, and likewise Nygren cannot explain how Agape and Eros, being wholly opposed to each other and having nothing in common, are yet answers to the same ultimate question. Perhaps if Nygren had made more room for Nomos, not confining it to a context of Jewish legalism,[23] and had been prepared to reckon with the sense of 'ought', he might have come within sight of the problem, if not of its solution; but as it is he is content to represent Agape and Eros as two diametrically opposed ultimates which are yet quite arbitrarily described as different answers to the *same* ultimate question.[24]

In the second place, when Nygren describes the subject of the Christian life as not man but God he approaches the heteronomous determinism which we have already found reason to criticize in both Emil Brunner and Karl Barth, and in the context of his own thought it is no more credible than it was in theirs. So far from being a possible account of the Christian ethic it really eliminates ethics from Christianity. Nygren claims the authority of St Paul's words to the Galatians, 'no longer I, but Christ liveth in me'; but as I have elsewhere written in a rather different context, it is to be noticed that St Paul speaks the words, referring to himself in the first person and to Christ in the third; and what St Paul says must on no account be interpreted in a way that is logically at odds with the fact that he says it.[25]

Besides these two criticisms of Nygren's position there seem to me to be three other points at which his teaching is open to serious question. Consistently he speaks of Agape as creating values where there were none before, and yet he represents Paul as giving to Agape 'its highest and, in a sense, final expression'[26] by bringing together the theme of Agape and the theology of the Cross.[27] The theology of the Cross, however, cannot be made to cohere with the thought of Agape defined as creating values, for the whole point of that theology is, not that God poured out his love upon those who from the standpoint of value were utterly neutral, but much rather that 'while we were yet sinners' – that is, having a *dis*value, a negative value – 'Christ died for us'.[28] Thus in Nygren's very conception of Agape there is a confusion between the theme of redemption and the theme of creation which is seriously in conflict with the Pauline theology of the Cross; and it is not difficult to see that there is a corresponding problem for Karl Barth's theology.

A closely related point is that Nygren is very greatly concerned to represent Agape as in conflict, not just with 'vulgar Eros', the sensual type of Eros, but with 'the heavenly Eros'. It is the latter which presents a problem, not by any means the former, and this, not at all because it is empirically more widespread than the other (that in any case would be extremely doubtful), but because in its own way it 'shines with the light of heaven' and is 'the highest form of Eros'.[29] Clearly, however, a principle of evaluation has here been introduced for which Nygren's account has really no room.

Finally, there must be laid against Nygren's account of Agape the criticisms already made of those who seek to build an entire Christian ethic upon love alone, forgetting that love is the fulfilment, not the replacement, of law, that love by itself is without direction. Nygren at one point in his discussion quotes Luther's statement that love seeks to 'confer *good* upon the poor and needy';[30] but if this word 'good' introduces a moral criterion it means that the truth about ethics has overflowed Nygren's considered statement of the case, while if it does not but simply points to the psychological category of need, then love even as Agape is without defence against its own fanaticisms and its own sentimentalization.

The truth is that, whether in ethics or in Christian ethics, the moral life cannot be grasped exclusively in terms of love, self-love, love of neighbour, love of God, even God's love. Indeed, on the contrary, apart from the moral consciousness and moral principles, love becomes a purely psychological category and is not applicable to God at all. On the other hand, much – not by any means the whole – of the ethical discussion within Christianity has traditionally been in terms of love and Nygren's book is a great help in coming to terms with it.

In the light of this critical analysis it is interesting and important to take account of another substantial, indeed a massive, contribution to the subject from Lutheran thinking, namely, *Theological Ethics* by Helmut Thielicke. This book is peculiarly relevant to the present discussion because, although it shares to a very considerable extent the basic view to be found in Nygren, it does not on the face of it exhibit the chief weakness of the latter's position, which is that he treats Nomos as a phenomenon of Judaism and therefore as a minor rival to Agape which it is safe virtually to ignore. Thielicke, on the contrary, regards the Law as an indispensable theme in Christian ethics, and accordingly he moves clearly in the direction required by what has been the main criticism of Nygren. What remains to be seen is whether he moves far enough in this direction to achieve a stable position.

The substantial common ground he shares with Nygren is evident in two principal respects. In the first of these it is plain that Thielicke too regards human life as held between two possibilities which he designates self-love on the one side and love of God on the other. 'The specifically "Christian" element in ethics', he insists,[31] 'is . . . to be sought explicitly and exclusively in the motivation of the action'; but he is careful to point out that this does not place Christian ethics in the class of ethics of disposition, for in the last resort there are for Christian ethics only two possibilities, the love of self and the love of God, and the latter only as a gift so that 'I can love only where I know that I am loved, where I am dealing with the heart of God'.[32] Accordingly, he says, 'what is involved is not a "disposition" at all, but a totally new existence';[33] and in line with this he understands the New Testament incident of the rich young ruler as one in which 'Jesus aims to lift from him the mortgage of self-love which burdens and depreciates everything he does, and free him for the love of God'.[34]

The second important direction in which Thielicke's position is close and parallel to that of Nygren is virtually an extension of the first and relates to the latter's point that the subject of Christian behaviour is really God. For this affirmation likewise finds a place in Thielicke's thought. 'Our love and the acts which flow from it', he says,[35] 'are not just a response to the preceding love of God. . . . They are not just a reaction, a second act. On the contrary, they are actually the reverse side of God's love.'

In the light of such statements it is clear that if this were even no more than the main outline of Thielicke's thesis his position would not be substantially different from that of Nygren; but in fact this is not so, for in comparison the peculiar merit and interest of the former's discussion derive from his refusal to dismiss law as a somewhat unimportant rival to love, and from the persistence with which he wrestles with the problem posed by law and the various orders within which man lives whether he be Christian or not. If he were to follow what he takes to be the traditional framework of dogmatics he would dismiss this problem; but, he considers, it is no longer possible to ignore the 'human-historical reality which secularization has warped almost beyond recognition but nonetheless brought squarely to the center of attention'.[36] The Christian has no choice in this matter. Whether he likes it or not he may not be *of* the world but he is at the same time *in* it, and Thielicke can even say that 'the problem of ethics is all wrapped up in this *simul*'.[37] 'Ethics has its place therefore precisely in the field of tension between the old and the new aeons, not in the old alone, nor in the new alone.'[38] That being so, the problem of law and of everything that can be brought under that rubric, such as conscience, is altogether inescapable, and it is greatly to Thielicke's credit that he recognizes this fact. On the other hand, the problematical character for him of this quite central problem should not be underestimated, for he can also say that 'evangelical ethics is completely different from all natural or philosophical ethics. Indeed the two lie on wholly different planes . . .'[39] The trouble is that if the core of the Christian ethic is to be seen in the gift of a new nature from which the appropriate fruits flow and the appropriate consequences follow (not just, quite explicitly, are 'to be drawn'[40]), if even more ultimately one can say that 'the point of the salvation event consists in God's change towards us rather than in our change towards God',[41] it does not seem possible to peg out a place for the imperative of law in conjunction with the far more important indicative of the Gospel;

but for Thielicke the former motif is present also in the teaching of Scripture and in the thought of the Reformation, so that the task of thinking the two motifs together, without detriment to the doctrine of justification by grace alone, may not be eschewed.

What makes this task exceedingly difficult is Thielicke's conviction that in our knowledge of the Law or of the orders and in conscience there is no awareness of the eternal will of God; and what imposes this conviction quite firmly upon Thielicke's thought is his belief that to allow such a knowledge of God's will apart from the Gospel is to introduce the idea of work-righteousness alongside, and therefore in contradiction of, the *sola fide*,[42] and also his tendency to assume that such a knowledge could only be suggested on the basis of the traditional Roman Catholic view of the *imago dei* in man as an inherent or ontic quality of man and not, as Thielicke himself believes, as a relationship in which man stands to God.[43] Accordingly his own view is that 'the doctrine of the Law must always be viewed against the background of the fall'.[44] In other words, 'it is the will of God as altered by the fallen world'.[45] 'Theologically', he says,[46] '. . . it is important to view the Law of God for this fallen world in terms of this constitutive relationship to sin.' To fail to do this and to think and speak instead of the timeless validity of the Law or of moral principles would indicate 'a crisis in the concept of history'.[47] It would be on Thielicke's interpretation to sit far too loosely to salvation history.

It follows from all this that whatever place is assigned to the Law it must be one between the Fall and the Consummation and that not just contingently, as it happens, but as belonging to the very essence of the matter. We cannot understand the place of the Law – this is Thielicke's argument – unless we understand it as a place and function in salvation history;[48] and this can perhaps be best seen in relation first to the beginning of the Christian life and then in relation to its continuation.

So far as the former is concerned Thielicke insists that 'the purpose of the imperative is not to intrude upon the automatic process and so declare that justification of itself is incapable of producing the "new creation". On the contrary, the imperative is rather a demand that we should attain to that starting point where the automatic process goes into operation.'[49] So far as the role of the Law in the already begun and continuing life of the Christian is concerned Thielicke seems to represent it by two main images of which the first is that of the 'gauze in the wound'. That is to say, whereas it is true that 'while we were yet sinners Christ died for us', 'the just for the unjust', it is also true that while we are justified by grace alone we remain in fact sinners,[50] and the Law has the job of not allowing us to forget this state of affairs and so of driving us again and again to the one and only source of our justification. As Thielicke puts it, 'the true function of the Law with respect to the Gospel is to serve as "gauze in the wound". There is no healing of this wound.'[51]

Yet it does not appear that that is the whole of what may be said, and Thielicke indicates the fact by the use of another metaphor, that of the sheep-dog 'whose purpose is to recall the members of the flock to the path of the shepherd',[52] and he speaks[53] of the 'pedagogic' significance of the Law, quoting Calvin's reference to its '"didactic role" for believers'.[54] If, however, the reader is tempted to breathe a sigh of relief, feeling that he now knows where he stands, that at long last the Law is being identified with the unchanging will of God, he should note very carefully that this is not so, that the Law is *not* being identified with the unchanging will of God, that Thielicke himself is very careful to retain the Law as some sort of *external* signpost and to insist that its pedagogic significance is not 'a normative significance' but 'a regulative significance'.[55] It is not indeed easy to know what is meant by a regulative significance as distinct from a normative one, but clearly it must be some sort of factual, non-normative significance; and yet this does not seem to make sense unless the Law can be deemed to have somehow dropped from heaven and to be able to command a completely blind and slavish obedience. The sheep-dog is not after all a very congenial addition to the biblical picture of the Good Shepherd and the flock.

Up to this point it may be thought that Thielicke has hardly mapped out for the Law a very credible role; but whether it be a credible role or not it suffers, up to this point, from one overriding defect, namely, that its significance has been represented exclusively with reference to the life of the Christian. Once again, however, Thielicke is aware of the difficulty, for he sees quite clearly that along his own line of thought, so far as the world outside Christianity is concerned, there seems 'no point in quickening the conscience, for everything is sin'.[56] On the other hand, to follow the alternative Roman Catholic solution would be to surrender justification by grace alone. 'We seem to be caught', he says,[57] 'on the horns of a real dilemma. We have arrived at what is a key problem in any discussion of the foundations of ethics.'

His way out of this dilemma is, first, quite boldly to say that in the moral actions and standards of men apart from faith we have 'manifestations of the human element, the *imago* in man',[58] and then, recalling his comprehensive division of human life between self-love and love of God he recognizes that such actions and standards may simply cloak the former and lead no higher than sheer hypocrisy. Yet he finds that he cannot allow that to be his last word, and he seeks for something 'more than mere hypocrisy'[59] in the morality of natural man. What in the end he professes to find is – not some, perhaps confused, awareness of God's will for his creation – but the 'affirmation that man is not his own legislator but has his place within a nexus wherein he is a subject'[60] – that and nothing more than that, a kind of ragged edge to human existence, whether his topic is conscience or natural law or the 'orders' of this world. If, however, this final thesis is to be understood as an ethical one and not merely as a psychological one about man's restlessness or homelessness, it leaves us in a position once again not very far removed from that of Karl Barth, for whom, as we have seen, man is exposed to the moral question from the outset though, apart from Christ, without any inkling of the reality which poses the question.

This is a puzzling end to a profound inquiry, and it is all the more so because Thielicke seems eminently sound in thinking of the *imago dei* in man in terms of a relation in which man stands to God. He is right when he says that 'the divine address constitutes the person'[61] and even that 'the continuous aspect of the relationship lies . . . in the divine promise, in God's loving will';[62] but when he adds the word 'exclusively' to the latter sentence one may well doubt whether there is any sense left in speaking of a completely 'negative mode of the divine likeness'[63] – as if the relationship had been cut down the middle but still survived. It looks as if what is required is a more positive doctrine, not of natural law, but of natural morality. Yet Thielicke insists that the doctrine of justification by grace alone must not be infringed. It may be, however, that while he has outgrown the other-worldliness of earlier outlooks he is still imprisoned by their individualism.

Bishop Nygren's contribution to Christian ethics may be seen, I have said, as the development within Lutheranism of a position similar in certain respects to that of Karl Barth within the Reformed tradition; and it would certainly be an error to regard either of these, in so far as they fail, as merely individual aberrations of particular thinkers, for both are rooted in the traditions out of which they have come and contrive to bring to expression what is implicit in them, the one in the Reformed emphasis upon the sovereignty of God and the other in the Lutheran doctrine of justification by grace alone. The great weakness of Nygren's position, I have suggested, is the cavalier treatment it accords to Nomos and its lack of a doctrine of natural morality (which Thielicke's preoccupation with Nomos fails in the end to supply); and indeed one of my main theses in this essay has been that it is impossible to make sense of Christian ethics without some such doctrine. It may therefore be not inappropriate at this point to take cognisance of the fact that within the Anglican tradition, in contrast both to the Reformed and to the Lutheran, a place has frequently been found, not just for a doctrine of natural morality, but for a doctrine of natural law, sometimes in obvious reliance upon the traditional doctrine and sometimes in a more exploratory fashion.

The doctrine of natural law seems to have three distinctive features the absence of any one of which makes a theory so far different from the traditional theory of natural law. The first is that the law is derived from the *nature* of man as such;[64] the second is that it is rationally so derived without the aid of revelation and may consequently be expected to command something like universal assent; and the third is that it serves as a foundation for the special requirements of the Christian ethic which is then a supplement to it or a second storey erected upon it. Much of this traditional conception has appeared in Anglican thought down the centuries from Richard Hooker in his *Of The Laws of Ecclesiastical*

*Polity* through the Caroline theologians Robert Sanderson and Jeremy Taylor to Kenneth E. Kirk and Lindsay Dewar in the present century. None the less there are three difficulties in this approach to Christian ethics or moral theology which nothing seems to lessen. The first is that the concept of human nature seems much too static and abstract to throw any clear light upon the concrete problems of human living. The second is that it is difficult, if not impossible, to isolate any definite laws which are universally agreed; and thirdly, if God was in Christ reconciling the world to himself, that reconciliation is very imperfectly portrayed by the idea of a supplement. Indeed these difficulties, perhaps in varying degrees, so far from becoming more tolerable, seem instead to have become more acute. In particular, the presupposition of the traditional doctrine that human nature is a stable reality seems no longer credible.

At any rate this point receives sympathetic notice in two recent attempts within Anglicanism to restate the doctrine of natural law in modern terms. Thus, in his essay 'Towards a Rehabilitation of Natural Law', Dr I. T. Ramsey, the Bishop of Durham, acknowledges freely the changed situation of modern man,[65] while Professor John Macquarrie, having referred to 'moral foundations that belong to our humanity as such'[66] and having suggested that the concept of natural law 'seems to me to be acquiring a fresh importance, and it offers the most likely basis on which to establish secure moral bonds between Christians and non-Christians',[67] goes on immediately to insist that the man who must be considered in this connection is 'the man of the modern age, caught up in rapid change',[68] and later holds that since man's self-understanding is part of himself we must admit 'that the existent, man himself, changes too'.[69] 'The traditional moral theology', he says,[70] 'was too strongly tied to the notion of a fixed, essential human nature, set in the midst of a static hierarchically ordered universe. Yet its basic method of approaching the problem of ethics was correct . . . through the study of man.'

In his attempt to re-think the doctrine of natural law Dr Ramsey leans quite heavily on the treatment offered by Professor H. L. A. Hart in his book *The Concept of Law*, and like the latter attempts to build upon the 'tacit assumption that the proper end of human activity is survival'[71] but as 'a mere contingent fact' rather than a metaphysical necessity. He quotes with approval Hart's point that 'we could not subtract the general wish to live and leave intact concepts like danger and safety, harm and benefit, need and function, disease and cure';[72] but as it stands there are two obvious weaknesses in this presentation of the case. For one thing there is a quite unexplained and therefore entirely arbitrary leap from the will to survive to the recognition of the rights of others to survive themselves and even to have our assistance in the effort. The illicit leap is comparable to that taken by John Stuart Mill in his famous argument about what is desirable – unless indeed we are being offered something like the crude cynicism of Thomas Hobbes. Secondly, it seems clear that if this difficulty could be overcome it would still be the case that in terms of bare survival only a minimal morality could be contemplated. Perhaps Dr Ramsey sees something of these two weaknesses, for he says that 'if survival is to be basic to a new natural law, there must be a *moral necessity* about survival'.[73] It is not altogether clear what he means by this, but if, as I suspect, he is saying that the ultimate here is already moral in character he has, I think, unwittingly moved the basis from the nature of man as such to the actual morality of men, not just their behaviour but their actual moral judgments – a step in the right direction, no doubt, but away from a doctrine of natural law.

Professor Macquarrie is even more clearly aware that for a revised doctrine of natural law human nature must be conceived in dynamic, not in static terms; and he spends a good deal of time in describing the various images which express modern man's understanding of himself, for example, a Being-on-the-way, a Being-in-the-world, a Being-with-others, Man as agent, and Man come of age. While, however, there is much ethical significance in these characterizations of modern man this part of the discussion seems to fall somewhere *between* the examination of specific moral problems *and* the formal analysis which is the fundamental task both of ethics and of Christian ethics. Yet when Macquarrie comes to this latter problem there is an unfortunate ambivalence in what he says. Thus he seems to find acceptable Sir David Ross's work in philosophical ethics and in particular Ross's recognition of 'some half-dozen *prima facie* duties'.[74] 'I am inclined to agree with Ross', he says,[75] 'that there is this kind of fundamental moral knowledge, given with human existence itself. Although he does not use the expression "natural law," I would think it quite appropriate.' But is it? Only, I think, if we are prepared to water down the concept and eliminate from it the derivation from the nature of man. For Ross this fundamental moral knowledge took the form of moral intuitions and was certainly not derived from some concept of human nature. He might very well have held that our concept of human nature is coloured by our fundamental moral knowledge but not vice versa.

Yet as Macquarrie's discussion proceeds it becomes clear that he is not prepared to eliminate from the concept of natural law the element of derivation from the nature of man, provided that nature is dynamically, not statically, construed. On the contrary, he lays it down that 'if man's nature is to *exist*, then he exists moşt fully when he *goes out* of himself. Here', he says, 'we strike upon the paradox of the moral life, perceived in many traditions – that the man who would "save", that is to say, preserve it as a static possession, actually loses it . . .'[76] Clearly, however, even italicized existence is no more able than bare survival to open the door upon the moral situation of actual men and women. Here again there is a quite unexplained, and therefore totally arbitrary, leap from the natural to the moral – but in this case the moral is not unambiguously so, for what Macquarrie says seems quite consonant with the condemnation of the miser and the acclamation of the spendthrift. It is true that Macquarrie has sought strenuously to correct the intolerably static character of the traditional concept of human nature, but in doing so he has rendered it even more abstract.

So far as the specifically Christian ethic is concerned Bishop Ramsey holds that its relation to the morality of natural law must be either that of identity, opposition or supplementation; and he is quite insistent that 'the whole Catholic tradition at any rate would seek for supplementation'.[77] He does not consider – what the present essay has argued – that there is a more complex fourth possibility according to which Christian morality reaffirms *and* redeems the natural morality of men, nor does he consider the obvious criticism that in terms only of supplementation there can be offered only a poor portrayal, rather a caricature, of reconciliation. These must remain the two large questions which Ramsey's discussion poses, although there are others which mainly arise from his general standpoint of radical empiricism.[78]

Ramsey does say, 'I cannot see any Christian granting absolute identity between the key-ideas of Natural Law and Christian ethics';[79] but it must be allowed that Professor Macquarrie comes very close to that 'impossible' position. 'Christian moral teaching', he says,[80] 'is an unfolding of the "natural" morality of all men.' The specific contribution of Christianity, as Macquarrie understands it, appears to be found in attitudes of faith and hope 'that may accompany all the other moral virtues – attitudes which, I think it may be claimed, can strengthen these virtues and supply a moral dynamic'.[81] Even so he almost at once adds, 'Surely no one will claim that faith, hope, and love are found exclusively in the context of Christianity.'[82] It seems impossible to avoid the conclusion that any unique claim on the part of Christianity has been whittled away until there is nothing left but the confidence and hope recognized by Macquarrie's former colleague, Paul Lehmann – with the difference that the former 'founds ethics on the doctrine of creation rather than on the doctrine of redemption'.[83]

Yet the truth seems to be that there is both continuity and discontinuity between natural morality and Christian morality. Bishop Ramsey and Professor Macquarrie are not wrong in emphasizing continuity in their different ways just as the Lutheran theologians already considered are right in emphasizing discontinuity. Where both sides err is in failing to recognize the validity of the other side; but both sides can be held together only by a doctrine of natural morality as the creative though sinful response of men within the constitutive relationship to ultimate reality in which they are held as men. The articulation of this doctrine does not proceed in terms of an abstract human nature, whether statically or dynamically conceived, but in terms of actual men and women bound together in their concrete societies and forming the world which God so loved 'that he gave his only begotten Son, that whosoever believeth in him should not perish, but have everlasting life'.[84] In other words, within the broken fellowship of man – and a broken fellowship is *not* an aggregate of self-centred and isolated units – God has established the fellowship of his kingdom which summons the children of men to faith and hope

and love that are rooted and grounded in God.[85] Only moral
beings could savour the grace of this gospel, the miracle of this
divine faithfulness;[86] and the truth of the doctrine of justification
by grace alone is that while we do not have moral resources to
build this kingdom, by grace it has been given to us to receive it.

# NOTES

1 *The Christian Message in a Non-Christian World*, Edinburgh House Press, London, 1938, pp. 134f.
2 *What is Christian Civilization?*, Oxford University Press, London, 1945, p. 45.
3 Ibid., p. 46.
4 Ibid., pp. 46f.
5 *The Christian Message in a Non-Christian World*, p. 87.
6 Ibid., pp. 85f.
7 Ibid., p. 87.
8 *God Was In Christ*, Faber, London, 1948, p. 107.
9 *Church Dogmatics*, T. & T. Clark, Edinburgh, 1957, II, 2, p. 524.
10 *Christianity and Ethics*, Duckworth, London, 1914, p. 2.
11 *Church Dogmatics*, II, 2, p. 528.
12 Ibid., p. 529.
13 *Amor Dei*, Hodder & Stoughton, London, 1938, p. 49.
14 Ibid., p. 29.
15 *Institutes*, SCM Press, London, 1961, Bk. III, Ch. VII.
16 Ibid., Bk. III, Ch. I.
17 Ibid., Bk. III, Ch. II.
18 Ibid., Bk. II, Ch. VIII.
19 Ibid., Bk. III, Ch. VII.
20 Ibid., Bk. III, Ch. VI.
21 John 6: 29; Luke 24: 26.
22 *The Interpretation of Religion*, T. & T. Clark, Edinburgh, 1929, p. 299.
23 *The Person of Jesus Christ*, T. & T. Clark, Edinburgh, 1912, p. viii.
24 *Utilitarianism*, Ch. II.
25 Ibid., Ch. II.
26 H. D. Lewis, *Morals and the New Theology*, Gollancz, London, 1947, p. 68.
27 *Christian Morality*, Oxford University Press, London, 1936, p. 3.
28 Ibid., p. 58.
29 Ibid., p. 296.
30 Ibid., p. 305.
31 *Christianity and Ethics*, p. 24.
32 Ibid., p. 25.
33 Ibid., p. 26.
34 *The Ethics of the Christian Life*, Williams & Norgate, London, 1909, p. 3.
35 *Christianity and Ethics*, p. 25.
36 *Christian Ethics*, T. & T. Clark, Edinburgh, 1894, p. 13.
37 Ibid., p. 10.
38 *The Ethics of the Christian Life*, p. 127.

39 *Christianity and Ethics*, p. 128.
40 *The Ethics of the Christian Life*, p. 112.
41 Ibid., p. 114.
42 Similarly, the phrase 'the perennial philosophy' contains within itself a violent contradiction. The only perennial philosophy possible is the determination to philosophize and to follow the wind of the argument wherever it may lead.

CHAPTER 2

1 Matthew 7: 9–11; cf. Romans 2: 15.
2 Cf. *The Knowledge of God and the Service of God*, Hodder & Stoughton, London, 1938, p. 143.
3 *Nicomachean Ethics*, 1094a.
4 J. H. Muirhead, *Rule and End in Morals*, Oxford University Press, London, 1932, p. 6.
5 Op. cit., Q.xciv., Art. 2.
6 *The Christian Philosophy of St Thomas Aquinas*, Gollancz, London, 1957, p. 264.
7 *Leviathan*, Pt. i, Ch. 6 (italics mine).
8 Ibid., Pt. i, Ch. 13.
9 W. D. Ross, *Foundations of Ethics*, Oxford University Press, London, 1939, p. 171.
10 G. E. Moore, *Principia Ethica*, Cambridge University Press, Cambridge, 1903, p. 147.
11 *Grundlegung*, translated by T. K. Abbott, *Kant's Theory of Ethics*, Longmans, Green, London, 1927, p. 13.
12 In ethical theory too Kant's day is by no means done; and it is interesting to note that even R. M. Hare, whose earlier book, *The Language of Morals* (Oxford University Press, London, 1952), certainly did not reflect a Kantian point of view (cf. *infra*, pp. 62ff.), none the less comes very much nearer such a perspective in his later book, *Freedom and Reason* (Oxford University Press, London, 1963), for although he holds that he has not changed his view the critical reader may well conclude that the new emphasis upon the principle of universalizability cannot be contained in the old linguistic schematism.
13 *The Divine Imperative*, Lutterworth, London, 1937, p. 18.
14 *Sermons*, XI.
15 Professor W. G. Maclagan has suggested (*The Theological Frontier of Ethics*, Allen & Unwin, London, 1961, p. 59) that certain theological writers, such as W. R. Matthews, John Baillie, and Paul Tillich, have erred in confusing the moral and the non-moral in this way; and although, as in all such conflicts, as we shall see later, the ethical criticism may not provide the last word, it is at least *relevant* and presents a prima facie case to be considered.

16 Op. cit., p. 34.
17 Ibid., p. 35.
18 Ibid., p. 35.
19 Ibid., p. 35.
20 Ibid., p. 44.
21 *Philosophy of Right*, Oxford University Press, London, 1942, p. 30.
22 In this connection it is worth recalling John Baillie's comment on the
   pre-war debate between Barth and Brunner on this and kindred topics.
   'Dr Barth's position', he said (*Our Knowledge of God*, Oxford University
   Press, London, 1939, pp. 30f.), 'seems untrue to the facts but clearly
   argued; Dr Brunner's position seems nearer the truth but, because it is
   not sufficiently far advanced beyond the other, to be involved in confusion and unreal compromise.' Cf. also R. Niebuhr, *The Nature and
   Destiny of Man*, Nisbet, Welwyn, 1943, II, p. 66, note.
23 *The Divine Imperative*, p. 36.
24 Ibid., p. 37.
25 Ibid., p. 40.
26 Ibid., p. 41.
27 Cf. my *Faith and Duty*, Gollancz, London, 1950, pp. 38f.
28 *Church Dogmatics*, T. & T. Clark, Edinburgh, 1957, II, 2, pp. 513–15.
29 Ibid., II, 2, pp. 516f.
30 Ibid., II, 2, p. 517.
31 Ibid., II, 2, p. 509.
32 Ibid., II, 2, p. 521.
33 Paul Weiss, *Man's Freedom*, Yale University Press, New Haven, 1950,
   and Oxford University Press, London, 1955, p. 179, quoted by Paul
   Lehmann, *Ethics in a Christian Context*, SCM Press, London, 1963,
   p. 207.

CHAPTER 3

1 *Language, Truth and Logic*, 2nd ed., Gollancz, London, 1948, p. 102.
2 Ibid., pp. 102f.
3 Ibid., pp. 105f.
4 Ibid., p. 107.
5 Italics mine.
6 Op. cit., p. 103.
7 R. M. Hare, *The Language of Morals*, p. 1.
8 Op. cit., p. 69.
9 Ibid., p. 69.
10 Ibid., p. 69.
11 Ibid., p. 69 (italics mine).
12 Ibid., p. 195.
13 Ibid., pp. 195f.
14 Cf. J. Baillie, *Our Knowledge of God*, pp. 181ff.

15 *Utilitarianism*, Ch. IV.
16 *Ethics*, Penguin, Harmondsworth, 1954, p. 36.
17 *Treatise*, Bk. III, Pt. I, Sect. i; quoted by Nowell-Smith, *Ethics*, p. 37.
18 *Ethics*, p. 42.
19 Ibid., p. 43.
20 Ibid., p. 48.
21 Ibid., p. 60.
22 Ibid., p. 65.
23 Ibid., p. 181.
24 Cf. R. M. Hare, *The Language of Morals*, pp. 195f. It may have been some awareness of this weakness which led Professor Hare in his later book, *Freedom and Reason*, to lay much greater weight upon universalizability and so (in spite of his own denial) to change his ground quite considerably.

CHAPTER 4

1 *Utilitarianism*, Ch. II.
2 *Morals and the New Theology*, p. 68.
3 *The Theological Frontier of Ethics*, p. 50.
4 *Utilitarianism*, Ch. II.
5 *Kant's Theory of Ethics*, p. 55.
6 Ethical subjectivism does seem parasitical in character, positing in a way the very thing it denies; and it is only on the basis of objectivism that one can really make sense of Barth's view of the moral question as the 'supremely critical' one or of R. M. Hare's declaration that 'moral principles are ... superior to or more authoritative than any other kind of principle'. (*Freedom and Reason*, p. 169.)
7 Op. cit., p. 51.
8 Ibid., p. 56.
9 Ibid., p. 57.
10 Ibid., p. 64.
11 *Mysticism and Logic*, Longmans, Green, London, 1918, pp. 56f.
12 In harmony with this way of thinking John Baillie, in one of his earlier books, was prepared to say that 'religion is a moral trust in reality'. (*The Interpretation of Religion*, p. 318.)
13 *The Theological Frontier of Ethics*, p. 63.
14 I do not wish to quarrel with this change from rationalism to what I have called empiricism. It is arguable that much modern thought is seeking a more adequate empiricism than the narrower philosophical school which claims the name is prepared to allow.
15 Quoted by J. Baillie, *Our Knowledge of God*, p. 159.
16 *The Theological Frontier of Ethics*, p. 64.
17 Ibid., p. 67.
18 Ibid., p. 68.

19 Ibid., pp. 67f.
20 Ibid., pp. 68f.
21 Ibid., p. 68.
22 Ibid., p. 68.
23 Ibid., p. 88.
24 Ibid., p. 63.
25 Ibid., p. 64.
26 Ibid., p. 69.
27 Ibid., p. 81.
28 Ibid., p. 82.
29 Ibid., p. 82.
30 Ibid., p. 82.
31 Ibid., p. 82.
32 *The Christian Doctrine of God*, Lutterworth, London, 1949, p. 248.
33 Ibid., p. 242.
34 *The Theological Frontier of Ethics*, p. 185.
35 Ibid., pp. 187f.
36 Matthew 7: 11.
37 Luke 23: 46.
38 *The Divine Imperative*, p. 71.
39 This form might be described as self-righteous moral complacency, and others might be self-indulgent moral laxity and high-principled humanism.
40 Cf. *The Interpretation of Religion*, p. 318; *Our Knowledge of God*, p. 3.
41 Job 42: 5, 6.
42 *The Divine Imperative*, p. 74.
43 Ibid., p. 56.
44 Ibid., p. 85; cf. p. 72.
45 Ibid., p. 86.
46 Cf. Karl Barth, *The Knowledge of God and the Service of God*, pp. 143f.
47 *The Theological Frontier of Ethics*, p. 71.

CHAPTER 5

1 *Christian Morality*, p. 32.
2 Ibid., p. 58.
3 *Conscience and Christ*, Duckworth, London, 1916, p. 23.
4 Ibid., p. 23.
5 Cf. Matthew 5: 31, 32, and Mark 10: 2–12.
6 *Conscience and Christ*, p. 29.
7 Ibid., p. 32.
8 Ibid., p. 24.
9 *Christian Morality*, p. 297.
10 W. S. Urquhart, *Humanism and Christianity*, T. & T. Clark, Edinburgh, 1945, p. 217, quoting A. E. Whithan, *The Pastures of His Presence*, Hodder & Stoughton, London, 1939, p. 16.

11 Galatians 2: 20.
12 1 John 3: 2.
13 Matthew 5: 21, 22.
14 Matthew 11: 28.
15 Matthew 16: 15.
16 Matthew 25: 31-36.
17 Matthew 5: 44.
18 John 4: 34; Matthew 19: 17.
19 *Pro Christo et Ecclesia*, Macmillan, London, 1900, p. 3.
20 Acts 14: 15.
21 Op. cit., pp. 63f.
22 John 6: 68.
23 Isaiah 59: 14.

CHAPTER 6

1 1 Corinthians 3: 11.
2 *Christian Ethics and Moral Philosophy*, Scribner's, New York, 1955, p. 102.
3 Ibid., p. 103.
4 Ibid., p. 103.
5 John 6: 29.
6 W. G. Maclagan, *The Theological Frontier of Ethics*, p. 50.
7 Romans 7: 12.
8 Cf. *Morals and the New Theology*, p. 76.
9 Cf. Anders Nygren, *Agape and Eros*, Westminster Press, Philadelphia, and S.P.C.K., London, 1953. Nygren places 'the main emphasis' on 'the rivalry' between the two ideas holding that 'even where the Eros motif prepared the way for Christianity, it prepared at the same time for a confusion of the two motifs'. (Op. cit., p. 162.) On this John Burnaby's comment is enlightening. 'One who believes that God's providence has never ceased to guide and govern the world He created would naturally draw the inference that if God has given Himself to men in Christ, it is because men need Him, and that consciousness of the need, so far from being an obstacle to acceptance of the gift, is its necessary condition. Nygren thinks that this is to obscure the real issue. Where others see a *praeparatio evangelica*, he is more disposed to find a *praeparatio daemonica*; for he is interested in Eros not as the simple expression of a need but as the spirit of a religion which has its own way of meeting the need, and therefore must be in rivalry to the Gospel.' (*Amor Dei*, p. 16.)
10 *The Christian Philosophy of St Thomas Aquinas*, p. 264.
11 Matthew 18: 21.
12 Romans 5: 8.
13 Cf. Matthew 5: 41.
14 *The Christian Philosophy of St Thomas Aquinas*, p. 349.

15 *Church Dogmatics*, II, 2, p. 509.
16 Ibid., II, 2, p. 511.
17 *The Divine Imperative*, p. 53.
18 Ibid., p. 53.
19 Ibid., p. 54.
20 Ibid., p. 59.
21 Genesis 18: 25.
22 Luke 7: 19.
23 *The Divine Imperative*, p. 56 (italics mine).
24 *The Ethical Teaching of Jesus*, Macmillan, New York, 1924, p. 57.
25 Ibid., p. 58.
26 *The Divine Initiative*, SCM Press, London, 1921, p. 99.
27 Ibid., p. 100.
28 Ibid., p. 107.
29 *The Person and the Common Good*, Geoffrey Bles, London, 1948, p. 9. A similar point is made by Richard Niebuhr, *The Meaning of Revelation*, Macmillan, New York, 1960, p. 70. 'Human association', he says there, 'also differs when regarded from the external or internal points of view. The external knower must see societies as made up of atomic individuals related to each other by external bonds. . . . In internal history, on the other hand, society is a community of selves. Here we do not only live among other selves but they live in us and we in them. Relations here are not external but internal so that we are our relations and cannot be selves save as we are members of each other.' Further, while this more cohesive view of human association may be understood in a way which is amoral and which has left behind all thought of obligation, this is not necessarily so, and St Paul is to be found basing the duty of truth-telling upon our membership one of another. 'Wherefore putting away lying, speak every man truth with his neighbour: for we are members one of another.'
30 'Some Ethical Foundations of Christian Theology', *Union Seminary Quarterly Review*, January 1960, p. 101.
31 Cf. William Temple's discussion in *Nature, Man and God*, Macmillan, London, 1934, pp. 57ff. and the comment of John Baillie that 'the only way to get out of the egocentric predicament is never to get into it'. (*Our Knowledge of God*, p. 152.)
32 Op. cit., p. 84.
33 Ibid., p. 87; cf. pp. 190–2.
34 Psalm 25: 14.
35 Matthew 25: 29.
36 Isaiah 59: 4, 14, 15.
37 John 10: 10.
38 *Basic Christian Ethics*, Scribner's, New York, 1950, p. 34.
39 Ibid., p. 44.
40 Ibid., p. 57.
41 Ibid., p. 160.
42 Ibid., p. 162.

43 Ibid., p. 243.
44 *The Good Will*, Allen & Unwin, London, 1927, p. 310, quoted *Basic Christian Ethics*, p. 160.
45 *Basic Christian Ethics*, p. 330.
46 Ibid., p. 13.
47 Cf. ibid., p. 346.


CHAPTER 7


1 H. J. Paton, *The Categorical Imperative*, Hutchinson, London, 1947, p. 180.
2 *Morals and the New Theology*, p. 33.
3 Ibid., pp. 33f.
4 Ibid., p. 35.
—5 *The Theological Frontier of Ethics*, p. 72.
6 *Institutes of the Christian Religion*, Bk. III, Ch. VI, 1.
7 Op. cit. (1st British ed.), p. 51.
8 Psalm 51: 10.
9 Matthew 22: 36–39.
10 Galatians 2: 20.
11 This is not to say that Scripture has no place in the Christian life. On the contrary, it has a very large place and that life would be inconceivable without it. But it does not function in the Christian life simply as a precept out of a book. If that were so we might well gather its precepts together beforehand and carry them about in our pocket, as a traveller may carry the everyday phrases and easy sentences of some foreign language. Rather, as a whole Scripture functions as that which points away from itself, bearing witness to and spotlighting, as it were, the sovereign centre of Christian life, while in its parts it may function as a command and directive *from above*. In this event, it is not the objective situation in which a man finds himself which merely by the criterion of relevance selects one particular precept out of the sum-total of precepts; it may be the living Spirit of God to whom in faith a man has committed his life and all his ways and to whom Scripture in all its parts bears witness.
12 Cf. *supra*, pp. 26ff.
13 *The Ethics of the Christian Life*, pp. 3f.
14 Cf. *Christianity and Ethics*, p. 25.
15 *The Ethics of the Christian Life*, p. 126.
16 *Christianity and Ethics*, p. 26.
17 Ibid., pp. 25f.
18 *The Ethics of the Christian Life*, p. 126.
19 *Christianity and Ethics*, pp. 127f.
20 Ibid., p. 218.
21 Ibid., p. 219.

22 *The Christian Faith*, T. & T. Clark, Edinburgh, 1928, p. 50.
23 *Types of Modern Theology*, Nisbet, Welwyn, 1937, p. 60.
24 T. & T. Clark, Edinburgh, 1920, XI, p. 237a.
25 *Towards Belief in God*, SCM Press, London, 1942, p. 42.
26 It is noteworthy that even Karl Barth who so often stressed the discontinuity between the nineteenth and twentieth centuries in theology yet came to speak of *the humanity of God*, and always regarded theology as a function of the Church.
27 *Ethics in a Christian Context*, pp. 41f., note 3.
28 Ibid., p. 262.
29 Ibid., p. 266.
30 Ibid., p. 266.
31 Ibid., p. 267.
32 Ibid., p. 266.
33 H. R. Mackintosh, *Types of Modern Theology*, pp. 144f.
34 Ibid., p. 148.
35 Ibid., p. 145.
36 Ibid., p. 155.
37 *The Ethics of the Christian Life*, p. 3.
38 Cf. ibid., p. 18.
39 Ibid., p. 19.
40 Ibid., pp. 126f.
41 Ibid., p. 22.
42 Ibid., p. 4.
43 *The Doctrine of the Word of God*, T. & T. Clark, Edinburgh, 1936, p. xiv.
44 *The Theological Frontier of Ethics*, p. 72.
45 'For no law, apart from a Lawgiver, is a proper object of reverence. It is mere brute fact; and every living thing, still more every person exercising intelligent choice, is its superior. The reverence of persons can be appropriately given only to that which itself is at least personal.' (William Temple, *Nature, Man and God*, p. 254.)
46 Cf. *The Christian Doctrine of God*, p. 125. The passage is worth quoting. Some people, says Brunner, 'want to keep their minds closed to all that comes to them from outside the sphere of reason, the sphere, that is, which they can control by their own thought; they do not wish to see it opened from outside. They recognize only the truth which they already know, and that which can be verified by means which are at man's disposal. They have no intention of admitting that there could be such a thing as "given" truth. They will accept as truth only that which they can attain for themselves, but not that which approaches them from without. They will only receive – and this is the same thing in the end – monological and not dialogical truth, only truth which is preceded by the words: "I think", but not that which is prefaced by the words: "Here it is!" that is, truth which they can only receive in this way. Thus this habit of thought is rooted in the self-sufficiency of the isolated "I": *Cogito, ergo sum.*'
47 A similar suggestion was made by John Baillie, *Our Knowledge of God*,

pp. 35ff., 75ff.; but the insight is not necessarily tied to the particular terms in which he expressed it or to the conclusions he drew from it.

48 *Christianity and Ethics*, p. 22.
49 John 10: 10.
50 Matthew 11: 28–30.

CHAPTER 8

1 Mark 9: 24.
2 Luke 17: 10.
3 Galatians 2: 20.
4 *The Divine Imperative*, pp. 56f.
5 Ibid., p. 58.
6 Ibid., p. 55.
7 Ibid., p. 86.
8 Ibid., p. 58.
9 Ibid., p. 58.
10 Ibid., p. 61.
11 Ibid., p. 69.
12 Ibid., p. 69.
13 Ibid., p. 59.
14 Ibid., p. 18.
15 *Church Dogmatics*, II, 2, pp. 516f.
16 *The Divine Imperative*, p. 53.
17 *Church Dogmatics*, II, 2, p. 509.
18 *The Divine Imperative*, p. 71.
19 *Church Dogmatics*, II, 2, p. 518.
20 Ibid., p. 517.
21 Ibid., p. 532.
22 Ibid., p. 510.
23 Ibid., p. 538.
24 Ibid., p. 536.
25 D. Cairns, *A Gospel without Myth?*, SCM Press, London, 1960, p. 110.
26 J. Macquarrie, *The Scope of Demythologizing*, SCM Press, London, 1960, p. 12.
27 It is to be noted that for Bultmann the divine source of the Christian faith and life is the act of God in Jesus Christ, the eschatological event, and that this event is *repeated* whenever the Gospel is *preached*.
28 Cf. *The Theology of the New Testament*, SCM Press, London, 1952, I, pp. 268f., 329f., 336.
29 *Radical Obedience*, Epworth Press, London, 1965, p. 95.
30 Cf. *The Theology of the New Testament*, I, pp. 314, 317.
31 Ibid., II, p. 203.
32 Ibid., I, p. 325.
33 Cf. *Radical Obedience*, pp. 28ff.
34 Ibid., p. 36; cf. p. 56.

35 Ibid., p. 123.
36 Thus Paul Tillich makes a sound point when he says that 'ultimately love must satisfy justice in order to be real love' and to avoid what he calls 'chaotic surrender'. (*Love, Power and Justice*, Oxford University Press, London, 1954, pp. 12, 14; cf. pp. 68, 82f.) 'Love, in the sense of *agape*, contains justice in itself as its unconditional element and as its weapon against its own sentimentalization.' (*Morality and Beyond*, Routledge & Kegan Paul, London, 1964, p. 39.)
37 *Jesus Christ and Mythology*, SCM Press, London, 1960, p. 41.
38 Ibid., pp. 41f.
39 Ibid., p. 43.
40 Ibid., p. 42.
41 *The New Man*, SCM Press, London, 1956, p. 32.
42 Ibid., p. 45.
43 *Radical Obedience*, p. 120.
44 Cf. what Oden says and what Bultmann says, respectively, ibid., pp. 130f., 142f.
45 Ibid., p. 36 (italics mine).
46 Quoted ibid., p. 36 (italics mine). But cf. Paul Tillich, *Love, Power and Justice*, p. 79: 'it may well be that one wants to receive benefits which contradict the justice towards oneself and which would contradict equally the justice towards the other one, if he received them.'
47 *Radical Obedience*, p. 63.
48 Ibid., p. 62.
49 *The New Man*, p. 46.
50 *An Interpretation of Christian Ethics*, SCM Press, London, 1936, p. 79.
51 *Ethics*, SCM Press, London, 1955, p. 61.
52 Ibid., p. 77.
53 Ibid., p. 59.
54 Ibid., p. 61.
55 Ibid., p. 77.
56 Ibid., p. 81.
57 The same difficulty is to be encountered in Gregor Smith's argument in *The New Man* where, on the one hand, he held that Christianity must be seen, not as a religion 'which imposed standards and norms upon society', but as 'the very substance of society', and yet, on the other, he declared that it contains 'a critical dissolvent element' which represents human culture 'as ridden with sin and imperfection', as well as 'a positive hopeful element' – although Gregor Smith did seem to suggest that the criterion implied is to be found in *'unlimited'* or *'absolute* openness', an *'unreserved* togetherness with others', and it may be that the corresponding criterion in Bonhoeffer lies in the character of the world as a totality, a unity, a reconciled whole. (Cf. *The New Man*, pp. 44, 6of. – italics mine.) Such criteria, however, are in themselves natural rather than normative, and, even when combined with an exclusive emphasis upon the demand of love without law, of a 'normless' love, they cannot

make contact with the genuinely ethical but can lead only to some form of naturalism.

58 *The Divine Imperative*, p. 74.
59 *Ethics*, pp. 142f.
60 Ibid., p. 73.
61 Cf. ibid., p. 252.
62 *Creation and Law*, Oliver & Boyd, Edinburgh, 1961, p. 30. Later Wingren refers with approval to the work of Regin Prenter who 'does not accept the so-called "orders of Creation" ... as being divine institutions, but acknowledges them as freely chosen "pacts" which have a historical existence, and which are thus essentially variable. This', he adds, 'is what we mean by the works of the Creator. The act of Creation is not limited to a single beginning, but is still going on.' (Ibid., p. 155, note 10; cf. also Reinhold Niebuhr, *Man's Nature and His Communities*, Geoffrey Bles, London, 1966, pp. 24f.) It should be noticed, however, that, while it has been possible to quote Professor Wingren in support of the two criticisms already made of the conception of 'orders', this is no longer the case when the argument moves on to what is the third and major criticism. Instead, what Wingren puts in place of the orders, namely, God's use of 'the Law' to restrain the effect of human sin and to give to man some sense of the accusation against him, may very well be open to precisely the same criticism. Thus where Brunner refers to 'a standard of law which is totally different from that which is known by faith' Wingren speaks of 'the indelible difference between the order of earthly government at its best ... and ... the attitude of Jesus – the proper object of our imitation – to evil'. (*Creation and Law*, p. 144.) See *infra*, pp. 210ff.
63 Ethics, p. 80.
64 Ibid., p. 81.
65 Ibid., p. 83.
66 *The Divine Imperative*, p. 148.
67 Ibid., p. 150.
68 Ibid., p. 335.
69 Cf. *The Misunderstanding of the Church*, Lutterworth Press, London, 1952, pp. 84, 90, 109.
70 Op. cit., p. 44.
71 Ibid., p. 44.
72 Ibid., p. 23.
73 Ibid., p. 45; cf. p. 25.
74 Ibid., p. 45.
75 Cf. ibid., pp. 126, 278ff.
76 Ibid., p. 152.
77 Cf. ibid., p. 174.
78 Cf. ibid., pp. 190ff.
79 Cf. ibid., p. 143.
80 Ibid., p. 14.
81 Ibid., p. 16.

82 Ibid., p. 45.
83 Ibid., p. 47.
84 Ibid., p. 124.
85 Ibid., p. 131.
86 Ibid., p. 131.
87 Ibid., p. 159.
88 Ibid., p. 159.
89 Ibid., p. 120.
90 Ibid., p. 152.
91 Ibid., p. 152.
92 Ibid., p. 16.
93 Ibid., pp. 139f.
94 Matthew 5: 16.
95 *Ethics in a Christian Context*, p. 159.
96 Ibid., p. 77.
97 Ibid., p. 159 (exclamation mark Lehmann's own).
98 Ibid., p. 117.
99 Ibid., p. 121.
100 Ibid., p. 54.
101 Ibid., pp. 54f.
102 Ibid., p. 121.
103 Ibid., p. 54.
104 Ibid., p. 96.
105 Ibid., p. 277; cf. pp. 152, 268ff.
106 *The Divine Imperative*, p. 18.
107 *Ethics in a Christian Context*, p. 145.
108 Ibid., p. 145.
109 Ibid., p. 147.
110 The phrase seems originally due to Dr J. H. Oldham. Cf. 'Such broad
     assertions as that Christians are bound to obey the law of love or to
     strive for social justice do not go far towards helping the individual to
     know what he ought to do in particular cases. On the other hand, there
     is no way by which he can be relieved of the responsibility of decision
     in concrete situations. To give him precise instructions to be literally
     carried out is to rob him of his moral responsibility as a person. ...
     Hence between purely general statements of the ethical demands of the
     Gospel and the decisions that have to be made in concrete situations
     there is need for what may be described as middle axioms. It is these
     that give relevance and point to the Christian ethic. They are an attempt
     to define the directions in which, in a particular state of society, Chris-
     tian faith must express itself. They are not binding for all time, but are
     provisional definitions of the type of behaviour required of Christians
     at a given period and in given circumstances.' (Visser 't Hooft and
     J. H. Oldham, *The Church and its Function in Society*, Allen & Unwin,
     London, 1937, pp. 209f.)
111 *Ethics in a Christian Context*, p. 152.
112 Ibid., p. 152.

113 Ibid., p. 284n.
114 There *is* a way in logic from general to particular, even if the resultant conduct is ethically unreal; and if real ethical conduct is marked by 'a certain *kind* of reality possessed by the concrete' the general has not after all been avoided.
115 Cf. ibid., p. 152, quoted *supra*, pp. 206f.
116 'Art thou he that should come? or look we for another? ... Go your way, and tell John what things ye have seen and heard; how that the blind see, the lame walk ...' (Luke 7: 19–23.)
117 *Ethics in a Christian Context*, p. 154.
118 Ibid., p. 155.
119 Ibid., p. 154.
120 Ibid., p. 157.
121 Ibid., p. 157.
122 Ibid., p. 158.
123 *Theology of the New Testament*, I, pp. 190, 270.
124 Cf. *The Christian Doctrine of God*, pp. 271ff.
125 *De Incarnatione Verbi Dei*, para. 44.
126 *Creation and Law*, p. 191; cf. pp. 6f., 89, note 15, 132.
127 Ibid., p. 52.
128 Ibid., p. 53.
129 Ibid., p. 81, note 85.
130 Ibid., p. 157.
131 Ibid., p. 157; cf. p. 12.
132 Cf. ibid., pp. 118, 168.
133 Ibid., p. 57.
134 Ibid., p. 58.
135 Ibid., p. 151.
136 Cf. ibid., pp. 162ff.
137 Ibid., p. 42 (italics mine).
138 Ibid., p. 86.
139 Ibid., p. 20.
140 Ibid., p. 21.
141 Ibid., p. 177.
142 Ibid., pp. 94f.
143 Cf. ibid., pp. 57ff.
144 Ibid., p. 60.
145 Ibid., p. 124; cf. p. 195.
146 Cf. ibid., p. 144.
147 Ibid., p. 183.
148 Ibid., p. 117.
149 Ibid., p. 192
150 Ibid., p. 55.
151 Cf. *The Christian Doctrine of God*, pp. 248ff.
152 *Ethics in a Christian Context*, p. 322.
153 Cf. my *Faith and Duty, passim*.
154 Matthew 25: 40.

155 Op. cit., p. 29.
156 Ibid., p. 31.
157 Such a firm distinction seems lacking from John Baillie's presentation of the thesis that there is no nature devoid of grace. Cf. *Our Knowledge of God*, pp. 75–104.
158 Ezekiel 29: 3.
159 *Ethics in a Christian Context*, p. 120 (italics mine).
160 Cf. John Baillie's suggestion that there is a belief in God 'in the bottom of all men's hearts' (*Our Knowledge of God*, p. 101), and the careful criticism of this thesis by Professor H. D. Lewis in I. T. Ramsey (ed.), *Christian Ethics and Contemporary Philosophy*, SCM Press, London, 1966, pp. 172ff.
161 Op. cit., p. 251.
162 Ibid., p. 254.
163 Ibid., p. 255.
164 Ibid., p. 278; cf. p. 280.
165 R. G. Smith, *The New Man*, p. 45.
166 R. G. Smith's book *The New Man* carries the sub-title 'Christianity and Man's Coming of Age'; but the suggestion that autonomy as the whole truth is 'one inescapable consequence of any doctrine of the Incarnation, of God becoming man' (p. 43) seems to reverse the movement of the Incarnation. This may avoid docetism but it runs headlong into a very radical adoptianism – and beyond it.
167 Joel 2: 25, 28, 32.

CHAPTER 9

1 *Nature, Man and God*, p. 317.
2 Harvey Cox, *The Secular City*, SCM Press, London, 1965, pp. 105ff.
3 This is the traditional term to characterize that which is distinguished from grace, and it is probably the most convenient one; but, it should be noted, its use carries no commitment to naturalism. Natural man is, if I am not mistaken, moral man; but naturalism misunderstands this condition by losing sight of the normative character of the moral and by assimilating it to the actual.
4 Cf. E. Brunner, *The Divine Imperative*, p. 150.
5 Whether his theory has room for the recognition or not Professor R. M. Hare describes moral principles as 'superior to or more authoritative than any other kind of principle'. (*Freedom and Reason*, p. 169.)
6 The Pauline injunction 'come out from among them, and be ye separate' (2 Corinthians 6: 17), when properly understood, is not in conflict with that of Isaiah, 'hide not thyself from thine own flesh' (Isaiah 58: 7).
7 Romans 13: 1.
8 *Moral Theology in the Modern World*, Mowbray, Oxford, 1964, p. 17.
9 *The Divine Imperative*, p. 76.
10 Ibid., p. 80.

323

11 Ibid., p. 81.
12 Ibid., pp. 68f.
13 Ibid., p. 74.
14 Ibid., p. 81.
15 Cf. 'The personal is the true supernatural.' (H. H. Farmer, *The World and God*, Nisbet, Welwyn, 1936, p. 6.)
16 *The Divine Imperative*, pp. 345ff.
17 Ibid., p. 80.
18 Ibid., p. 74 (italics of final sentence mine).
▶ 19 Cf. R. Gregor Smith, *The New Man*, p. 45.
20 *Honest to God*, SCM Press, London, 1963, pp. 119f.
21 Op. cit., p. 61.
22 Cf. *Letters and Papers from Prison*, 3rd ed., SCM Press, London, 1967, pp. 114ff.
23 Ibid., pp. 120f.
24 Cf. Bultmann's volte-face in *Jesus Christ and Mythology*: 'It is, of course, true that de-mythologizing takes the modern world-view as a criterion' but the 'stumbling-block is that the Word of God calls man out of all man-made security. The scientific world-view engenders a great temptation, namely, that man strive for mastery over the world and over his own life.' (Pp. 35, 39.)
25 *The Theology of Dietrich Bonhoeffer*, SCM Press, London, 1960, pp. 270f.
26 Ibid., p. 270.
27 Quoted ibid., p. 272.
28 Ibid., p. 270.
29 A half-way house towards full secularization can be found in some of the writings of Professor William Hamilton who, on the evidence of an article 'The Death of God' in the *Playboy* magazine, August 1966, certainly wishes to stress that 'the death of God ... moves straight into' such things as politics and revolutionary change but who also wishes to find in such human experiences as suffering and sex what he calls sacred events.
30 Op. cit., p. 112.
31 Ibid., p. 17.
32 Ibid., p. 109; cf. p. 119.
33 Ibid., p. 116.
34 Ibid., pp. 116f.
35 Ibid., p. 32. But it seems inconsistent to say much later of 'The Girl' in modern life that 'like every idol she is ultimately a creation of our own hands and cannot save us' (ibid., p. 197); and it is, to say the least, extremely doubtful whether ethical relativism can be reconciled with what the same author has to say in condemnation of Nazi atrocities. Cf. *On Not Leaving It to the Snake*, SCM Press, London, 1968, pp. 151ff.
36 *The Secular City*, p. 41. Is not Paul Tillich more Christian when he holds that creative justice demands 'at least that even in the most impersonal relations the other one is acknowledged as a person'? (*Love, Power and Justice*, p. 85; cf. p. 119.) In themselves there may not be much to choose

between the two statements, but everything depends on whether one is on the way up or on the way down.

37 *The Secular City*, p. 58.
38 Ibid., p. 60.
39 Ibid., p. 61.
40 Ibid., p. 154.
41 Ibid., p. 36. Cf. 'After all, it is God – not The Girl – who is God. He is the center and source of value.' (P. 199.)
42 Ibid., p. 247.
43 Ibid., p. 241.
44 Ibid., p. 243.
45 Ibid., p. 254.
46 Ibid., p. 254.
47 Ibid., pp. 264f.
48 Ibid., p. 266.
49 It ought to be noticed that in his later book, *On Not Leaving It to the Snake*, Harvey Cox does pay attention, not to Heraclitus, but to certain movements in modern theology which stress the future as the element of transcendence in the human situation (cf. op. cit., pp. 9, 62). He does not indeed surrender his thoroughgoing relativism (cf. pp. 22ff., 94), but it no longer prominently provides the framework for what he has to say; and he introduces a different but genuinely theological note in his suggestion that the confidence of contemporary man stems from a faith that history will prove itself accommodating (cf. ibid., p. 20). It is, however, hardly credible that such a faith in the future is given to us now *by* the future in divorce from the past.
50 *Situation Ethics*, SCM Press, London, 1966, p. 158.
51 Ibid., p. 41.
52 Ibid., p. 157.
53 Cf. ibid., p. 11.
54 Ibid., p. 26.
55 Ibid., p. 43; cf. the same author's *Moral Responsibility*, SCM Press, London, 1967, pp. 7, 29, 34, 73.
56 Ibid., p. 44.
57 Ibid., p. 45.
58 Ibid., p. 61.
59 Ibid., p. 60.
60 Ibid., p. 58.
61 Ibid., p. 64.
62 Ibid., p. 95.
63 Ibid., p. 95.
64 Op. cit., p. 54; cf. p. 56.
65 Ibid., p. 57; cf. pp. 78, 239f. Paul Tillich, however, seems nearer the truth when he recognizes that we 'can achieve justice without creating a relationship' and suggests that 'love becomes the ultimate moral principle, including justice and transcending it at the same time'. (*Morality and Beyond*, pp. 38f.)

66 In a context of relativism what can Fletcher possibly mean by 'the moral claims of our neighbors' (*Moral Responsibility*, p. 238) as distinct, presumably, from the arbitrary importunities of all and sundry?
67 *Situation Ethics*, p. 96.
68 Ibid., p. 70.
69 *Christian Freedom in a Permissive Society*, SCM Press, London, 1970, pp. 15f.
70 Cf. ibid., pp. 12, 17, 23f., 30.
71 Ibid., p. 24.
72 Ibid., p. 13.
73 Ibid., p. 13.
74 Ibid., p. 4.
75 Ibid., p. 5.
76 Ibid., p. 5.
77 Ibid., p. 5.
78 Ibid., p. 5.
79 Ibid., p. 12.
80 Ibid., p. 12.
81 Ibid., p. 26.
82 For example, by Bultmann and Tillich: cf. *supra*, pp. 187, 189, 319.
83 *Christian Freedom in a Permissive Society*, p. 39.
84 Cf. ibid., pp. 5, 32, 56; *Honest to God*, pp. 119f.
85 Cf. *Christian Freedom in a Permissive Society*, pp. 31ff.
86 Ibid., p. 40.
87 This concentration supports the atomism well, as indicated by the popular song, 'If you were the only girl in the world and I were the only boy'. To do Dr Robinson justice, however, it must be added that his concentration on the sexual problem is very different from the obsession with sex which makes some so-called television celebrities barely distinguishable from smutty schoolboys suffering from arrested development. The tragedy is that the moving picture becomes a stream which carries along the unthinking mind; and here there is a critical question for contemporary educators who use similar devices. Are they educating or are they conditioning? If they do not see the difference someone some day must undertake the task of educating the educators.
88 *Creation and Law*, p. 48.
89 In M. E. Marty and D. G. Peerman, *New Theology*, Macmillan, London, No. 3, p. 70.
90 Cf. also his *Secular Christianity*, Collins, London, 1966.
91 Op. cit., p. 45.
92 Ibid., p. 46.
93 Ibid., p. 49.
94 Ibid., p. 44.
95 Quoted by J. Baillie, *The Interpretation of Religion*, p. 312.
96 *The New Man*, p. 44.
97 Ibid., pp. 59f.
98 Ibid., p. 65.

99 Philippians 2: 12, 13.
100 Cf. *supra*, Ch. 3.
101 *Jesus Christ and Mythology*, pp. 41f.
102 Is Bultmann seriously suggesting a fall at a particular point of history between ancient times and modern? The fall is, surely, neither an event *in* history nor one *beyond* (or before) history, but a continuing character of the world's life. Cf. my *Faith and Duty*, pp. 143ff.; *Christ and Conscience*, Nisbet, Welwyn, 1956, pp. 31f., 63ff.
103 *Ethics in a Christian Context*, p. 218.
104 Ibid., pp. 287f.
105 Ibid., p. 320.
106 *Man's Freedom*, p. 179, quoted by P. Lehmann, *Ethics in a Christian Context*, p. 207.
107 *The Secular City*, p. 1.
108 Matthew 12: 20.
109 Matthew 5: 20.
110 John 3: 16.
111 To reject this solution is not to deny the quite different thesis that in fact Christianity has exercised an influence upon the ordinary moral consciousness.
112 Cf. *supra*, pp. 170ff.
113 *Ethics in a Christian Context*, p. 16.
114 Ibid., p. 25.
115 One can recognize that this is a moral, not just a technical, argument without agreeing with it. Indeed, without impugning the moral character of the argument, one may hold that it is mistaken on the ground that, on the one hand, it fails to distinguish between the objective orientation of the act and the agent's intention (and so is committed, for example, while condemning the minister who does not visit his parishioners, at least to excusing his colleague who makes a point of calling and leaving his visiting-card when he knows there is no one at home), and, in the case of birth-control, that, on the other hand, it can retrieve itself from this absurd situation only by laying great weight upon what is *natural* and what is *unnatural*, and so by laying itself open to the charge that it has committed the naturalistic fallacy.
116 *Ethics in a Christian Context*, p. 33.
117 'It is not a difference of being outside of Christ and so under judgment as distinguished from being inside with Christ and so under grace. Judgment and grace in Christ belong to the humanity which is common to all men in him. The difference between believers and unbelievers, both of whom are involved in the new humanity, is rather the difference between being in a situation which is hidden and being in one which is open. This openness is a matter not only of knowledge as against ignorance but also of behavior expressive of confidence and hope as against anxiety and despair, of behaving with abandon rather than with calculation, of being all things to all men rather than ... "pursuing selfish advantage ... compiling statistics of evil".' (Lehmann, *Ethics in a*

*Christian Context*, p. 120.) But surely this final characterization of unbelief does not distinguish it from belief, for the Christian too may err and stray.

118 *The New Man*, p. 64.
119 *Ethics in a Christian Context*, p. 25 (italics mine).
120 Ibid., p. 47.
121 Ibid., p. 100.
122 Ibid., p. 152.
123 Ibid., p. 141.
124 For example, it makes a difference if my neighbour happens to be, so to speak, my neighbour's wife.
125 Paul Tillich, *Morality and Beyond*, p. 38.
126 Luke 17: 10.
127 When Professor Harvey Cox refers to 'The Girl' as an idol he is certainly not mistaken, but he may be elliptical. She is first an image in this sense, an abstraction, perhaps a female figure; and then she may become an idol.
128 Characteristically, because of his indifference to the question of knowledge, Professor Gustaf Wingren says that 'Israel's actual history takes place between the primal act of God in the Creation of the world, and the unfulfilled act of God in the Consummation' and that 'the history of each individual Christian . . . lies between the same two divine acts'. (*Creation and Law*, p. 146.)
129 *Man's Nature and His Communities*, p. 63.
130 *The Secular City*, pp. 48f.
131 Isaiah 43: 6, 7.
132 1 John 4: 10.
133 *Mysticism and Logic*, pp. 56f.
134 Jeremiah 12: 1.
135 *Church Dogmatics*, II, 2, p. 585.
136 Mark 2: 7.
137 Op. cit., Bk. III, Ch. VII, 6.
138 1 John 4: 10.
139 Romans 5: 8.
140 Matthew 11: 28; 28: 19; 26: 11; 25:40.
141 John 13: 14.
142 Luke 23: 34.
143 On this point in general, cf. Paul Ramsey, *Basic Christian Ethics*, pp. 16ff.
144 *An Interpretation of Christian Ethics*, pp. 113ff.

APPENDIX A

1 *Systematic Theology*, Nisbet, Welwyn, 1964, III, p. 283.
2 Ibid., p. 284.
3 Ibid., p. 285.
4 Ibid., p. 284.

5 This method of procedure is bound to affect, not only ethics, but the whole range of theology.
6 Ibid., pp. 13ff.
7 Ibid., p. 15 (italics mine).
8 Ibid., p. 283.
9 *Morality and Beyond*, p. 22; cf. *Systematic Theology*, III, p. 42.
10 *Morality and Beyond*, p. 14.
11 *Love, Power and Justice*, p. 82.
12 Ibid., pp. 56f.
13 Ibid., p. 66.
14 Op. cit., p. 87.
15 Ibid., p. 88.
16 Ibid., p. 89.
17 *Love, Power and Justice*, p. 68; cf. pp. 82f., and *Morality and Beyond*, pp. 93f.
18 Ibid., p. 71.
19 *Morality and Beyond*, p. 26.
20 Ibid., p. 59.
21 *Love, Power and Justice*, p. 25.
22 *Morality and Beyond*, p. 46.
23 *Love, Power and Justice*, p. 48.
24 Ibid., p. 24.
25 Ibid., p. 27.
26 Ibid., p. 109.
27 Ibid., pp. 111f.
28 *Morality and Beyond*, p. 49.
29 Ibid., p. 40.
30 Cf. ibid., p. 61.
31 *Systematic Theology*, III, p. 292; cf. *Morality and Beyond*, pp. 47ff.
32 *The Divine Imperative*, p. 74.
33 *Morality and Beyond*, p. 60.
34 *Love, Power and Justice*, p. 98.
35 Ibid., p. 50.
36 Ibid., p. 26.
37 Ibid., p. 49.
38 *Systematic Theology*, III, p. 286.
39 Ibid., p. 290.
40 *The Protestant Era*, Nisbet, Welwyn, 1951, p. 150.
41 *Morality and Beyond*, pp. 59f.
42 Ibid., p. 60.


APPENDIX B

1 Op. cit., p. 46.
2 Cf. ibid., p. 37.

3 Cf. ibid., pp. 39f.
4 *Creation and Law*, p. 172.
5 *Agape and Eros*, p. 51.
6 Ibid., p. 84.
7 Ibid., p. 231.
8 Ibid., p. 722.
9 Cf. ibid., p. 210.
10 Cf. ibid., p. 219.
11 Cf. ibid., pp. 94, 125f.
12 Ibid., p. 129.
13 Ibid., p. 133.
14 Ibid., p. 48.
15 Quoted ibid., p. 91.
16 Cf. ibid., pp. 215f., 731.
17 Quoted ibid., p. 733.
18 Ibid., p. 734.
19 Ibid., p. 559.
20 Ibid., p. 561.
21 Ibid., p. 562.
22 Cf. ibid., p. 160.
23 Cf. Wingren, *Creation and Law*, p. 172, note 50.
24 Cf. *Agape and Eros*, pp. 160f.
25 In *Journal of Theological Studies*, Vol. XX, Part I, 1969, p. 199.
26 *Agape and Eros*, p. 143.
27 Cf. ibid., pp. 115ff.
28 Romans 5: 8.
29 *Agape and Eros*, p. 51.
30 Quoted ibid., p. 736 (italics mine).
31 *Theological Ethics*, A. & C. Black, London, 1968, p. 20.
32 Ibid., p. 25.
33 Ibid., p. 26.
34 Ibid., p. 31.
35 Ibid., p. 66.
36 Ibid., p. 36.
37 Ibid., p. 41.
38 Ibid., p. 43.
39 Ibid., p. 51.
40 Ibid., p. 65.
41 Ibid., p. 68.
42 Cf. ibid., p. 78.
43 Cf. ibid., pp. 83, 151.
44 Ibid., p. 147.
45 Ibid., p. 147.
46 Ibid., p. 148.
47 Ibid., p. 149.
48 Cf. ibid., p. 149.
49 Ibid., p. 93.

50 Cf. ibid., p. 94.
51 Ibid., p. 125.
52 Ibid., pp. 131f.
53 Ibid., p. 126.
54 Ibid., pp. 134f.
55 Ibid., p. 134.
56 Ibid., p. 196; cf. p. 251.
57 Ibid., p. 197.
58 Ibid., pp. 260f.
59 Ibid , p. 269.
60 Ibid., p. 269; cf. pp. 298–320, 429–33.
61 Ibid., p. 164.
62 Ibid., p. 163.
63 Ibid., p. 167.
64 Cf. 'the essential characteristics of human nature', Dewar and Hudson, *Christian Morals* (Hodder & Stoughton, University of London Press, London, 1945), p. 36; and 'the alleged constitution of human nature', Dewar, *Moral Theology in the Modern World*, p. 142.
65 In I. T. Ramsey (ed.), *Christian Ethics and Contemporary Philosophy*, pp. 382ff.; cf. pp. 383f.
66 *Three Issues in Ethics*, Harper & Row, New York, 1970, p. 19.
67 Ibid., p. 20.
68 Ibid., p. 21.
69 Ibid., p. 45.
70 Ibid., p. 42.
71 *Christian Ethics and Contemporary Philosophy*, p. 386.
72 Ibid., p. 387.
73 Ibid., p. 388.
74 *Three Issues in Ethics*, p. 105.
75 Ibid., p. 105.
76 Ibid., p. 109.
77 *Christian Ethics and Contemporary Philosophy*, p. 393.
78 Cf. my paper 'Mystery and Logic', *Canadian Journal of Theology*, Vol. xv, Part 1, 1969, pp. 30ff.
79 *Christian Ethics and Contemporary Philosophy*, p. 392.
80 *Three Issues in Ethics*, p. 110.
81 Ibid., p. 132.
82 Ibid., p. 137.
83 Ibid., p. 145.
84 John 3: 16.
85 *Contra* J. Macquarrie, *Three Issues in Ethics*, p. 137.
86 *Contra* H. Thielicke, *Theological Ethics*, p. 314.

# ACKNOWLEDGMENTS

The author and publishers wish to acknowledge their indebtedness for permission to reproduce copyright material as follows: from *Christianity and Ethics* by A. B. D. Alexander, published by Duckworth, London; from *Language, Truth and Logic* by A. J. Ayer, published by Victor Gollancz Ltd, London; from *God Was in Christ* by D. M. Baillie, reprinted by permission of Faber and Faber Ltd, London; from *Church Dogmatics* by Karl Barth, published by T. & T. Clark, Edinburgh; from *Ethics* by Dietrich Bonhoeffer, published by SCM Press, London, and the Macmillan Company, New York; from *The Christian Doctrine of God* by Emil Brunner, published by Lutterworth Press, London; from *The Divine Imperative* by Emil Brunner, published by Lutterworth Press, London; from *Jesus Christ and Mythology* by Rudolf Bultmann, published by SCM Press, London, and Charles Scribner's Sons, New York; from *Amor Dei* by John Burnaby, and used by permission of the publishers, Hodder and Stoughton; from *The Secular City* by Harvey Cox, published by SCM Press, London, and the Macmillan Company, New York; from *Situation Ethics* by Joseph Fletcher, published by SCM Press, London, and the Westminster Press, Philadelphia, Copyright © MCMLXVI, W. L. Jenkins. Used by permission; from *The Language of Morals* by R. M. Hare, by permission of the Clarendon Press, Oxford; from *The Christian Message in a Non-Christian World* by Hendrik Kraemer, published by the Edinburgh House Press, London; from *Ethics in a Christian Context* by Paul Lehmann, published by SCM Press, London, and Harper & Row, New York; from *Types of Modern Theology* by H. R. Mackintosh, published by James Nisbet, Welwyn; from *The Theological Frontier of Ethics* by W. G. Maclagan, published by Allen & Unwin Ltd, London; from *Ethics* by P. H. Nowell-Smith, published by Penguin Books Ltd, Harmondsworth; from *Basic Christian Ethics* by Paul Ramsey, published by Charles Scribner's Sons, New York; from *Conscience and Christ* by Hastings Rashdall, published by Duckworth, London; from *The Church and its Function in Society* by W. A. Visser 't Hooft and J. H. Oldham, published by Allen & Unwin Ltd, London; from *Man's Freedom* by Paul Weiss, published by Yale University Press, New Haven, reprinted by permission of Southern Illinois University Press, Carbondale; from *Creation and Law* by Gustaf Wingren, published by Oliver and Boyd, Edinburgh.

332

# INDEX

333

# INDEX